4.18 bc

W9-ABN-532

Home Automation Made Easy

Do It Yourself Know How Using UPB, INSTEON, X10, and Z-Wave

Dennis C. Brewer

800 East 96th Street

Indianapolis, IN 46240

Home Automation Made Easy: Do It Yourself Know How Using UPB, INSTEON, X10, and Z-Wave

Copyright © 2014 by Pearson Education, Inc.

All rights reserved. No part of this book shall be reproduced, stored in a retrieval system, or transmitted by any means, electronic, mechanical, photocopying, recording, or otherwise, without written permission from the publisher. No patent liability is assumed with respect to the use of the information contained herein. Although every precaution has been taken in the preparation of this book, the publisher and author assume no responsibility for errors or omissions. Nor is any liability assumed for damages resulting from the use of the information contained herein.

ISBN-13: 978-0-7897-5124-9

ISBN-10: 0-7897-5124-0

Library of Congress Conrol Number: 2013951117

Printed in the United States of America

First Printing: October 2013

Trademarks

All terms mentioned in this book that are known to be trademarks or service marks have been appropriately capitalized. Que Publishing cannot attest to the accuracy of this information. Use of a term in this book should not be regarded as affecting the validity of any trademark or service mark. Home Automated Living (HAL) is a registered trademark.

Warning and Disclaimer

Every effort has been made to make this book as complete and as accurate as possible, but no warranty or fitness is implied. The information provided is on an "as is" basis. The author and the publisher shall have neither liability nor responsibility to any person or entity with respect to any loss or damages arising from the information contained in this book.

Bulk Sales

Que Publishing offers excellent discounts on this book when ordered in quantity for bulk purchases or special sales. For more information, please contact

U.S. Corporate and Government Sales
1-800-382-3419
corpsales@pearsontechgroup.com

For sales outside of the U.S., please contact

International Sales
international@pearsoned.com

Editor-in-Chief: Greg Wiegand

Executive Editor: Rick Kughen

Development Editor:
Brandon Cackowski-Schnell

Managing Editor: Sandra Schroeder

Project Editor: Mandie Frank

Copy Editor: Cheri Clark

Indexer: Lisa Stumpf

Proofreader: Debbie Williams

Technical Editor: Tim Shriver

Editorial Assistant: Cindy Teeters

Designer: Mark Shirar

Compositor: Jake McFarland

Contents at a Glance

Introduction   1

Chapter 1   Home Wiring and Electrical Fundamentals   7

Chapter 2   Using a Windows Computer as Your Home Automation Platform   33

Chapter 3   Introduction to Control Protocols and Automation Process   59

Chapter 4   Project 1, Installing HALbasic Software on Your PC   69

Chapter 5   Project 2, Controlling Appliances, Lights, and Devices   89

Chapter 6   Project 3, Controlling Lighting: Indoors and Outdoors   127

Chapter 7   Project 4, Linking Video to Your Security System   157

Chapter 8   Project 5, Upgrading the Home Automation Platform to HALultra   183

Chapter 9   Project 6, Installing a Home Automation Voice Portal Modem in Your Computer   191

Chapter 10   Project 7, Getting Green and Managing Your Home's Climate   207

Chapter 11   Project 8, Adding New Controllers and Interfaces: Z-Wave, INSTEON, and More   225

Chapter 12   Project 9, Automating the Home Entertainment Center's Music Management   241

Chapter 13   Project 10, Connecting and Using the Home Automation Platform over the Internet   257

Chapter 14   Controlling Your Home with iOS and Android   273

Chapter 15   Evaluating Broadband and Telecom Home Automation Offerings   287

Chapter 16   Adding Future Self-Designed Home Automation Projects   297

Index   305

DEC 15 2016

Table of Contents

Introduction   1

Value Proposition of a Central Home Automation Platform   2

Solving Place and Time Problems   2

Maximizing Convenience   2

The "Wow!" Factor   2

Neutralize Physical Challenges   2

Going GREEN (Getting to Reduced Energy Expenditure Now)   3

Safety and Security   3

How This Book Brings Automation to Your Home   3

Free HAL Software Download   4

About HALBasic   4

Chapter 1   Home Wiring and Electrical Fundamentals   7

Safety Tips   7

Terms to Know and Understand   10

DC (Direct Current)   11

AC (Alternating Current)   11

Single-Phase AC Circuits   12

Three-Phase AC Circuits   12

Transformer Connections   13

Delta-Connected Three-Phase Transformers   14

Wye-Connected Three-Phase Transformers   14

Ohm's Law and the Power Formula   15

Voltage (E)   16

Resistance (R)   16

Amperage (I)   16

Watts (P)   16

Watt Hours (kWh)   16

Power Distribution Transformers   17

Inverters   18

Converters   19

Household Electrical Power   19

Household AC Wiring and Devices   19

Hot Wire   20

Neutral Wire   20

Ground/Bonding Wire   20

Phone   24

Cable TV/Satellite   25

Microphones   25

Thermostats   25

Common Legacy Electric Controls   25

Switches   25

Dimmers and Dimmer Switches   29

Timers   29

Clock Timers   29

Motion Sensor Switches   30

Heat Sensor Switches   30

Alternative and Backup Power Sources   30

Battery Backup Power Supplies   30

Backup Generators   30

Definitive Information Source—NEC   30

Schematic Diagrams   31

Chapter 2   Using a Windows Computer as Your Home Automation Platform   33

Details and Choices   34

First Choice: Shared, Dedicated, or Networked?   35

Shared Computer Option   35

Dedicated Computer Option   35

Networked Computer Option   36

Second Choice: Buy Preconfigured or Build Your Own   36

Purchase a Preconfigured Home Automation PC   37

Have a Home Automation System Professionally Installed   37

Purchase a New or Used PC   37

Most Important Characteristics for Your Home Automation Platform   38

Computer Case   38

Computer Operating System   38

Processor (CPU)   39

Memory   40

Storage Drive(s)   41

I/O Ports   41

Optical Drive   41

Video Card   41

Ethernet Port   42

Monitor   42

Sound Card   42

Additional Hardware   43

Planning the Computer's Installation Location   43

Book Prototype Computer   43

Setting up Your Computer   45

Updating the Operating System Software   45

Updating the Security Software   51

Creating Recovery Media and Diagnostics   56

Surge Protection and Battery Backup   56

Chapter 3   Introduction to Control Protocols and Automation Process   59

Control Methods   59

Reasons for Using Automated Control   60

Time Based   60

Need Based   60

Event Based   61

Communication Based   61

Protocols and Standards   61

Physical-Layer Communication   62

Imposing Messages on the Physical Media   63

Automation Processes are Trigged by an Event   67

Process Actions   67

Chapter 4   Project 1, Installing HALbasic Software on Your PC   69

Starting Point   70

Security Software   70

Beginning the HALbasic Install   71

Modify OS Security Setting   72

HALbasic Installation Steps   75

Activation   82

Register with HAL   86

Exploring HALbasic   86

Chapter 5   Project 2, Controlling Appliances, Lights, and Devices   89

Connecting the Hardware   89

Connecting the Control Adapter to the PC   90

Setting up the Control Modules   93

Setting up Plug-in Control Modules 95

Setting up Hard-wired Outlet Control Modules 98

Configuring Control Modules Identities in HALbasic 100

Control—Time-Based Routines 115

Control—Voice Commands 122

Chapter 6   **Project 3, Controlling Lighting: Indoors and Outdoors**   **127**

Switching for Indoor and Outdoor Lighting Circuits 128

Existing Multilocation Switching 129

Deciphering Existing Home Wiring 131

Lighting Fixture Switched from a Single Location   *131*

Lighting Fixture Switched from Two Locations   *132*

Lighting Fixture Switched from Three Locations   *133*

Lighting Fixture Switched from Four or More Locations   *134*

Existing Home Wiring Adapted for UPB Controls 135

Single-Location UPB-Controlled Lighting Fixture   *135*

Two-Location UPB-Controlled Lighting Fixture   *138*

Three-Location UPB-Controlled Lighting Fixture   *139*

Making the Wiring Connections 143

Connecting the UPB Control Adapter to the PC 145

Setting up the UPB Control Modules   *147*

Configuring Control Modules' Identities in HALbasic   *148*

The Remote Wall Switches   *156*

Chapter 7   **Project 4, Linking Video to Your Security System**   **157**

Linking in HAL Video Capture Features 158

Surveillance Camera Selection 159

USB Cameras   *159*

Internet Protocol Security Cameras   *160*

Deciding How Many Cameras Are Needed 162

Installing and Locating the Cameras 162

The One-Web-Camera (USB) Solution 162

USB Camera Installation   *163*

The Multiple-Camera Solution 163

IP Ethernet Camera Installation   *164*

Assigning IP Addresses for Cameras on Your Network   *171*

Registering the Cameras in HALdvc Setup   *173*

Setting Up Camera Security Actions with HALultra 178

Chapter 8   **Project 5, Upgrading the Home Automation Platform to HALultra   183**

Upgrading to HALultra   184

Administrative Steps   184

Back Up HALbasic   184

Installing   186

Activating   187

Testing   187

Explore New Features   189

Chapter 9   **Project 6, Installing a Home Automation Voice Portal Modem in Your Computer   191**

Installing the Voice Portal Modem   193

Connecting the Voice Portal in the Operating System   197

Voice Portal Installation with the HAL Setup Wizard   199

Chapter 10   **Project 7, Getting Green and Managing Your Home's Climate   207**

Getting Green   207

Managing Temperature and Energy Consumption   207

Heating and Cooling System Links   208

On/Off Devices   208

Thermostats   208

Deploying Gauges, "Triggers," and Sensors   209

Using Time-Based Heating/Cooling Control   209

Installing a HALultra-Compatible Thermostat   210

Installing an In-line Fan/Light Control   216

Setting up the Interface in HALultra   218

Chapter 11   **Project 8, Adding New Controllers and Interfaces: Z-Wave, INSTEON, and More   225**

Additional Interfaces for HALultra   225

ZigBee   225

Infrared   226

HVAC   227

Security   228

Input/Output   229

INSTEON   229

Z-Wave   229

Setting up a Z-Wave Network   232

Using a Laptop with the Leviton RF Installer Tool   233

Chapter 12 Project 9, Automating the Home Entertainment Center's Music Management   241

The Changing Landscape of Home Electronics   241

Select Sound Reproduction Equipment   242

Digital Sound Reproduction Quality   242

Digital Music File Formats   243

Download and Install HALdmc   246

Setting Up HALdmc   246

Using HALdmc   250

Using Voice Commands with the Digital Music Center   254

Chapter 13 Project 10, Connecting and Using the Home Automation Platform over the Internet   257

Preparing the Internet/Intranet Connection for HALultra   257

Internet Service   258

Setup and Tweaks on the Modem-Router-Firewall-Switch   258

Setting up the HomeNet Server   259

Enabling the HomeNet Web Server   259

Logging In to HomeNet   262

Using HAL on the Internet   262

Collecting Internet Data   262

Viewing Internet Data Collected by HAL   268

Controlling HAL over the Web   270

Chapter 14 Controlling Your Home with iOS and Android   273

Interactive Device Server Applications   273

Apple App   274

Android App   274

Using Smart Phones and Tablets to Control HAL   274

Enabling the "Interactive Device Server"   274

Using HALids with iOS   275

Using HALids with Android   281

Checking the IDS Log   285

Chapter 15 Evaluating Broadband and Telecom Home Automation Offerings   287

Selection Criteria for Monitoring and Managed Service Providers   288

Market Service Area   288

Proprietary Technology   288

PC or Controller Based   289

Initial Installation Cost   289

Cost Model 1   290

Cost Model 2   290

Cost Model 3   290

Cost Model 4   290

Monthly Service Fees   291

Commitment Term   291

Level of Ongoing Service Support   291

Installer Competence and Tech Support Quality   291

Monitoring/Management Center Location   292

What Is Being Monitored?   292

What Is Being Managed Versus Offered?   293

Miscellaneous Concerns   294

Expected Future Offerings   294

Mainstream Companies with HA and Monitoring Systems or Services   294

Chapter 16   Adding Future Self-Designed Home Automation Projects   297

Design Steps   297

Popular Home Automation System Add-ons   299

Growing Your Automation System with Additional UPB Devices   299

Expanding the Reach of Your Control with INSTEON Controls and Kits   300

Enlarging the Control Zone with Additional Z-Wave Devices   301

Remoting with IR   302

Improving Security Reactions with Interfaces to Home Automation   302

Setup Correlations   302

Summation   303

Index   305

About the Author

Dennis C. Brewer is a technology enthusiast who has been associated with electrical and electronic projects since attending Washington Middle School in Calumet, Michigan.

His early technology experience included testing for and receiving an FCC commercial radio broadcast engineer license that allowed him to become a solo station operator announcer/engineer for WMPL AM/FM radio in Hancock, Michigan,. and finished service as a Chief Petty Officer Interior Communications Electrician to pursue a Bachelor of Science degree.

Dennis attended Michigan Technological University (MTU) and served simultaneous membership in the Michigan Army National Guard as a communication Sergeant First Class and a Cadet in the Michigan Technological University Army ROTC program. Upon graduation he was commissioned and a first Lieutenant, Combat Engineer Branch US Army Reserve.

Mr. Brewer's employment in government service included the State of Michigan as a computer technology specialist with assignments in the Department of Military and Veterans Affairs, Department of Management and Budget, and Department of Information Technology. During his 12-year career in State of Michigan Government as a Novell (CNE) certified network engineer and information technology specialist, his experience included hands-on hardware, administration, network management and troubleshooting, consulting and planning services for state agencies, establishment of enterprise-level standards and procedures implementation, data security, and identity management. After retiring from state government, Dennis continued to pursue his interests in technology as an author and independent consultant.

Published books by Dennis C. Brewer include:

Build Your Own Free-to-Air (FTA) Satellite TV System, by Dennis C. Brewer (McGraw-Hill: Nov 8, 2011)

Wiring Your Digital Home For Dummies, by Dennis C. Brewer and Paul A. Brewer (For Dummies/Wiley: Oct 9, 2006)

Security Controls for Sarbanes-Oxley Section 404 IT Compliance: Authorization, Authentication, and Access, by Dennis C. Brewer (Wiley: Oct 21, 2005)

Picture Yourself Networking Your Home or Small Office, by Dennis C. Brewer (Course Technology PTR: Dec 2, 2008)

Green My Home!: 10 Steps to Lowering Energy Costs and Reducing Your Carbon Footprint, by Dennis C. Brewer (Kaplan Publishing: Oct 7, 2008)

His magazine writing credits include topics on disaster recovery, defining adequate security controls, free satellite TV, and Sarbanes-Oxley controls.

For more information about this author and his current technology and writing projects, visit http://www.DennisCBrewer.info.

Dedication

This book is dedicated to individuals who face mobility challenges of any kind with everyday living; particularly those individuals who sacrificed for their nation during times when leadership, foreign policy, and diplomacy failed.

Acknowledgments

I'd especially like to thank the persons, instructors, and professors who made a positive impact on my education as a writer and as a critically thinking person. There are many, but among the many are a few who made a significant and memorable contribution. The first of these is my mother, Verna W. (Sembla) Brewer [1910–2006], who taught me to read as a very young child from the pages of the *Daily Mining Gazette* while sitting on her knee. My father, Leslie Brewer [1903–1951], who sacrificed to make sure I had access to volumes of the classics at home. Fast-forward to my time at Michigan Technological University (MTU) to thank and recognize the person from whom I received the first sincerely positive and constructive feedback on a piece of my writing: Arlene Jara Strickland, an instructor in a freshman Humanities class. I also wish to confer thanks to Professor George Love (MTU), who taught me to appreciate the full communicative power of the words found in our English language. Sincere thanks are also due to Melissa Ford Lucken, who provided post-college lessons in creative writing and taught me the intricate anatomy of good stories and the elements necessary for a respectable book, and provided a personal example as someone who not only professes the skills of writing but also is a very accomplished author in her own right.

My thanks go out to, and this book is dedicated to, those who helped in so many ways to make it a success. My agent Carole Jelen at Waterside Productions. Tim Schriver, the CEO at Home Automated Living and Technical Editor of this text. Rick Kughen, the acquisition editor for knowing there was a need for this book. Many thanks to the entire Pearson/ Que editing and production team, including: Mandie Frank, Project Editor; Todd Brakke, Development Editor; Brandon Cackowski-Schnell, Development Editor; Cheri Clark, Copy Editor; Jake McFarland, Layout; Debbie Williams, Proofreader; and so on for turning my rambling text into a respectable book. Thanks everyone.

We Want to Hear from You!

As the reader of this book, *you* are our most important critic and commentator. We value your opinion and want to know what we're doing right, what we could do better, what areas you'd like to see us publish in, and any other words of wisdom you're willing to pass our way.

We welcome your comments. You can email or write to let us know what you did or didn't like about this book—as well as what we can do to make our books better.

Please note that we cannot help you with technical problems related to the topic of this book.

When you write, please be sure to include this book's title and author as well as your name and email address. We will carefully review your comments and share them with the author and editors who worked on the book.

Email: feedback@quepublishing.com

Mail: Que Publishing
         ATTN: Reader Feedback
         800 East 96th Street
         Indianapolis, IN 46240 USA

Reader Services

Visit our website and register this book at quepublishing.com/register for convenient access to any updates, downloads, or errata that might be available for this book.

Introduction

The term "home automation" or its inverse "automated home" may mean different things to each reader. Some homeowners would think of one-off devices such as time clocks controlling a lamp as home automation. Others would consider home automation to be a managed service, essentially a virtual "big brother" that monitors events in the home and makes adjustments when necessary. Others would envision high-end systems where a virtual Jeeves handles all of the repetitive chores. None of these views would be wrong. However for the purpose of this book, home automation is made easy for the do-it-yourselfer by employing computer software that will become the artificial intelligence to manage controllable tasks through currently available technologies. The projects in this book will allow a DIYer the opportunity to have that high-end home automation system one increment at a time and expand his or her system as time and budget permits.

There are about four million households in the United States using some level of partially to fully integrated home automation features.

This is a surprisingly small number given how long these features have been available to the consumer. We use our voice to control our phones, so why not use it to control the entire home?

For many decades it has been possible, even easy, to control one-off devices such as lights, thermostats, and appliances with single, non-integrated automatic and remote controls. On the one hand, these one-off automation devices save effort and energy, but on the other hand, even modest adjustments are inconvenient and require the user to be present and knowledgeable enough to make the change. In the past consumers have expressed a reluctance to adopt home automation technologies because of a lack of a standard solution that can be extended to perform every task they might envision. Implementing twenty-first-century home automation with the projects described in this book can eliminate a majority of the negative issues associated with one-off remote control devices and bring full automation and increased levels of control to nearly all the fixtures, equipment, and appliances in the home. Best of all, this platform is centralized and extensible, and it can interface with nearly all the latest control technologies.

Value Proposition of a Central Home Automation Platform

Home automation features are no longer reserved only for the wealthy or highly technical. Anyone with a few hundred dollars, a Windows computer, and some time can leverage this technology into their living space. Why take this step? What's to gain? The benefits, as you're about to read, are numerous and wide-ranging!

Solving Place and Time Problems

Have you ever wanted to make your home look lived in while you were away on vacation for a week? The old solution was a lamp and a clock timer switch to turn the lamp on and off at preset times. Over a few days this routine turning on and off can be noted by someone with ill intent, leaving your home vulnerable with little psychological deterrent to trespass or break into your home. It is difficult with ordinary controls to overcome the problem of being away from home. Automation allows you to manage many aspects of your home environment, from any location in the world, with phone/cell phone service, by speaking simple voice commands.

Maximizing Convenience

Some home dwellers do not mind the drill of operating everything manually, whereas others want to maximize convenience and save time. After your home automation platform is in place, you can eventually control nearly every electrical appliance and electronic convenience in the home. Security systems, watering systems, entertainment systems, and more can all be conveniently controlled by programmed routine or modified as needed by an event or a voice command.

The "Wow!" Factor

Being the first in your neighborhood to automate your home might be more fun than being the first one in the area to install a home theater system. This is technology that brings "oohs" and "aahs" from viewers who have seen it on TV. Just imagine how your guests will be impressed when you say a command such as, "House: TV on," or, "House: tune to Weather Channel," and it happens in an instant. There is a perception, however, that something this cool and technologically involved must be way too difficult or expensive to do. It is not difficult or expensive, and readers of this book will learn that anyone who can handle a pair of pliers and a screwdriver, operate a computer keyboard, and pay attention to some details and safety rules can easily implement this technology in their home or office by following the projects covered in this book.

Neutralize Physical Challenges

If you are an able-bodied adult, it might be difficult to fully appreciate how difficult it can be for some physically challenged home occupants to perform a task as simple as turning on a light switch. For those readers who are faced with mobility or dexterity challenges the idea of living in a fully automated home can add extra value. Voice-controlled home automation features can bring efficiency and added independence.

Going GREEN (Getting to Reduced Energy Expenditure Now)

All the functions intrinsic to home life use costly energy either directly or indirectly. Each home and the occupants' lifestyles set a baseline of energy consumption that cannot be reduced without modifications to the home or drastic changes in the occupants' habits. The remaining margin of energy consumption contains a usually substantial portion that can be more efficiently managed with home automation features. Within the automated home, energy costs can be minimized by leveraging all the home automation features that directly or indirectly impact energy use. These features are used to ensure that the energy used in the household does not go unnecessarily wasted.

Safety and Security

Achieving the maximum level of safety and security in a home has moved way beyond the timer and lamp stage to give a home a lived-in look. Smart phones and the Internet can now be tied into the home automation communications loop to allow for system control from anywhere in the world for nearly instantaneous feedback when something goes awry.

How This Book Brings Automation to Your Home

This book is written for the total novice to home automation.

This book covers wiring basics and safety before moving on to preparing your PC for home automation software, installing the HALbasic home automation platform, and leveraging this software to control X-10, UPB, and other devices for various home automation needs. If you don't know what all of that means, don't worry. You will. After you have your projects complete, I cover touch-controlling your home from your smart phone and tablet, as well as automation services offered by telecom and broadband companies.

This book concentrates on being a reference for the ordinary homeowner to understand home automation technology and provides hands-on instruction for 10 do-it-yourself home automation projects.

With HAL Automated Living software as the core control software, anyone with a computer and a modest budget for controls should be able to begin the tasks necessary to automate some functions in their home. This title is focused on getting the information, getting the parts/pieces together, and getting home automation projects done. Hopefully you'll have some fun along the way and the taste of home automation that this book provides will spur your imagination on to further automation projects.

Free HAL Software Download

Congratulations! Your purchase of this book entitles you to a FREE, no obligation, fully functional home automation program, HALBasic—an $89 value!

To download your free copy:

1. Make sure that you have your book in hand or open on your e-reader, then visit http://www.automatedliving.com/QueBasic.aspx.

2. You will be asked to flip to a random page number and supply a piece of information from that page. For example, it might ask you to enter the last word that appears in the third paragraph from the top of the page. The challenge questions are randomly generated.

> **Note** **There is a Time Limit** You have two minutes from the time the challenge question is asked to enter the correct answer. If you do not enter the correct answer, you are redirected to the main HAL page and must start over.

3. After you have entered the correct answer, you are taken to a shopping cart page where you will see the free version HALbasic with a cost of $0 in your cart.

4. Complete the checkout procedure, during which time you will enter an email address to which a link to download the software will be sent.

5. When the email arrives, open it, click the link and download your free software.

About HALBasic

Home Automated Living (HAL) provides consumers with the freedom to control their homes and all the wonderful technology within by voice or by Internet from anywhere.

To achieve that goal, HAL produces software and hardware at affordable prices that enable the consumer to speak to the technologies in the home—whether traditional technologies like lights, appliances, security, and thermostats—or new technologies like IP Cameras, digital music, and Energy management hardware.

HAL software taps the power of your existing PC to control your home. Once HAL is installed on your PC, it can send commands all over your house using the existing highway of electrical wires inside your home's walls or wirelessly using radio signals. No new wires means HAL is easy and inexpensive to install.

HAL's voice interface makes HAL easy to use. You can pick up any phone in the home, press the # key, and then tell HAL to dim the dining room lights or close the garage door. It's a two-way conversation, with HAL confirming that it has, indeed, performed the requested action.

HAL turns your PC into a personal Voice Portal. Is there an easier way to turn on the front door lights when you're returning home late at night than to call ahead and tell HAL, "Turn on the front door lights"? With HAL, any phone—anywhere in the world—enables you to step inside your home and control it as if you were there. And you can ask HAL to read you your email, give you a stock quote, or a sports score or a TV listing—because HAL automatically harvests Internet information for use when you want it.

HAL makes home control affordable for everyone. Users can choose the HAL product with the appropriate feature set to deploy as little or as much home control as they want. Choose among products that will allow users to control lights, appliances, devices, tele-phones, home theatre, security, and the Internet. HAL will schedule your house to suit the way you live.

HAL's HomeNet web interface enables you to control and interact with your home from any browser. HAL also has interfaces for Android and Apple iOS devices, giving you added control from anywhere.

HAL has been featured on popular television shows and networks, such as *Modern Marvels*, *Extreme Makeover*, *Oprah*, *Man Cave*, *Home & Garden TV*, *The Learning Channel* and others.

HAL software has won numerous awards such as "Best of CES," "Mark of Excellence," and "Coolest Product" to name a few.

HAL is also part of the Smithsonian Institution's Permanent Research Collection on Information Technology Innovation.

Chapter 1

Home Wiring and Electrical Fundamentals

This chapter is intended for those with very little understanding or experience working with electrical circuits and installing end-use devices. It covers some basics about safety and gives a brief primer on electricity. This chapter provides an understanding of how the home automation devices work with your home's wiring to achieve your home automation control goals. It is not possible to cover all the details of electricity as used in homes in one chapter, but this chapter can provide a basic understanding of electrical terms sufficient to tackle the projects outlined in this book.

Even if you intend to hire a professional electrical contractor, it is still nice to have some basic knowledge to improve your communications with the contractors and technicians doing the installation. Taking the time to read this section will also give you some insights to both the challenges and the opportunities for automated controls available in your existing home wiring system.

Safety Tips

One should respect, but not fear, electricity while always exercising due caution when working with it.

Safety begins with proper thinking about avoiding or minimizing inherent risks regardless of the activity. Working with electricity can be dangerous; it can kill you, burn you, shock you, or even trigger a heart attack—always respect its power. For starters, as a novice, you should always turn off the power to the circuit or device before you touch any part of the wires or connections.

To improve your chances of avoiding injury when working with electrical circuits and devices, first apply the following four safety steps to each task in the project:

- **Think things through**—Ask yourself what could go wrong and take steps to prevent these things from happening or take steps to minimize their impact.

- **Visualize**—Imagine going through each step of each task before you begin it, and ask what could go wrong.

- **Reduce risks**—Take steps to reduce or eliminate those things that can go wrong from your mental list of potential risks before you begin to do the work.

- **Take deliberately measured actions**—Think it through and then do; take your time between tasks and subtasks and evaluate your level of safety as you go.

As a homeowner, you'll find that there is rarely, if ever, any reason to work with energized electrical circuits in your house. Before installing any switches or outlets, isolate the circuit you are working on and either turn off the circuit breaker or remove the fuse to ensure that the power is off before handling the wires or making new connections. *Almost all manufacturers warn against wiring a device while the circuit is still energized "hot," for safety reasons as well as to avoid potentially causing damage to the switch or device being installed.*

There are a few ways you can go about being sure you have turned off the breaker or have removed the fuse for the circuit you intend to work on. For example, if you are working on replacing a light switch, use the switch to turn on the lights; then go to the fuse box or breaker box and turn off the breakers or unscrew the fuses one at a time until the lights go out. After you have identified and turned off the circuit breaker, tag it as "turned off" so that no one else will turn it on. Putting a piece of tape holding the breaker in the off position will also discourage anyone else from turning the breaker back on. A similar approach can be used to identify an outlet that you might want to upgrade to a control device. Plug in any electrical device and turn it on, go to the breaker box, and turn off breakers or unscrew the fuses until the device turns off. To be confident that you got it right, you might want to repeat the process twice. Another way to be sure is to use a multimeter as shown in Figure 1.1 to measure the voltage before and after you have the circuit's breaker off: It should be zero volts when you turn off the circuit breaker in the distribution panel. Set the scale switches on the meter to AC 250 volts to have the proper scale to measure the voltage. The expected voltage on a house circuit in the United States is between 110 and 120 volts. Be sure to use the proper setting because using too low a setting on the multimeter can ruin the meter.

Figure 1.2 shows the meter's probes in an outlet and the meter reading of 117 volts. If you get an abnormal reading, say, way above 120 or below 90 volts, that would be cause to seek out a licensed professional to find the problem. Also, if you insert the probes with one on the neutral (the wider connection in the outlet) and the other on the circular bonding connection, the voltage must be zero: any reading above zero identifies a problem that will need a licensed electrician to find and correct.

Figure 1.1   *An inexpensive multimeter purchased from nearly any hardware store for under $20.00.*

As shown in Figure 1.2, the meter's probes are in the outlet slots and the meter is showing a reading of 117 volts. Before you can safely work on any circuit, the voltage reading must be confirmed to be zero or no voltage. With the circuit turned off and tagged out of service, it is safe to remove a standard outlet and replace it with an appliance or a lamp control outlet. More details on this procedure can be found in later chapters.

If you are not comfortable doing any of this type of work, hire a licensed electrician to make the connections and install the new devices for you. Maintaining your personal safety throughout the duration of your home automation projects is the most important task you have.

Figure 1.2 *Notice that the voltage reading is 117 volts AC on the meter.*

Terms to Know and Understand

Trade jargon can be overwhelming to someone new to the field. Home automation is no exception, because doing HA projects crosses over parts of many trades so there are some terms that would be nice to know and understand as you plan out and do your home automation projects. The list presented next is a good start for getting some HA jargon into your personal lexicon.

At the simplest level, an electrical current is the flow of electrons through a circuit. When we talk about amperage and voltage, what we're talking about is the number of electrons in motion (the current) and the pressure of the electrons in motion (the voltage). In order for electrons to flow through a substance, it needs to be a conductor. In the case of your home's wiring, the most common conductor is copper; however, aluminum is also used in some circumstances. If you think about the flow of electricity as similar to the flow of water, it becomes easy to visualize where the flow is going and what needs to be in place to let this flow continue.

DC (Direct Current)

DC is shorthand for direct current. A flashlight battery, a car battery, and the battery in your cell phone store and produce direct current electricity. Direct current flows in one direction through a conductor. DC flows from a source that is oversupplied with electrons to a place that is undersupplied. The two plates in a battery provide the source and the destination for the electrons. One plate has extra electrons and the other plate is undersupplied. In your flashlight the electrons flow from the negative plate though the light bulb and then come to rest on the positive plate completing the circuit. Car batteries and other rechargeable batteries are resupplied with extra electrons by forcing the current to flow in the opposite direction, again creating an oversupply of electrons on the negative plate. The recharged battery can be used as an energy source again. Over time the plates in rechargeable batteries become contaminated from use and will no longer be fully rechargeable. If you were to graph DC with an oscilloscope, it would appear on the scope screen as a steady straight line at some voltage above zero, as shown in the graph in Figure 1.3.

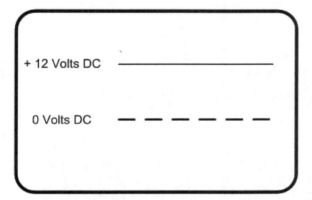

Figure 1.3 *The graph show DC at 12 volts, represented by a straight solid line.*

AC (Alternating Current)

AC is the shorthand term for alternating current. The power plant supplying energy to your house uses alternating current generators. Unlike DC from batteries, which always flows in one direction through a conductor, AC flows first in one direction and then another, meaning that the polarity is reversed at some determined interval. In the United States that cycling of AC electricity is 60 times per second. It is therefore called 60 cycle AC current. If you were to graph AC with an oscilloscope, it would appear on the scope screen as a sine wave line peaking at some voltage above zero and then alternating to the same voltage below zero, as shown in the graph in Figure 1.4. This phenomenon in which for a moment in time the voltage is zero is important to running control signals over a home's existing wiring. This point where there is no source electricity flowing just as the decay to zero occurs provides an opportunity in time to induce a control signal on the home's wiring that the control devices can recognize and act on.

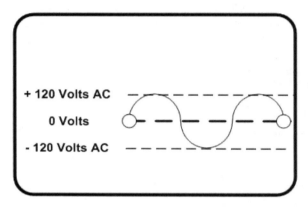

Figure 1.4   *One-and-a-half cycles of single-phase AC house current at 120 volts as it would appear on an oscilloscope screen.*

Note   AC or DC?   The dominant electrical power in your home is alternating current with available nominal voltages of 120 and 240 volts. Major power appliances such as electric stoves, electric clothes dryers, and electric water heaters are often powered by 240-volt circuits.

Single-Phase AC Circuits

Single-phase electric power is created in a two-wire circuit when the north and the south pole of a single magnet are passed across a single coil of wire in the generator, creating the AC power discussed in the preceding section. Household circuits predominately use single-phase AC power.

Three-Phase AC Circuits

Three-phase power is created when a generator has three coils in the generator's stator, and the north and south poles of the rotating field magnetic coils pass by them in turn.

The physical layout within the generator's stator would typically separate the three independent coils by some number of degrees of rotation, and therefore the current that is produced is also typically separated by 120 degrees if graphed. There are two common ways to wire in and connect three-phase power in the distribution lines, in the line transformers, and at the building or home's point of service. Figure 1.5 is a representation of three-phase electric currents as they would appear on an oscilloscope screen.

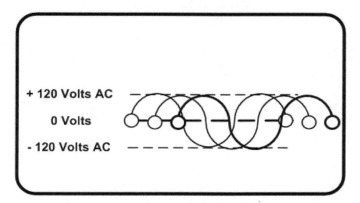

Figure 1.5 *One-and-a-half cycles of three phases of AC current as it would appear on an oscilloscope screen.*

Three-phase power is frequently used to supply energy to large high-torque motors such as air compressors or on large air conditioners. It is rare for three-phase AC to be used to power residential houses but is fairly common in offices and commercial buildings. Bringing automation into the three-phase environment presents some challenges with some of the technologies, such as with legacy X-10 installations. In any case, it is important to know whether any of your projects will be implemented in a three-phase AC power environment.

Transformer Connections

Transformers are used to change voltage and current ratings on a large power distribution system, to reduce the voltage for your home electrical service, or to provide a needed voltage level within an electrical or electronic device. Single phase transformers are simple and have only two coils or windings. One of those windings, the supply side, is connected to the source of electric power. The secondary, or load side, is connected to power the load. Three-phase distribution systems can use one of two connection schemes, because each of the three phases requires its own supply and load coils within the transformer or three separate transformers are used. The two connection schemes for three-phase transformers are called Delta and Wye.

Delta-Connected Three-Phase Transformers

In a delta three-phase transformer connection the ends of the coils are connected as shown in Figure 1.6 to form a triangle. When this configuration is used at a building service entrance, one of the transformer's coils is center tapped to produce 120/240 VAC (volts AC).

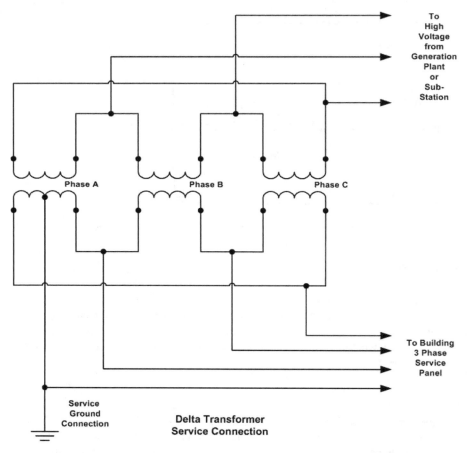

Figure 1.6   *This diagram represents the delta connected transformer configuration.*

Wye-Connected Three-Phase Transformers

In wye-connected generators, and the same is true for transformers, one end of each of the coils of the three-phase stator is connected together. At the typical home service entrance this wye connection method results in a voltage of 120/208 volts instead of the

120/240 as shown in the transformer setup for three-phase wye-connected transformers providing a building service, as shown in Figure 1.7. When the phase-to-ground voltage is measured, it will be a nominal 120 volts AC. When the phase-to-phase wire voltage is measured, it will be a nominal 208 volts AC because the reading is the collective non-competing energy of the two coils as the net result shown on the meter.

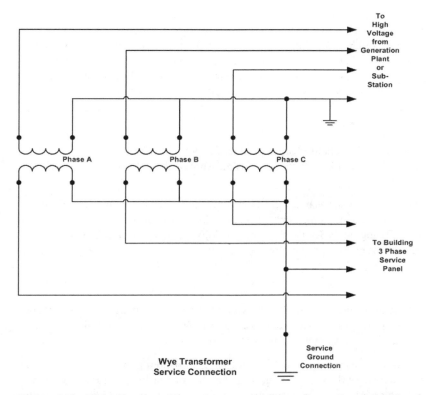

Figure 1.7   *This diagram shows the connection configuration for 120-volt secondary windings on the three-phase service.*

Fortunately, for simplicity and economy reasons most homes and small apartments are powered by single-phase alternating current circuits.

Ohm's Law and the Power Formula

Electricity in a circuit always behaves by a set of rules that can be quantified mathematically by Ohm's law:

$E = I \times R$, or $I = E/R$, or $R = E/I$

Ohm's law expresses in mathematical terms how those moving electrons behave in an electrical circuit. In the next few sections the most common terms are explained.

Voltage (E)

Voltage is the term used to express the relative force of the electricity available in a circuit. It is a measure of the force the electrons carry. If you think of a circuit as a water hose, with electrons as the water, voltage would be the water pressure. One volt (1.0 volts) is the basic unit of measure of electrical force.

Resistance (R)

As electrons flow through a material, it is easier or harder for them to move from atom to atom depending on the characteristics of the material. When the electrons find it harder to move though a conductor, they are said to encounter resistance. This resistance to the flow of electrons is measured in ohms.

Amperage (I)

An amp (ampere) is the basic unit of measurement to show the relative volume of electricity in a circuit; essentially, it is an instantaneous measure of the volume of electrons moving though the circuit.

There are thought to be twice as many electrons moving though a two-amp circuit as compared to a circuit drawing one amp of power. Think of this as a measure of the rate at which the work is being done. To use the water analogy, amperage would be similar to a flow rate expressed as gallons per minute.

Watts (P)

Power (in watts) = amperage (I) multiplied by voltage (E). If you substitute terms algebraically between the power formula and the basic Ohm's law formula, most unknowns can be calculated from any two known variables about the circuit.

Power consumption in electrical circuits and devices is measured in watts. One volt moving one amp of electricity through a circuit is using one watt of power. It is an instantaneous measurement of the rate of consumption of electricity. In your home, a light bulb might be rated between 40 and 60 watts and a hair dryer might be rated at 2100 watts.

Watt Hours (kWh)

Unlike watts, which are instantaneous measurements, watt hours are a measure of how much electricity is being consumed over a period of time. Electricity is metered and billed to your house using kilowatt hours. Kilowatt hours, abbreviated kWh, means that over the course of one hour, 1000 watts were consumed or any combination that reaches 1000. For example, if you were not home and just left 500 watts' worth of lighting on, it would take two hours to consume a kilowatt hour of electricity. It would be typical for a four-person household to average about 888 kWh per month, or about 30 kWh per day. Figure 1.8 shows a typical watt hour meter for a residential home.

Figure 1.8 *This meter shows that the dwelling has used 64214 kWh since its installation.*

As we look at ways to use home automation features to reduce energy usage in future chapters, it is a good idea to quantify your annual and each month's average home energy consumption to establish a baseline for later comparison. It is better to not use a dollar amount for comparison because prices fluctuate over time. Always use kWh for electricity and gallons for propane and cubic feet for natural gas.

Having a basic understanding of Ohm's law and the Power Formula allows you to calculate for the unknowns in a circuit and help make needed calculations for component size and specifications.

Power Distribution Transformers

The purpose of transformers is to change the voltage and current in an electrical power delivery system. Due to the impracticality of distributing the low-voltage electricity used in your home over large distances, transformers are used to transform the high-voltage electricity leaving the power plant or substation into the low-voltage electricity used in your home.

Figure 1.9 shows a 25 kVA transformer with two service drops to two homes connected to the same transformer. With some home automation technologies this type of connection can cause the signals to "bleed over" or "cross talk" to actuate a neighbor's control device, such as a lamp or an appliance module. Sharing the transformer is the cause of this issue when nearby homes are automated with similar technologies and the neighbor's house lights respond to your "all lights on command" or vice versa. There are work-arounds if you become aware of this problem. Begin exploring workarounds by coordinating your house codes with the neighbor so you are using different codes. The extreme fix is to move to a different control protocol.

Figure 1.9   *A 25 kVA transformer with two service drops connected to two neighboring homes.*

Note   One Final Note About Transformers   In some neighborhoods, transformers can support multiple homes via underground wires. As we discussed before, if those other homes are also using home automation technology, cross talk between your system and their system can occur. To prevent such a thing from happening, contact your electrical company to find out whether your home shares a transformer with other homes.

Inverters

Inverters are electronic devices that take power from DC batteries and create AC voltages with either true sine wave form or modified (saw tooth) sine wave electrical power. Common input voltages would be 12 or 24 volts DC from a storage battery and common outputs would be 120 or 240 volts AC to run electronics in your house or motor home. Inverters are rated for how many watts they will handle under a constant load.

The job of an inverter device is to make AC electrical power from a DC power source such as an automobile battery or RV "house" battery. Many road warriors plug small inverters into the cigarette lighter outlet in their automobile to supply AC power to a notebook or laptop power supply.

Controlling circuits supplied by an inverter generally requires that the control module be plugged into that circuit. Be sure that your inverter is a pure sine wave inverter and not a modified sine wave inverter when using home automation control devices for inverter supplied lamps and appliance. RVs and remote camps and cabins are often powered by inverters. Off the grid power installations generate DC to store in batteries and use inverters to supply the standard household appliances and electronics.

Converters

The work of a converter is to provide DC power for charging batteries or powering low voltage DC circuits and devices from an AC power source. Converters are used in travel trailers and motor homes to recharge the batteries and supply power to DC lights and appliances. Your cell phone is recharged by a very small converter when you plug it in at home.

Household Electrical Power

Homes in the U.S. are typically serviced by single-phase 60-cycle AC power with available nominal voltages of 120/240 volts at amperage ratings between 60 and 200 amps. The most common service is 100-amp electrical service. A smaller percentage of homes are supplied by three-phase power offering available voltages of 120/208 or 120/240. Countries with 220-volt 50 cycles typically have only the one voltage available in single phase.

Always check the specification when using a new appliance, device, or home-electronics product to make sure that its specifications match your available electrical power.

Household AC Wiring and Devices

If you have ever looked at your household wiring, you might have seen plastic-coated cable with three copper or aluminum wires inside of it. The correct term for this wiring product is "nonmetallic sheathed cable." It is often referred to by its trademark brand Romex. Those wires are color-coded by the sheathing on the individual strands of wire. Most frequently the wires are black, white, and either bare metal or green. The color-coding when the cable is properly installed to the NEC code on a household circuit tells you the purpose of the wire. A striped and peeled-back nonmetallic sheathed cable ready to be wired to an outlet is shown in Figure 1.10.

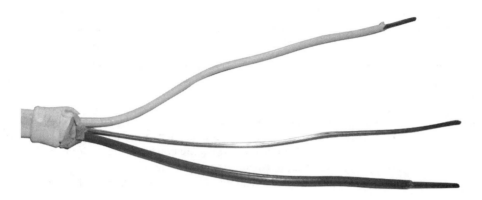

Figure 1.10   *Wires in a nonmetallic sheathed cable.*

Hot Wire

The hot wire, AKA the current-carrying conductor in household circuits, is typically black, red, or blue in prewrapped cables. The same color-coding applies generally speaking when wires are run in metallic or nonmetallic conduits. Nonmetallic sheathed cable that has a total of four wires, one red, one black, one white, and one bare, is used frequently for 240-volt circuits.

Neutral Wire

The neutral wire is color-coded white and provides the return path for the electrical power flowing through the load. The load refers to any electrical device drawing electricity from the circuit.

Ground/Bonding Wire

The purpose of the bonding wire (sometimes inappropriately called the ground wire) is to help prevent electrical shock and to blow the fuse or shut off the circuit breaker when the circuit is overloaded by drawing too much amperage. Overloading a circuit means that a device faulted out and could cause damage or start a fire. The bonding wire in household circuits is a bare wire or is color-coded with a green sheath. Under normal operation of an electrical circuit supplying power to a device or an appliance, there is no current flowing through the bonding wire. If there is current through the bonding wire, it means there is a problem with the connected device or an error in the wiring. This will become important in the discussion of GFCI outlets in later sections.

There is a lot of unnecessary confusion between grounding and bonding. Antennas, satellite dishes, and other outdoor equipment such as FM or Wi-Fi antennas need to be grounded with a ground wire in the event that lightning bolts strike them or objects nearby. That energy from the lightning, unless brought to ground potential, can do great damage and harm. The confusion comes in with the term bonding wire simply because in a properly wired home or building the service neutral and the bonding wire are both connected to ground. Although the bonding wire is at ground potential when properly installed, its purpose is to bond stray currents back to the service neutral to help trip a breaker or fuse or to protect an occupant using equipment from electrical shock when there is a fault on the equipment.

Circuit Loading

Circuits in your home are protected from overloading with circuit breakers or fuses. The circuit breakers are rated for carrying a certain number of amps. Common amp ratings are 10, 15, 20, and 30. When a circuit is overloaded by appliances or devices or if a fault occurs, the circuit breaker will trip. Circuits should not be loaded at their full capacity and a margin of 10 to 20 percent of the rated current should not be exceeded. To find the number of amps you are connecting to a household 120-volt circuit, add up the watt ratings of all the lights and appliances that will be connected to or plugged into that circuit and divide by 110 volts.

Compare your result with the circuit breaker's rating to ensure that your loading of the circuit is under the rating of the breaker or fuse.

GFCI/GFI

Although *GFCI* (ground-fault circuit interrupter) is technically the correct term, *GFCI* and *GFI* (ground-fault interrupter) are used interchangeably. The GFCI feature shuts off the flow of electricity whenever a fraction of the power on the downstream circuit cannot be measured as returning on the neutral wire. This means that some of the electrical power is escaping from the conductors or the appliance or power tool on that circuit. The circuit cutoff point for a GFCI device occurs when the energy difference between the hot (current-carrying) conductor and the neutral conductor approaches five milliamps. That means that some of the electrical energy has found an alternative return path to the service ground. Anyone on that path runs the risk of electrocution.

There are three common circumstances in which a GFCI will trip the circuit to off status: (1) A person or some other path to ground has come in contact with the hot (current-carrying) conductor, (2) the device, tool, or appliance is faulting from a short (unintended circuit) to the case, or (3) water has found its way to a conductor and is providing a path for some of the electricity. A fourth but uncommon circumstance in which a GFCI will trip off is when a GFCI is used on the end of a long cord and another long cord is plugged in to provide power to the load. It is an anomaly but it does happen.

This GFCI feature is intended to save lives and prevent injury when humans inadvertently become part of an electric circuit. The National Electric Code dictates where GFCI must be used in new construction and in remodels/rehabs to meet code requirements. Homeowners can choose to add GFCI devices in situations not dictated by code. Do not replace a GFCI outlet with a home automation controlled outlet; you will lose the GFCI protection, subjecting yourself and other residents to dangerous electrical shock.

If a GFCI is to be automated, it must be a GFCI-protected "downstream outlet" or supplied by a GFCI circuit breaker. Never replace a GFCI outlet such as one found in a bathroom with an automated control device because you will lose the GFCI protection. The GFCI protection is there because the building safety or NEC code required it.

In addition to GFCI outlets, GFCI circuit breakers can supply protection for all outlets on the breaker; however, in this situation, when the breaker trips, every device on that protected circuit will cease functioning rather than just the affected outlet. Finally, an in-line GFCI adapter can provide protection to an extension cord or a device by plugging the device into the adapter and plugging the adapter into a nonprotected outlet.

Surge Suppressors

Every now and then, an event up the power distribution lines causes a spike in the voltage supplied to your house. Each circuit's devices can handle small fluctuations in supply voltage, but spikes over 600 volts can ruin just about any device attached and turned on at the time of the spike. Televisions, radios, and computers are frequent casualties of overvoltages. These overvoltage spikes can be caused by lightning, a poor connection on a high-voltage line, a car-to-power-pole collision knocking wires together, and problems at the power source. There is a device to protect your whole home and individual circuits against the ravages of power spikes: a surge suppressor. A surge suppressor does nothing and does not conduct electricity when the supply voltages are within a normal operating range. When the voltage goes over a predetermined value, say, 330 volts as an example, the surge suppressor sacrifices itself as a low-resistance alternative path to the higher voltage and provides an easy path for the excess voltage to flow though, thus protecting the device or devices downstream. The voltage where the surge suppressor begins conducting is referred to as the "clamping voltage" or the "let through voltage." That refers to the voltages it will let through itself; lower voltages flow to and through the connected device(s). When the surge suppressor is working, it does two things. It shunts some of the current to ground (the return path) and converts some of the electrical current into harmless heat energy when an overvoltage event occurs. It is not uncommon for a single surge-protected circuit to absorb enough additional current to trip the circuits' breaker or blow a fuse. It is important to match the capacity of the surge suppressor to the load it will protect.

Fuses

Fuses are devices used to protect the circuit wiring from carrying current above the circuit or devices rating. A fuse works by providing some amount of resistance to the flow of electricity in the circuit. When a current above the fuse's amperage rating tries to flow though the circuit, it does; however, when it meets the added resistance provided by the fuse, the additional current causes the fuse wire to heat up and melt away, thus opening the circuit so that no more electricity can flow though the wiring. Fuses are made from metals with a low melting point. If the overcurrent is a minimal amount, it might take a while for a fuse to heat up sufficiently to melt away. The higher and more instantaneous the overcurrent is, the quicker a fuse will blow.

Circuit Breakers

Circuit breakers perform much the same purpose as a fuse but have the advantage that they simply need to be reset to be used, not replaced as a blown fuse would be. A circuit breaker works by having a magnetic force that works against spring tension. When the current exceeds the operating amperage, the magnetic field increases enough to overcome the spring tension and the circuit turns off. After the fault is removed, the breaker can be reset for future use.

Solenoids

Solenoids are devices used to convert an electrical current into mechanical energy. That mechanical energy can be used to turn a water valve on and off, flip a power switch, or do things like open a door lock.

Relays

A relay is a switch that is activated (turned on or off) by another electrical circuit. Often relays are used to control heavier loads, allowing smaller wire sizes or different voltages to the switching circuit.

A relay is simply a switch that is operated by electricity from a remote location. Relays are used instead of in-line switches to turn on electrical circuits for three reasons. The first reason might be that it is desirable to use a lower voltage or a lower current for the control wiring than the in-line circuit that needs to be controlled. Lower voltages in control circuits are often desired because they are inherently safer than higher voltages. Lower currents used in the relay controls allow the controls to be wired in with smaller-diameter and lower-cost wiring. The next reason to use relays is that it allows for control to take place from an alternative location, which is a major goal for automating a home. The third reason is to hand off control to another logic device or nonhuman entity, such as a computer, as we do with home automation. The final reason is to meet an "if-then do" situation, an example being that if the outside temperature is over 80 degrees, then do allow the air conditioner to turn on; if not, then do not allow the air conditioner to power up.

Motors, Electric

Electric motors serve the purpose of turning electrical power into a mechanical action (usually a rotational force) to do work such as moving air, pumping water, or opening and closing valves.

Arc Fault Breakers

Arc fault breakers are circuit breakers that trip off-line when an arc (spark, temporary short) is detected down-line. Arcing is a potential fire starter, and tripping off the breaker when an arc fault occurs reduces the opportunity for a fire to start, thus reducing the risk of a fire.

Infra-Red Remotes

If you have a TV remote, a DVD/VCR remote, or a sound system remote, the odds are that it performs its control function by imposing a short digital signal on an infrared carrier signal. If you look closely at an infrared remote, the end you point at the television has a small light bulb on the end that needs to point at or "see" the receiver eye on the appliance you intend to control. The coded signal is processed by the TV and acted on to change the channel, adjust the volume, or perform many other functions. One cannot see the bulb lighting up on a remote with the naked eye when a key is pressed, but your digital camera can. To test an infrared remote for infrared output, hold it in front of a digital camera, turn it on, take a picture as you or someone else presses the remote buttons, and observe the output on the camera screen. Your eyes can't see infrared but the camera's "eye" can and when you look through the camera screen you can see the infrared rendered on the screen.

Household Low-Voltage Wiring Types and Devices

Many applications around the house take advantage of low-voltage wiring. Often bell wire or Cat5 cable is used for thermostat control wires, remote microphones, doorbells, telephone connections, and so forth. Low-voltage wires are considered less dangerous than household voltages, and the requirements for their use are less stringent in the NEC code book.

Phone

Phones (landlines) are wired by using four conductor bell cables or by using Cat3 or Cat5 cable. In most homes the wiring to phone outlets is serial, meaning that the wire travels from the entry box to each outlet in turn. When wiring in your HAL voice portal (modem), you will need to have the landline phone wire go to the Line In on the Hal voice portal first and then from the handset out of the Hal voice portal to the respective phone downstream. To do this you might need to do some phone-line rewiring.

Cable TV/Satellite

Cable TV/satellite wiring should be RG6 cable. RG6 wiring brings the signal to your TV from the cable company's entrance box. With satellite TV the signal travels from the satellite dish's LNB to your satellite receiver.

Microphones

Microphones are devices that convert sound energy, such as from your talking, into electrical energy. The electrical energy produced from a microphone matches (but on a smaller energy scale) the frequency and amplitude of the sound from your voice. If that energy is amplified and connected to speakers, it can be a much stronger energy than your talking is. Speakers convert that electrical energy back to sound energy, in effect moving air with a similar frequency and relative amplitudes of your voice box. When you move up to Hal voice controls, you will want to have microphones located throughout your house. The voice portal has an input for sound, so you will need to use a microphone mixer to control many microphones located throughout a larger home.

Thermostats

Thermostats are nothing more than temperature (heat) activated switches. Thermostats operate on low voltages connected to relays within the furnace or air conditioner.

Common Legacy Electric Controls

In this section, the devices you find as manual controls in any existing home we will call legacy controls and explain a little bit about them. In later chapters you will learn how to replace or rewire the legacy devices in order to control them with home automation controls instead of simple switches.

Switches

Common household switches and switch arrangements include simple on/off, three-way, and four-way. The details presented in the next sections will help you figure out which ones you are dealing with in your home.

On/off switches, the simplest of switches, have two connections for the wires and a single contact inside the switch. In the "on" position the contacts connect the two connection points to allow electrical current to flow through the switch. A typical on/off (SPST {single pole/single throw}) switch is shown in Figure 1.11.

Figure 1.11   *A simple single-pole on/off switch has two connections, usually on the same side.*

Single-point switches can be wired one of two ways. In the first way the hot, neutral, and bonding wire are run from the distribution panel to the switch box first. Then the hot wire is connected though the single-pole switch and is run with the neutral and bonding wire to the light, load, or device. In this situation, in-wall controls that require a neutral connection can be located in the switch box.

The second method is called a "switch drop." In this situation the hot, neutral, and bonding wires are run from the distribution panel to the light or load first. Then a two-wire and bonding wire are brought down to the switch location, where the bonding wire provides the ground connection on the switch mounting and the two conductors connect to the switch. A "switch drop" is what you have when only two insulated conductors are in the switch box. In this situation control devices that require connections to the neutral cannot be used in the box without rewiring.

A three-way switch such as the one shown in Figure 1.12 is used to control a light from two different switches. It has three connections and a contact that connects the common connection to either of the other poles as the switch is moved from one position to the other.

To switch a light from two locations, two three-way switches are used, connected with an extra set of wires, called runners. These runners connect the poles of the two switches. In the case of a three-way switch, a line is run from the distribution panel to the first switch and is connected to the common connection on the first switch. From this switch to the second switch, a four conductor with one of them being a bonding wire, cable is run to the second switch. The white wire is connected through to the next switch, as is the bonding wire, and the two hot wires, usually black and red, are each connected to their own noncommon connector on the first three-way switch. At the second three-way switch location, the travelers are each connected to their own noncommon connection on the switch. At the second switch box a cable with two conductors and a bonding wire are connected. The hot (black) wire is connected to the common connection on the switch and the neutral, and bonding wire is wired through to the light, device, or other load being switched.

Figure 1.12 *Notice that the single colored common connection is toward the top of this three-way switch.*

To switch a light or a load from more than two locations, a four-way switch is used, such as the one shown in Figure 1.13.

Figure 1.13   *A four-way switch has four contacts plus the bonding tab contact.*

A four-way switch circuit uses two three-way switches and a specialized four-way switch with four contacts that is installed between the runners of the two three-way switches. Each additional switch location beyond the first three requires use of the specialized four-way switch, but there is theoretically no limit to the number of locations a load or a light can be controlled from. The four-way switch connections are typically labeled input and output, as shown in Figure 1.13. In the default position the connection on the left is connected straight through to the other connection on the left, as is the case with the connections on the right side. What makes a four-way switch unique is that when the switch is flipped to the opposite (nondefault) position, the connection labeled "input" on the left is connect to the "output" on the right as the "input" connection on the right is connected to the "output" connection on the left. Do not confuse a two-pole aka double-pole single throw switch with a four-way switch; they both have four connection points but the alternate position of a double pole simply opens both connections.

Remember that a three-way switch allows control of the same light or appliance from two switch locations. A four-way switch allows for control from three or more locations.

The contact screws on a four-way switch are color-coded as shown in Figure 1.14: two dark black and two brass color. Connect the set of two runners from each of the three ways to its own color.

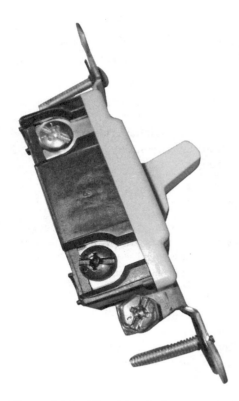

Figure 1.14   *The side of a four-way switch with the bonding tap.*

Dimmers and Dimmer Switches

Dimmer switches are used exclusively with incandescent lighting circuits to vary the brilliance of the lighting. Specialized dimmers can be used with compatible fluorescent and LED lighting fixtures.

Timers

Timers are switches operated by a mechanism or a digital circuit and are used to control the amount of time a circuit will stay on.

Clock Timers

Mechanical or digital circuit timer clocks turn circuits on or off based on the time of a 24-hour day. Seven-day models are also available to vary the routine on and off times based on the day of the week.

Motion Sensor Switches

Motion sensor switches turn on circuits or cameras or alarms when movement is sensed. The movement could be a car, a person, an animal, or any other things in motion near the sensor.

Heat Sensor Switches

Heat sensor switches detect the heat given off by the body at infrared ranges to turn on circuits. An example would be the Leviton PR180-1LW Decora 500W Incandescent, 400VA, Passive Infrared Wall Switch Occupancy Sensor.

Alternative and Backup Power Sources

Building a backup power source into your home automation might be expensive but necessary for those relying on HA to overcome physical challenges. On a smaller scale, if the utility power goes out and you plan to have security features and rely on them in your HA solution, a day's worth or more of backup power might be a priority.

Battery Backup Power Supplies

Along with using an end-point surge protector for your home automation computer, it is wise to use a battery backup power supply. Choose a model that can be used with an automated software routine to shut down the computer gently when power outages occur.

Backup Generators

Generators convert mechanical energy, usually rotational into electrical energy. Residents in areas prone to storm damage and frequent power outages often have emergency back-up generators to run at least a minimum number of critical electrical loads in their home. Automated controls can be employed along with automatic transfer switches to start a generator and switch the home's distribution panel to run on the generator instead of the electrical grid. For long-term use, natural gas power or propane-powered backup generators have significant advantage over any emergency generator using gasoline or diesel fuel and burn much cleaner (pollute less) in operation. Also, at least in theory, the potential exists for a natural gas line to supply the generator for months if needed.

Definitive Information Source—NEC

Builders, licensed electricians, and code enforcement agencies all use the latest revision of the National Electrical Code to determine what rules and regulations need to be followed. The latest edition of NFPA 70, commonly referred to as the National Electrical Code (NEC) Softbound, is the 2011 Edition with revised versions coming out every three years. Always use the most recent code book when checking whether your current or proposed wiring situation is up to code.

Schematic Diagrams

A schematic diagram is the road map that shows how a circuit is wired or how the interconnections are made within an electronic device such as a radio or stereo amplifier. Standard symbols are used for the components in schematic diagrams. A collection of standard schematic symbols can be found at http://electronicsclub.info/circuitsymbols.htm.

Schematic diagrams are used in later chapters as required by connection details. The diagrams are project specific and as simple as possible.

The terms and concepts presented in this chapter are used in Chapters 2 through 16, usually without further definition. Refer to this chapter whenever necessary for clarification. As stated in the beginning of this chapter, this is not a complete course on electricity; it is an introduction for the novice do-it-yourselfer who needs a starting point to complete the DIY projects in later chapters.

Chapter 2

Using a Windows Computer as Your Home Automation Platform

A Windows-based computer is in many ways the most logical and easy choice for a computer platform on which to build a home automation system. There is a plethora of inexpensive Microsoft Windows operating system–compatible hardware out there in the marketplace, both new and used.

New computers are available at record low prices, especially given their high-end performance. There is a vast knowledgebase in the user community as MS Windows is the dominant home, office, and portable computer operating system.

Big-box stores such as Office Max offer troubleshooting and technical support at many locations. Windows 8 OS is available in smart-phone offerings by many major Telcos' wireless services, and Windows phones can play a role controlling the home's automation features.

It is so easy to forget that the phone's first job is to make and receive telephone calls. So much of what is done on smart phones is web-based these days, and to some degree the underlying OS for the phone becomes irrelevant to most end users as long as the phone meets their basic needs.

The same is true of computers having the bells and whistles: It is nice but a workhorse that does the basic job you want it to do and fairly quickly is all you are really after in your home automation platform.

There is a range of Windows-compatible personal computer manufacturers and vendors with offerings across price points from $300 to $3,000 and more. Major retailers including Best Buy, Walmart, Office Max, Staples, and other regional retailers will often have bundled PC packages that include decent monitors in the $400–$600 range. Factory-refurbished or reconditioned computers are often available beginning at about $200. For a home automation computer platform, the focal point of the purchase decision should simply be functionality and expectation of reliability. Stated another way, will the computer allow you to put it in a corner of your home and handle the home automation for at least two to four years? You would benefit from using a Windows

7, 32 bit software OS as your home automation platform for ease of use and economy on price. Consider that as the probable best price versus value option as it is frequently available on used and reconditioned computers.

For those computer users without a lot of experience, there are Windows-associated computer classes available via community school programs, community colleges and universities, libraries, and community service organizations. If you have no experience with using computers, it would be a good idea to take an introductory course in using a Windows operating system–based computer.

To successfully install and use home automation software on your home automation platform computer, you do not need to be a power user. A few elementary skills are necessary, such as using the keyboard and mouse, booting up the system, launching applications, and installing new software and performing periodic software updates. You will need to know how to tab or mouse-click between data entry fields within the home automation application. You will also need to input labels and device codes composed of numbers and letters using the keyboard into the home automation software screens. These basic keyboarding and mouse operation skills are those that should be included in any introductory computer course you would take.

This chapter shows you how to make your home automation system software and applications work in a simple and straightforward fashion. However, I assume that you have mastered a few of the very basic skills needed to operate a computer. If you can start a computer, load a CD to play music, play solitaire, log on to the Internet to check your email, post to Facebook, or use a spreadsheet or simple word processing program, you can probably be quite successful at installing, setting up, and using computer-centered home automation software without taking any more courses. If these things are foreign to you, you should consider taking a basic computer skills course.

Because Windows is relatively inexpensive, readily available, and widely used, it is a great choice for your home automation computer.

Note   **Budget Estimate Information**   Throughout this book, I include how much I spent on each item in 2013 prices. The budget numbers offered in this book are intended to make clear what items are necessary and about how much you can plan on spending for those items as you budget for your own unique home automation system.

Details and Choices

Choosing a computer for your home automation platform can be likened to buying a car. As with a car or any purchase, there is the minimum feature set necessary to provide personal transportation. Beyond those minimum features are the nice to have but not totally necessary features. Lastly, there is the cost-is-no-object category for the ultimate level of features, sophistication, and convenience.

For the purposes of this book, I focus on the necessities for getting the job done. I occasionally include the nice-to-have specifications and features, but because I intended this book to be a beginner's guide, I didn't delve into the super cool (and expensive) options and features.

First Choice: Shared, Dedicated, or Networked?

As you plan your home automation system and envision using it, you will have to consider whether you want to control your system from a shared, dedicated, or networked computer.

Shared Computer Option

Windows will handle the HAL software in the background, meaning that the computer can still be used for other routine computing tasks. However, this shared use will place an operating burden on the computer's processor and memory and will tend to slow the responsiveness for both HAL software and the person using the computer for other tasks. This performance degradation will vary significantly depending on how memory- and CPU-intensive the applications are. If all you do on the computer is check email and Facebook, a shared computer option may work just fine.

It is fine to use HAL and share the computer with other users as long as you recognize that response times and performance will be slowed down somewhat. With a very robust high-speed CPU chipset and sufficient RAM (memory), the impact of having simultaneous users on the computer might be hardly noticeable. On slower CPU processors with nominal RAM memory, the impact might be quite distracting for users and degrade the response time for the Automated Living applications software. If you own only one computer that you use and you plan to use it for HAL software as well, just know that it might be slowed down a bit by the simultaneous use.

Dedicated Computer Option

Using a dedicated computer might be the very best option for those who can justify the expense.

Keep in mind that when you use your home automation platform for appliance and energy (lights, heating, and cooling) management, you might see some savings in electric, natural gas, or propane bills. Over time, the savings could easily recover the full cost of implementing a home automation platform. This is particularly true in larger homes or in homes that are unoccupied for long intervals. In these cases, the investment cost for a dedicated computer could be recovered very quickly.

Note   **More on Reducing Energy Costs**   I discuss using home automation for saving energy costs in more detail in Chapter 10, "Project 7, Getting Green and Managing Your Home's Climate."

I personally favor using a dedicated computer and passing every possible repetitive or routine task it can do over to the home automation system with a focus on doing the energy-saving projects first. The added benefit is that the more the home automation platform does, the more time you will have available for the other things you enjoy.

Networked Computer Option

There are some advantages to connecting the home automation control computer to a home network. Among these advantages is the capability to set up automatic software and data backups (to another computer, a networked hard drive, or, for advanced users, a dedicated server). Backups can prevent the loss of data (email, photos, movies, music, work files, and so on) and are huge time savers if you are forced to reinstall everything after a data loss.

A home network also provides you with extra storage space and increased levels of data organization. For example, an older computer could be dedicated to the function of storing all of your music, photos, and video files. That same computer could be set up to automatically back up to a networked hard drive or server. That means when you copy a CD of music files to one computer, the files are automatically backed up to the networked drive or server. Keeping multiple copies of your data is a great way to reduce the risk of ever losing them due to a mechanical or software failure.

Another advantage to having the home automation platform computer connected to a home network is that it can also access the Internet and be accessed from the Internet.

Tip   **Control HAL via the Internet**   I will discuss using the Internet for home automation purposes in more detail in Chapter 13, "Project 10, Connecting and Using the Home Automation Platform over the Internet." To do this you will need a feature on the Internet modem and router set up that allows opening a certain "port" or passage for the communication to take place across the Internet.

Second Choice: Buy Preconfigured or Build Your Own

If you don't already have a computer lined up to control your home automation software, you have two choices: buy off the rack or roll your own. The hobby reader might want to have the fun and gain the experience of buying a bare-bones computer kit and building from that point. Others might want to skip the hassle of building a computer and just buy one that's ready to go. Some might allow their budgets to drive the decision. In the next subsections we will discuss each of these options.

Purchase a Preconfigured Home Automation PC

If you want to be up and running quickly, or if you simply have no interest in building your own, the good folks at www.AutomatedLiving.com will be happy to sell you a preconfigured computer that you can plug in, set up, and use as your home automation platform.

A preconfigured computer will perform all the tasks outlined in this book. The instructions and setup routines in the individual project chapters to set up and build out the rest of your home automation system still apply.

Have a Home Automation System Professionally Installed

You also have the option of having a HAL system entirely installed by professional home automation experts. Many technologically astute local licensed electrical contractors and home builders can arrange for the setup and installation of a complete home automation system in a new home or as part of a remodeling project.

There are also nationally recognized companies that either provide a turnkey-managed service for home automation or can complete the installation and turn the day-to-day system operation back over to the homeowner. SaskTel subsidiary SecurTek, for example, offers a 24/7 Managed Service version of HAL called HALhms (Home Manager System). The system manages a home's heating, cooling, security, power, entertainment systems, and more.

Purchase a New or Used PC

When setting up your home automation system on a budget, you certainly can look into buying a used computer. However, the downside is you rarely get any sort of warranty ensuring at least some minimum months or years of use. When purchasing any new computer, you might get at least a year's worth of warranty but you will pay more for the computer than a used unit would cost.

You also generally have the option to purchase extended warranties for service and/or parts for an additional fee. For the computer used as the prototype for this book, I took a middle-of-the-road approach and spent $279 for what is essentially a used computer, but is referred to as a "factory reconditioned" or "factory refurbished" unit. The plus side is that the warranty is backed by HP itself, and for only $79 I was able to secure an additional warranty period, bringing my total cost for the computer to $375 with tax.

Note **Computer Cost** Computer cost from prototype budget: $279.
Extended warranty cost from prototype budget: $79.
Total so far: $375.

Most Important Characteristics for Your Home Automation Platform

When buying off the rack or building your own computer to use as your home automation control system, you need to keep several important things in mind. The following subsections outline those points.

Computer Case

Consider one of three case sizes for your home automation computer. As you will see, I recommend the small form factor cases:

- **Desktop**—The standard desktop case is fairly large and offers room for four to six drives and a half dozen expansion slots for add-in cards depending on the model of the motherboard installed. It is called the "desktop" because it takes up a lot of space on a desktop.

- **Tower**—This category includes tower computers in two flavors, small towers and large towers. Small towers have characteristics similar to desktops but are intended to sit vertically on the floor or desktop to save space. Large towers offer a larger number of options and space for including additional drives and add-in cards.

- **Small Form Factor**—A small form factor PC is preferable, in my opinion, because it offers a good price point and sufficient drive space and expansion card slots. The most important characteristic is its smaller size. Often the home automation computer is housed somewhere totally out of sight, and this case's small size makes finding a permanent hiding place for it in most homes or even apartments somewhat easier.

- **All-in-One**—I would be remiss if I did not mention the all-in-one style of computer, which features the computer and monitor in a single unit. If you used a Macintosh back in the mid-1980s to early 1990s, you probably remember the all-in-one design. Today, much more powerful computers with large monitors are available in all-in-one designs. The drawback with this style of computer is the limited space inside the computer case for expansion cards or slots. For example, it is hard to find one that will accept standard-size PCI add-in cards. Another drawback is the limited number of serial and USB ports. Even with their limitations, they can work in certain environments. Just be sure to consider the drawbacks before you decide on one of these units.

Computer Operating System

Any of the following versions of Windows will run HAL:

- Windows XP
- Windows 2000
- Windows Vista

- Windows 7 32-bit

- Windows 8 32-bit

Your hardware choices will dictate the range of options for running any particular MS Windows OS version. New computers and motherboards are not always backward or forward compatible with the various changes in versions of the operating system software.

Currently, versions of HAL home automation software will run on any of five Windows Operating Systems: the XP version, 2000, Vista, Windows 7, and Windows 8 in 32-bit. Home Automated Living's software will also run on 64-bit operating systems; however, the voice portal modem drivers are available only for 32-bit OS versions. A new HAL 64-bit voice portal modem is under development with no ship date as of yet. An alternative to internal voice portal modems using a USB port is undergoing testing for compatibility with HAL software in both 32-bit and 64-bit versions, so check with the HAL website for the lasted hardware compatibility before you make your hardware purchases. Having a USB fully functional voice portal would make the all-in-one TV option much more desirable.

Each of these operating systems has some innate limitations with regard to the hardware and software it would be compatible with. If you have an older computer running the operating systems before Windows 7 that you are not doing anything with now, it can still potentially make a fine candidate for getting your initial start into home automation.

The current target Microsoft operating system version that is recommended is the Windows 7 32-bit operating system. This would also likely be the most economical choice if you do not already have a computer cued up for home automation.

Processor (CPU)

I have a bias for computers with Intel processors because I have observed fewer problems when using Intel processors over processors of other manufacturers. Your experience might be different. There is less risk of compatibility issues between software and hardware when buying and using computers and components from top-tier vendors. When they produce computers with non-Intel processors, it is usually done to provide competitive products at a more affordable price point. The implication in the sale is that it will work so buying them is not a bad choice; it might just carry a little more risk.

Regardless of the brand, each processor will have a rated clock speed at which the processor performs its work. The speeds of the other components in the PC such as the video cards and hard drives also influence the overall speed of the computer's capability to perform tasks. Higher is generally better when it comes to processor speeds because the computer can do more work when it works faster in a given time frame. The OS software or application software can also influence the speed at which a computer will perform.

The *minimum* requirement to run HAL software is a processor running at 800MHz or faster.

The *recommended* speed is 1GHz.

A good *target* speed is a processor that runs in excess of 3.0GHz with 3MB of cache.

As stated earlier, faster is better; however, faster is typically more expensive as well. When choosing a processor, decide whether the price to squeeze out a few more instructions per second is worth the cost.

> **Note**   **Processor Comparison Tools**   To compare the speed, cache, cores, and processing threads for CPUs manufactured by Intel, visit this website: http://www.intel.com/content/www/us/en/processor-comparison/comparison-chart.html
>
> Or to go directly to a comparison of desktop processors, use this URL: http://www.intel.com/content/www/us/en/processor-comparison/compare-intel-processors.html?select=desktop

A computer dedicated to home automation does not have to be the fastest computer in your home. Its tasks rely on detecting events such as reading the computer's clock time or performing a task passed from an external trigger. Much of a dedicated home automation PC's time is spent waiting for some event so that the next actions can be triggered by the automation software. If the computer will be used to do other tasks or if you incorporate it into your home entertainment strategy, increased processor speeds can help juggle these other responsibilities.

The *prototype* computer used with the writing of this book has an Intel Pentium Dual-Core CPU E6700 Chip running at 3.20GHz with a cache size of 3.0MB. This processor has handled all the tasks within the projects covered in this book with more than adequate performance.

Memory

The *minimum* RAM (random access memory) necessary to run HAL software is 1GB. RAM size is related to a computer's overall performance and greatly impacts the overall speed of the computer's capability to process data. Not having enough RAM will bring a computer to a crawl.

The *recommended* RAM is 2GB. Each Microsoft OS covered in the earlier section has a maximum amount of RAM memory that can be used by the CPU.

Aside from RAM limitations placed on your system by your OS, your motherboard will have a physical limit as to how much memory it can hold. Finally, your budget might become a limit as well. Having said that, the *target* RAM memory for you should be to reach as close to the physical limit of the OS as your budget would allow; in the case of Windows 7 32-bit, that would be 4GB.

Our book *prototype* computer performs adequately with only the 2GB recommended RAM installed.

Storage Drive(s)

The storage drive, also referred to as the "hard drive," is where all of your operating system and application software is stored, along with the data files you load or create. The *minimum required* storage space on the drive for the installation of HAL basic is 250MB. If you plan to add HAL voices software, 400MB of disk space is necessary. Because the cost of hard drives is relatively low, a hard drive in the 250GB range offers a considerable amount of storage at a decent price point. Most computers will support the addition of a second hard drive if you find you need more storage space. If your PC has an extra USB port available, portable hard drives can easily expand storage without your having to open your PC's case.

The book *prototype* computer has a 240GB hard drive.

I/O Ports

Input/output ports are very important features on your home automation computer. The I/O ports are used to communicate with the devices that communicate with and control the appliances and lights in your home. They are also used to receive data from devices that are capable of interfacing with and communicating event-driven information as cues to the home automation software.

At a *minimum* the home automation computer should have one serial nine-pin connection (com port), referred to as com1, available in the Windows Device Manager properties. At least two USB ports would be needed to add additional control devices. Because parallel ports are rarely used, it is okay to have them, but it is unlikely that you would use them.

The *recommended* configuration would be to have two nine-pin serial com ports (com1 and com2) and four or more USB ports.

The *target* configuration would be to have five or more USB ports and two (com1 and com2) serial ports.

The *prototype* computer has one (com1) serial port and eight USB ports.

Optical Drive

Optical drives are the ones that read the CD music, software, and DVD movie or data removable media. Your home automation PC will require a DVD drive for reading software discs, so pick the drive that best fits your budget.

The book *prototype* computer has a factory-installed TS-H653T Lightscribe DVD drive.

Video Card

A video card or an integrated system board video capable of displaying at a resolution of 1280×720 is sufficient.

The *prototype* computer is displaying at 1600×900 through a system board integrated video card.

Ethernet Port

The Ethernet port is used to communicate over a network to other computers or over the Internet.

The *prototype* computer has a 10/100/1000 integrated Ethernet port.

Monitor

The question to answer is Do you want to connect the home automation computer to one of your TV's input jacks or use a standalone monitor?

Using a VGA input jack on the computer to connect to a TV is a viable option for a monitor for your home automation system, particularly if you plan to use your home automation PC as a home theater PC. You can save money with this option and it moves you toward the entertainment integration option at the beginning of the project. If you go the standalone monitor route, monitors with flat-screen sizes of 19 inches or more start at around $100. For the *prototype* monitor a new HP W2072a monitor measuring 20 inches was purchased on sale directly from HP on a free-shipping offer.

Note   Monitor cost from prototype budget: $109.
Total prototype cost so far: $485.

Sound Card

Most modern computers will ship with an integrated sound card or include an add-in sound card. Some will even ship with a set of speakers and a microphone to plug into the sound card. These are all features you will want to have for your home automation computer.

The prototype computer had an integrated sound card and I had an older compatible microphone and a set of external stereo speakers that came with an older computer. If I had to buy the speakers and microphone again, it would take about $60, so that number is included in the budget.

Note   Speakers and microphone estimated cost prototype budget: $60.
Total prototype cost so far: $545.

Additional Hardware

The HAL voice portal (vp300) requires that a compatible PCI slot is available on the computer's motherboard. Even if you are not planning to include the voice features now, be sure that the computer you choose will allow for the installation of this device or you will have to upgrade to a compatible computer later. The added convenience of being able to talk commands to the home automation computer is well worth the cost for most users. For many others it is the dominant reason to use home automation features to begin with. The HAL voice portal is also the interface for using a telephone landline to call the computer and issue commands. The product is HAL Internal PCI Voice Portal (vp300). To get an improved interactive voice control experience with your home automation system beyond the default voice, consider the addition of HALvoices. HALvoices is a software add-on to HAL that gives the home automation system a natural voice instead of the more typical computer-sounding text-to-speech engine. This software add on is available for purchase on the HAL website.

Note   HAL voice portal cost from prototype budget: $289.
Total prototype cost so far: $834.

Planning the Computer's Installation Location

Some of the things to keep in mind when planning for the computer's parking place in your home include access to outlets, good ventilation to keep it cool, safety from moisture, routes for access cables to network hub/router hardware, and a phone outlet. Further considerations will relate to being able to wire to microphones in various locations from the chosen location.

Each home or apartment presents its own opportunities for a place to permanently install the home automation computer. The best adage might be "out of sight, out of mind," particularly if your plan is to extend your home automation platform to include any home security functionality. Some fine points are easy access after installation, eye-level mounting, room and routes for the cables, and a space you can lock up. In a new build your architect or builder can include these features in the plans. On a retro-fit scenario do the best you can to place the computer in a convenient location.

Book Prototype Computer

To minimize the space needed for parking the home automation computer, I chose the HP Compaq small form factor 4000 Pro SSF PC with a Pentium Dual Core CPU with the E6700 Intel CPU running at 3.20GHz, with 2.0GB of installed RAM. The front of the computer is shown in Figure 2.1. The rest of this book is based on the author's experience with setting up this particular model as a home automation platform.

Figure 2.1   *Notice that the front of the computer has four USB ports that can connect to peripherals and control devices.*

An HP W2072A flat-panel monitor, as shown in Figure 2.2, was selected as the prototype monitor.

Figure 2.2   *The 20-inch monitor makes a great display for a home automation system computer.*

This monitor was selected for the home automation platform because it can be mounted to a swing arm or wall bracket after the installation of the home automation system is complete.

Setting up Your Computer

After you have your PC, you're ready to begin. Before you install your HALbasic software, there are steps to take to avoid headaches later. The key to maximizing your probability for long-term success with your home automation system is to be patient enough to go through the same steps the real pros would go through. Even if you buy a new computer right from the store, your computer is not "complete." Most likely your operating system will need updating to account for any patches released between when the system was built and when it was delivered. Your security software might be a trial version, and if it is a full version, it will suffer from the same update lag as your OS. Just as your car will occasionally need routine care, your computer will be in need of some routine preventive maintenance also. These tasks are not difficult, but they just require a little time and patience.

To complete the updates two download options are possible. The most practical alternative is to connect the computer that needs the updates to the Internet and then download the updates right to that computer and use the software supplier's update "wizards" to help do the updating operations. Alternatively, you can use another computer to download the patches and then transfer the patches to a CD or jump drive and load them to the target computer from the CD or jump drive. This might not be viable for all updates, though.

A direct Internet connection is the most efficient option, so this is the alternative that is covered in this section. Our prototype computer will be connecting to the Internet via a wireless connection made though a D-Link wireless dual-band Wi-Fi adapter connected via a USB port. Many hardware options are available for adding Wi-Fi to a PC that does not have a built-in Wi-Fi solution, so you're sure to find one that fits your budget. Simply follow the directions that come with the product and you will be connected in no time. If you'd rather make a direct connection between your PC and your router or modem, this is also a viable solution; however, keep in mind that it might limit the placement options for your home automation system.

Updating the Operating System Software

After the Internet connection is established for the computer that will become your home automation platform, the next step is to fully patch or "update" the operating system. In the case of our prototype computer, we are using Windows 7, the 32-bit version, so the next section walks through the steps to update/patch this OS. Taking a proactive approach to this is most important. Infrequent patching or loading application software without fully patching the OS can lead to glitches and performance issues.

In Windows 7, updating the OS begins with starting the Control Panel. To start the Control Panel, click the Start button on the left side of the taskbar. Then, from the resulting menu, select Control Panel. This brings up the Control Panel, as shown in Figure 2.3.

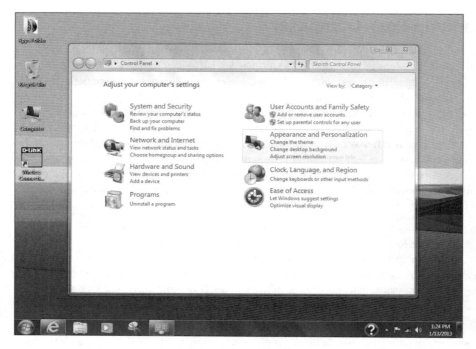

Figure 2.3   *Adjustments in eight categories begin at the menu choices within this window.*

Clicking on the System and Security choice brings up the window shown in Figure 2.4. In the fourth section, with the heading Windows Update, select the check action by clicking the Check for Updates option near the middle.

This action brings up the window shown in Figure 2.5, where the update status is presented. In this case on the prototype computer, the line "Most recent check for updates" correctly displays the status as Never, as does the line "Updates were installed," and both are correct. No updates have ever been loaded and this is the first time this computer has ever been connected to the Internet.

Figure 2.4   *The System and Security action items are displayed in this window.*

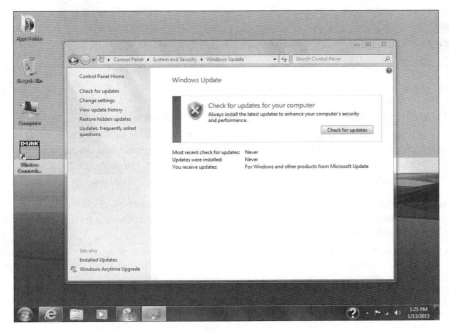

Figure 2.5   *This is the first Windows update for this computer.*

From here, click the Check for Updates button to begin the update process. In some cases, the updater must be updated before the OS can be updated. If this is the case for your system, you see the window shown in Figure 2.6. If this happens on your update, simply click the Install Now button.

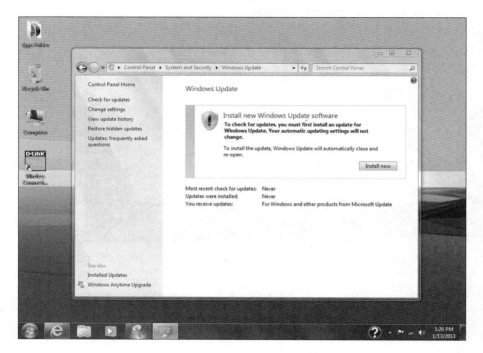

Figure 2.6   *Sometimes it is necessary to update the updater.*

After the updater has been updated, the status of the installation is displayed, as shown in Figure 2.7. Notice that since this OS was loaded on the hard drive at the factory, there have been 111 "important" updates published to the operating system and an additional 6 "optional" updates are available. From my experience it is best to consider the "optional" updates as necessary and to load them as well when they are made available.

Proceed with the important updates selected by the update process by clicking on the Install Updates button. The other updates can be selected on a return visit to the process. The default selections are most often the best option for immediate action. The next window to display asks you to agree to or decline the terms of the license agreement. You really have only one choice, and that is to click on the button I Accept the License Terms.

After you agree to accept the terms of the license agreement, the Finish button becomes available. Click it to begin the update process.

From this window you can review any additional important or optional updates available for installation and install them if necessary.

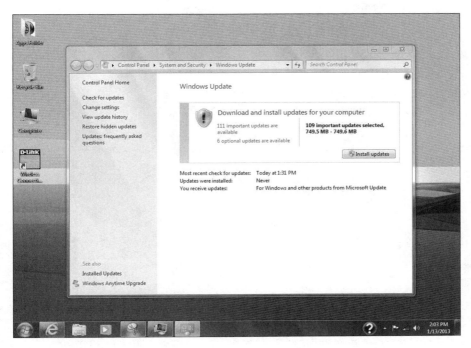

Figure 2.7 *The status shows the number and kinds of updates available.*

> **Note   Time Spent and Errors Found While Updating**   The amount of time needed
> to update your OS will depend largely on the speed of your Internet connection and
> the number of updates to be installed. It might take a few minutes, or it might take
> considerably longer. To further complicate matters, sometimes the update process
> fails to update the OS fully due to the need for a restart during the update process. To
> ensure that every update is installed correctly, check for available updates after every
> restart during the update process. If updates are still necessary, repeat the previous
> steps to install the updates.

After all updates have been installed, the update status window shown in Figure 2.8
appears. This is the window you are looking for, with a status of "Windows is up to date"
with checks for updates less than 24 hours old.

Now that the OS is updated, we need to take a look at the update schedule. Windows
7 will default to checking for and loading updates every day. It is okay to leave it at the
update default settings; however, there is a potential downside to allowing Windows to
manage the update schedule. Given the possibility of updates requiring a reboot, having
your home automation PC reboot at an inopportune time might not appeal to you. My
recommendation is to take control of the process by changing some of the automated
update procedures. From the previous screen, click Change Settings and then change the
Important Updates option to Download Updates but Let Me Choose Whether to Install
Them, as shown in Figure 2.9.

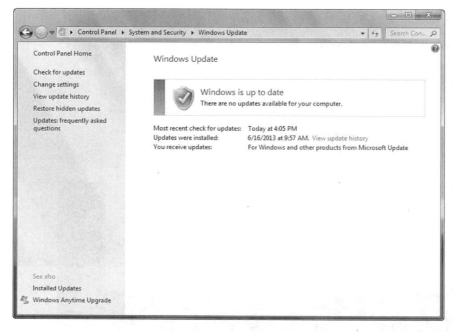

Figure 2.8   *This was our updating goal: "There are no updates available for your computer."*

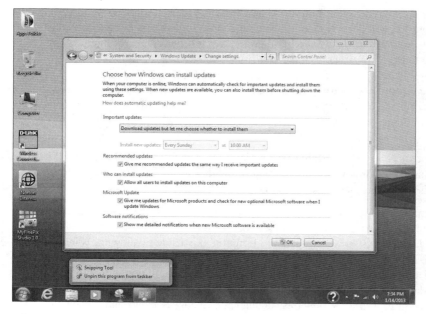

Figure 2.9   *Selecting a favored day for downloads and updates would also be possible.*

Now, your operating system is fully updated and any additional updates can be installed at your convenience.

Updating the Security Software

The prototype computer shipped with Norton Internet Security preloaded with a 60-day trial version. I happen to be a fan of the Norton security products because I have found them to be reliable and mostly trouble free. I have also been impressed with their product support. Not at all unlike the Windows operating system; any security software is also in need of daily updates. The security software needs the "virtual fingerprint" of the latest security threats on a daily basis so that it can compare the threats to what is being communicated to or from your computer or any removable media drives you might use. As a Norton fan, I upgrade the Internet security product, when the 60-day trial is up, to a more advanced product that does more: Norton 360. I happen to like the added features of Norton 360, and it is currently street priced at about $70 and can be loaded on three computers.

Regardless of your choice of versions of security software, it should be updated before you put the home automation platform computer into further setup and use. The update of Norton Internet Security is covered in the next section. Begin with the desktop displayed, as shown in Figure 2.10.

Figure 2.10   *The clear desktop is displayed with the taskbar showing at the bottom of the screen.*

Notice the up arrow at the right-hand side of the taskbar. Clicking on that up arrow brings up a small menu of icons, as shown in Figure 2.11.

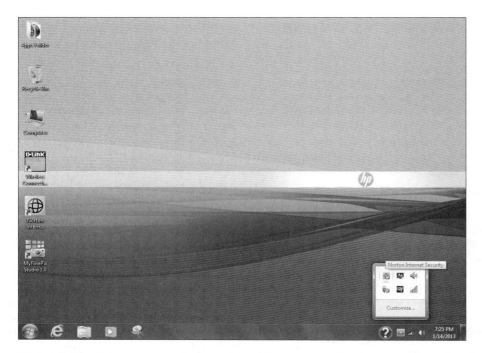

Figure 2.11   *Mousing over the icons identifies what application is associated with each icon.*

The Norton icon is in the upper-left corner of this little icon menu. Move the mouse over it and you can choose to click to bring the application window to the screen or right-click on it to bring up another mini menu, as shown in Figure 2.12.

After this menu appears, highlight and then click on Run LiveUpdate. Doing so will bring up the Norton LiveUpdate window, shown in Figure 2.13. Notice the three status lines: Check for Updates, Download Updates, and Process Updates. The status to the right will change as the update process proceeds.

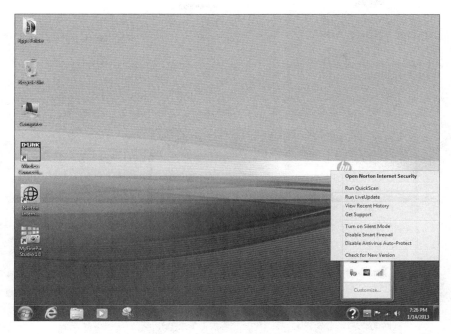

Figure 2.12   *Right-clicking gets you to the menu option you are looking for with fewer steps.*

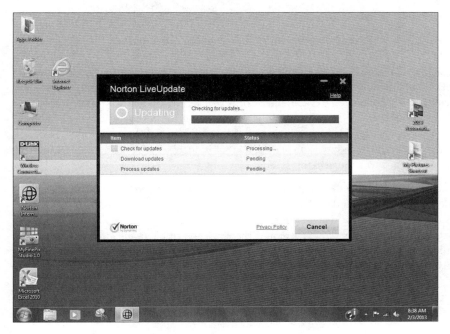

Figure 2.13   *Norton reports the status of the update process in this window.*

In the window shown in Figure 2.14, the status is changed as the process proceeds though each of the three updates in turn.

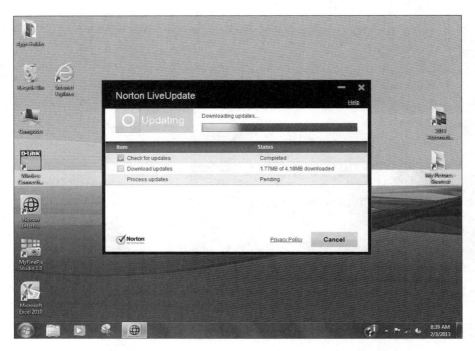

Figure 2.14   *The download is only partially completed in this window.*

The next figure, Figure 2.15, shows the desired endgame for updating the security software that is all downloaded and successfully installed. This process is necessary every day a computer is connected to the Internet or is sharing files in any way with others. Repeat this process every day or configure updates under the software settings heading. This is one of two possible windows that will display after the three update processes are completed. When this window is displayed, all that is necessary is clicking the OK button to clear the window off the desktop screen.

In the alternative scenario the window that displays after an update is shown in Figure 2.16. Here you are presented with the option buttons Restart Now and Restart Later. This applies to the OS, meaning that a computer reboot is required to fully load one or more of the updates into the operating system. If there are no critical home automation tasks happening right then or within the next five minutes, you should click the Restart Now button and let the computer begin the shutdown and reboot process.

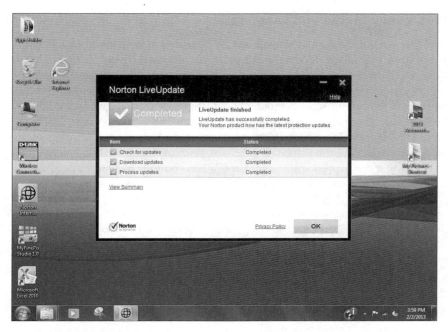

Figure 2.15   *The security update has completed successfully when all three lines show* *"Completed."*

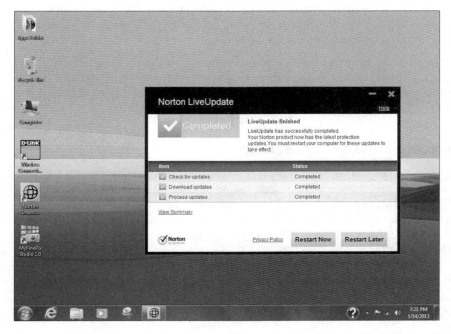

Figure 2.16   *The Restart Later option delays the shutdown and rebooting of the* *computer to a later time.*

Creating Recovery Media and Diagnostics

Computer system recovery approaches will vary by computer manufacturer. Take time to read the operating manual and follow the procedure for making recovery media or a snapshot of the system hard drive as recommended in the manufacturer's literature. Recovery media allows you to reinstall the operating system should there be serious problems with your computer in the future. Some computer brands ship with recovery media included in the box; others prompt you or at least provide a menu item for you to create DVDs or CDs to reinstall the operating system from a partition on the hard drive. Regardless of the approach this is an important step that gives you some insurance against some of the very bad things that can happen with a computer. When you follow the manufacturer's prompts or instruction book on creating the recovery media, be sure to label and store them in a safe place when they are finished being written to. If you have a boot-hard-drive fail, the recovery discs will let you reinstall the original OS. The OS update process to patch and update described earlier in this chapter will have to be followed if you ever have to use the recovery discs. The obvious reason is that anything committed to discs does not include the updates published since the time when the recovery tracks were recorded on the drive.

The same is true of the diagnostic programs for your computer. They might be included in the box when the computer was shipped, or you might have to use the manufacturer's menu on the computer to make one or more diagnostics discs. Diagnostics have testing software to test the CPU, hard drive, video card, and other subsystem components in the computer. If everything is working fine, you do not need to use them. At the first sign of serious trouble, run the diagnostic and it might find the problem. An advantage of using Norton 360 on your computer is that it can, when used properly, help prevent some of the issues that crop up during normal computer use.

If there are no disc recovery options for your computer, a visit to the manufacturer's website might lead you to find both under their downloads and support link. Take the situation seriously and take the time to equip yourself with both the recovery discs and the diagnostic programs.

Surge Protection and Battery Backup

In Chapter 1, "Home Wiring and Electrical Fundamentals," surge protection was introduced because no home automation system should be installed without surge protection. There are two alternatives for providing surge protection at the computer level, a simple plug-in surge protector or a more expensive battery-backup solution that provides surge protection and continued power in the case of an outage. An example of the latter is shown in Figure 2.17.

Note   APC battery backup cost from prototype budget: $64.
Total prototype cost so far: $888.

Figure 2.17   *This is the APC model 550 Battery Backup with surge protection used for the prototype installation.*

Whichever option you choose, follow the manufacturer's instructions for installing and using your surge protector. Often with more expensive surge protectors and backup systems, the manufacturer will provide insurance coverage for any connected devices lost to an electrical surge, so be sure to also fill out any included warranty information and keep any relevant documentation in a safe place. While you're at it, make sure that all PCs in the home are connected to some sort of surge protector. Many computers have ended up on the scrap heap because of power outages and power surges.

The steps covered in this chapter were time-consuming and tedious but necessary to increase the odds that the projects outlined in later chapters will go well and get you to your goal of a fully automated home. Taking these steps at the front end of the projects and maintaining the software updates and patches with some regularity will also contribute to the reliability of the home automation system.

Chapter 3

Introduction to Control Protocols and Automation Process

The home automation process involves changing the existing state or condition of a device, an appliance, a system, or an electronic component from an internal or external stimulus or event, by a person taking an action, or as the result of the movement of time. To achieve that state change through automation, a control message must be sent to the device to be acted on. The condition or state changes can be a simple switching to an on-or-off status, or can be a more complex adjustment such as dimming to a preset level; and that device modification can be an incremental on or variable or both. The control messages are sent via any one of a number of defined home automation protocols.

Control Methods

From infancy we test various methods and learn ways to control others to meet our needs. Crying is typically the first, then sounds, and before long we are crawling and moving about and can begin to make things happen on our own. Over time our individual skill set builds and we can interact with all the things around us. The simplest control method is human intervention, flipping a switch to turn on a light, for example. You know which switch to use, what it controls, and which direction to turn the target device, in this case a light, on or off. The process or steps for turning a light on or off includes the following mental and physical steps: disturbed–decide–poise–act–receive feedback–adjust if needed–feedback–satisfied. The nonhuman intervention automation process mirrors the steps a person would take. The total home automation process is similar except that the system can do everything but decide what to do. The deciding is left to the human, who must set up parameters in advance for consistent automated operation.

> **Note** **Humans as Automation Devices**   Literally each of the steps a person would do to control something can be automated:
>
> | A human would | the home automation platform does |
> |---|---|
> | Receive stimulus | receive event trigger |
> | Decide to act | check data base for instructions |
> | Poise to act | build control message for appropriate protocol controller |
> | Act to control | send out control message |
> | Receive feedback | wait for acknowledgment |
> | Adjust if needed | send new or repeat message from new event trigger. |

One-off devices to perform some of many home automation steps or functions have been around for some time, but with limitations that are not present in a completely automated computer-controlled environment. This chapter gives a basic understanding of how a novice home automation hobbyist can leverage diverse protocols and choose from myriad available products and technologies to control all the automation functions on one central home automation platform.

Reasons for Using Automated Control

The need for home automation technology comes from wanting to make a change in the condition of something: turning on a light or lowering the thermostat, for example. This need for change arises from four basic categories: time, need, event, and communication. In many cases, your home automation platform can take these actions based on the same stimuli that would spur a human to action with little or no need for human interaction.

Time Based

Time-based actions include actions based on a set amount of time passing, such as turning off a bedroom television after an hour of use so that the viewers can nod off and not worry, or actions based on a set time of day, such as turning on the coffee maker at the same time each morning. Time-based controls can be employed on any recurring interval, whether hours, day, week, day of week, and so on.

Need Based

Need-based events are just that, events that have to happen simply because we want them to. When your home gets too cold, you raise the temperature on the thermostat; when it gets too dark, you turn on a light. Not all events can be scheduled, so your home automation platform has to be able to process need-based actions as well. Human participation in initiating the control action can be an easy mouse click or two away or can be done by voice command with the HAL platform.

Event Based

Event-based actions are triggered based on an event, either predetermined or accidental. For example, you might set your thermostat to turn on the heat when the temperature dips too low, or have a trigger on your air handler shut off power to the unit if water is detected in the water pan.

Communication Based

Threaded through all of these prior circumstances to one degree or another is the desire we all have to stay informed. Some conditions, events, and actions we want to know about as fast as possible. Other events we don't need to know about but want handled as efficiently as possible and without our knowledge, In some circumstances we want to be able to find out later, by looking at a log entry, that the situation was handled. For example we might want to be notified by email to our smart phone if an aging parent called during our absence from the house.

The feedback loop is a very desirable and important feature of a modern home automation system for those of us who want or need to stay informed. Fortunately, unlike many products currently in use for home automation, the HAL platform has the capacity to keep us informed not only of those things happening in and about the home, but also of financial, weather, and communication information gathered from the Internet or localized weather equipment. We live in an age when the speed of access to information and communication is unparalleled, so leaving some of the recurring chores of keeping informed and in touch though leveraging some artificial intelligence in our home automation can increase our own communication productivity and at the same time free us to focus on other important matters.

The true beauty of the core automation product line discussed in this book is that the HAL software "communicates commands and processes device feedback" in enough of the commonly popular home automation protocols that it is possible to automate nearly every electrical, mechanical, and electronic device in your home environment.

The next section introduces highlights of the four very popular home device control protocols and standards. As a hobbyist, you'll find that it is important to know that there are differing protocols and that some are more suitable for certain tasks. By bringing diverse protocols into your home automation solution, you can have the best overall system with the lowest overall cost of implementation. Because the HAL software operates at the application layer in the control model, you are not locked into any particular protocol, brand of hardware products, or technology. It is truly a solution that allows combining best of the protocol breeds.

Protocols and Standards

When setting up processes to be completed with home automation technology, there are some relevant details to deal with for whatever protocol your control devices are using, but only during the initial setup or installation phase. After you have completed the device setups within the HAL software you will interact with HAL with language and words not protocols, but some readers will want to know about how those interactions take place. This section gives an idea of what is going on in the background to accomplish your control strategy.

Home automation standards are the set criteria for how home automation devices respond to a control signal and perform a function. There are many home automation standards, some of an open nature and others proprietary in nature.

Many consumers believe that implementing home automation is too expensive and available only to the very wealthy or technologically literate. Fortunately, the reality is that a complete home automation system is well within the reach of the ordinary home owner, provided that they have some spare time and a budget to build out a system. HAL software makes for a cohesive platform by integrating these various standards and protocols under one digital "roof." Not only does it act as the protocol communicator, but it also translates the users' needs into actions. After the devices and protocol interfaces are properly set up to work with HAL, the HAL software does the machine-level translating of the command to the physical. By using HAL software to control the various physical-layer communications, a home can have multiple types of devices installed and working together, even to the point of having a switch of one type activate a device of another, each using different control protocols.

The next few sections highlight some details of how the protocol adapters communicate with the devices.

Physical-Layer Communication

Because everything in home automation relies on electrical signals of one sort or another that carry a message to make the changes for us, we are limited somewhat by the physics or physical properties of electricity as discussed in Chapter 1, "Home Wiring and Electrical Fundamentals." Electrical signals can be of an analog or a digital nature. By using electrical, radio waves, or infrared light signals as our avenue or method of communication along the home automation control pathways, we are limited only by the physical properties of those signals. With electric power we can channel it to do work. By manipulating the properties of electricity we have the ability to communicate information to our advantage. We can use this communication property not only to control electrical and electronic things but also mechanical things like doors, locks, vents, and valves. This is accomplished by using the electrical controls and solenoids as our assistants to do the work from simple but highly defined message packets to control that work.

To borrow a page from biology, the control communication (electrical or wireless) pathway has to either sense and react to stimulus with a response or initiate a communication that will elicit a response or an action from a controlled device. Therefore, at the control pathway level or sensory level at the most primitive layer, there are only a few things that can happen with an electrical current to initiate or convey messages:

■ It can be turned off or on. Example: Voltage/no voltage.

■ It can be off, variable in voltage and/or current or frequency, or full on to the maximum. Example: high/low voltage; high to low frequency.

■ It can be measured within a low or high range for voltage, current, or frequency to compare or match desired presets. Example: 95 VAC to 130 VAC: Normal household voltage.

■ The sensed changes can be associated with time or timing cues to identify message start or end points.

These changes in the physical state are detected at the physical level (hardware, media level) and are interpreted as coded messages high up the application stack. They are used within the devices to execute the state change defined in the message.

Imposing Messages on the Physical Media

At the most basic physical level of the electrical wires or a wireless communication path, the medium used can carry an imposed signal of either an analog or a digital nature. The communication can be a one-way street; that is, sent only and received, or it can be two-way, with returned or reverse-direction message packets sent over the transmission medium from controller to device and back from the device to the controller. When an analog mode is used to communicate, the signal can be made to vary in amplitude or frequency so the resultant signal changes can carry frames of data.

In digital communications mode the signal can be chopped into time slices in which the amplitude of the signal is measured and is considered on or off in that time frame based on its strength, or measured as high or low in a time frame. These on/off states or high/low states of the electrical current or radio signal in digital mode are sensed or sent as changes in voltage, current, or frequency. They are used to represent zeros and ones or other numbers and are used as binary values that translate into data or information or are used as timing pulses to separate and keep track of chunks of the message. These representations of zeros and ones (or numbers) can be used at the distant end to represent anything necessary to perform the desired actions or convey the sought-after information. Parts of the message packets identify the target devices or all the devices or a group of devices through the encoding scheme used in the protocol. Timing pulses are used to define the beginning and end of the object communication so the communication packets maintain whole message integrity or are resent in two-way systems until the whole data packet is acknowledged.

One-way protocols cannot guarantee whole message delivery. A feature called "checksum" can be implemented as a part of a protocol to test the message for completeness and integrity by running a math formula against the packet's data bit and comparing that to the checksum value sent with the message packet. These fundamentals are implemented in various innovative ways, but at the most basic level the communication occurs because of these simple property state changes at the electrical signal level regardless of the physical media (wire, wireless, infrared, or fiber) used for the transmission of data. In the OSI seven-layer networking model this media layer is referred to as the physical layer. To do the home automation projects in this book, you do not have to delve too deeply into how networking and communications are accomplished or understand them fully. Awareness of some features of protocols covered in this rapid overview should be sufficient for trusting that unique control messages can be sent and received successfully to make the home automation device-level processes function to your benefit.

The four protocols of primary interest used in this book's projects include X-10, UPB, INSTEON, and Z-Wave. There are other protocols as well and likely there might be innovators in the future that will create other useful ways to communicate from controller to device. Some people talk about the network of things, a concept in which everything in your personal universe is identified by a unique communication's address, such as an IPV6 address, and everything is connected and reachable though that address. We are not quite there yet, even though many of the pieces are in place. We can, however, communicate right now to the components that matter most to us by using these protocols.

X-10

In X10 the data message frames are imposed on an AC current carrying wire at the point where the electrical power is dropping from 120 volts positive down to zero and before the second half of the sine wave that is moving in the opposite direction begins its half cycle.

The frequency of the transmission is 120KHz, and it occurs for only a very short span of time at a specific point in the 60-hertz current cycle, known as the zero crossing point.

There are 16 available House codes A though P, and 16 available Device codes 01 through 16, allowing for a maximum device count of 256 for X-10 devices.

There are seven change state commands to issue to one-way X-10 devices—on, off, dim, bright, all lights on, all lights off, and all units off—which are all sent via a 4-bit code.

There are seven additional command/info settings available to use in the devices and controllers capable of two-way X-10 communication: status on, status off, status request, pre-set dim, hail, hail acknowledge, and the extension code (or extension code itself).

The minimalist data messages sent as X10 communications are referred to as data frames and must include a start code signifying that an X10 command is about to be sent, a one-letter code signifying the "house" the command belongs to, and one function code. The binary for that could look like 1110 01001011 0001, carrying the information message start, house code letter K, and command "all lights on." It is a simple but limited protocol but is credited with beginning a trend in home automation implementation that did not require rewiring or additional control wiring.

UPB

Universal Powerline Bus is considered much more reliable than X-10. UPB communication messages are sent at speeds of a range of 120 to 240 bits per second.

In 60-cycle AC circuits each half cycle takes 8 1/3 milliseconds to occur. The UPB pulses are spikes in voltage placed on the power line at a precise time in each half cycle, the timing of which conveys a value from 0 to 3. Two bits of data are contained in each half cycle, and the data bits from four half cycles are grouped together and carry 8 bits of digital data, a UPB byte.

These bytes are combined into UPB communications packets sized between 7 and 25 bytes for interpretation and use by the device. Each message packet contains a preamble, a packet header, the data message, and a checksum byte followed by an acknowledgment frame. The header packets contain the information about network ID, device ID, source ID, and a packet control word. The data messages also contain the instructions for the device to perform.

One interesting element and what makes UPB different is that the information about the device ID, network ID, and so forth is stored in nonvolatile memory registers within the device.

INSTEON

INSTEON products operate by two communications over the media: over the home's wiring system and over a preset radio frequency. The devices forward the INSTEON protocol signals, extending the network range for up to three hops; the signal originally sent is hop count zero (0). The three-hop limit prevents endless looping of the command signals.

If the original signal is 0, then the first rebroadcast is hop 1; if the next device adds hop count 2, and the next device hop count 3, there are no more hop counts. So the original signal sent from the first device can travel though three layers of devices to the fourth device layer out in the distant network.

The RF signals are sent at frequencies of 915MHz in the U.S. The power-line protocol is transmitted at 131.65KHz over the wire.

INSTEON plays well with X10 devices although their protocols are different.

INSTEON is a dual-band communications protocol, meaning that its digital signals can travel over the home's wiring system and over radio frequencies.

There are about 200 available products that speak and understand INSTEON communications. Not that anyone would ever use that many but the core protocol can support more than 16 million devices per network.

The standard and smallest INSTEON message is composed of the following: from address (3 bytes), to address (3 bytes), flag (1 byte), command (2 bytes), and redundancy check (1 byte).

Z-Wave

Z-Wave is a wireless protocol and is very much a networking protocol supporting quality two-way communication, much like the Wi-Fi that supports your computers' connections to wireless networks. It operates at frequencies below 1GHz so it is mostly free from interference from the higher frequency Wi-Fi networks. A level of encryption of the data is supported to keep the communication between the devices secure and intact. Because it is at its core a networking protocol, it can support a version of IPV6 device addressing. It is a proprietary protocol but is supported by nearly 160 manufacturers making Z-Wave-compatible devices worldwide. There are nearly 700 available devices that speak and/or understand Z-Wave wireless messages.

A home Z-Wave network can support 232 devices, and more than one network can be bridged together at a higher layer to support more than 232 devices. This is rarely done in automated homes for two reasons. First, controlled device counts above 100 are rare, and second, other technologies can be used and might offer advantages in specific applications. When using HAL software as the hub command center, you are not limited to a specific technology as your home automation solution.

The Network ID (or Home ID) uses 4 bytes (32 bits) of the control message.

The Node ID uses 1 byte (8 bits) of the control message.

A single Network or Home ID can contain a total of only 232 nodes because some of what would be node IDs are co-opted for messages or performing exceptional functions. One has to accept that node IDs are identified from 000001 to 11101000 in binary or 0x1 to 0xe8 in hexadecimal.

Z-Wave's approved radio frequency operating range for the U.S. and Canada is set to 908.4MHz.

The devices emit low-power radio waves and the maximum transmit/receive ranges are considered to be 90 feet in buildings to 300 feet outdoors in the clear. Z-Wave presents a good option for controlling something located in outbuildings supplied or powered by a different electrical service because of the potential to send signals via radio wave to 300 feet.

Each Z-Wave network begins with at least one primary controller and a controlled node. New devices are brought into the network by a process called inclusion (or taken out by exclusions). After the network is set up, secondary controllers can join and can be brought into the network.

Two types of device nodes can take on one or more of three characteristics:

■ **Controllers**—Control other Z-Wave devices.

■ **Slaves**—Are controlled by other Z-Wave devices.

■ **Routing Slaves**—Pass messages to nearby neighbors, thereby extending the range of control of the entire network but adding modest time delays for the routing table lookups and retransmissions to each next available neighbor in turn.

Z-Wave presents two clear advantages because it is wireless. The first advantage is that you can control devices that are on nearby alternative wiring systems. The second is that you can use a handheld remote to control Z-Wave devices, again thanks to its wireless communication media.

Automation Processes are Trigged by an Event

Events that are common and vital to home automation process include these:

- Elapsed Time

- Arrived Time

- Occurring and Recurring Events

- Temperature Changes

- Voice Commands

- Proximity Sensing:

  - Motion Sensor

  - Heat Sensor

- Incoming Information Processing

- Outgoing Information Processing

After that the processes or pseudo-processes must be known and stored in the database for human like or referred control to occur from actions to be taken by the automation platform.

The object of control must have a name or an ID such as "Bedroom Lamp" that not only acts as a label for the process but also identifies the device or appliance being controlled. That name is then attached to the device name that is identified by the control interface within the protocol such as house and unit ID in X10.

The desired conditions or desired outcome of the automation process must be known and stored in the automation setup's database. One example would be that the desired new condition is to dim the lamp to a preset variable.

Any variable condition must be articulated and defined in the database, such as dim the lamp to 33 percent of total possible brightness.

A trigger or stimulus to set off the automation process is defined. This could be the ringing of the doorbell or the arrival of a clock time.

A human stimulus or automated sensor or predefined action then presses the predefined and stored steps into action through the controller sending out signals in various protocols to the devices that will be acted on.

Process Actions

When the control stimulus occurs, the automation process goes through these primary action steps:

1. Finds the named object device in the database.

2. Finds or collects the desired state or predefined condition.

3. Converts the device name to a recognized protocol name in the physical layer address scheme being used (example: X10).

4. Combines the object's physical-layer address with the control parameters.

5. Sends the control signal and parameters over a serial port or USB port, or to another type of control interface. It can also use the computer's own communications bus to convey commands such as playing music over the sound card.

6. The interface module converts the control signal into a physical layer message and sends it out on the wire (or RF) at the appropriate time.

7. The physical media (house wiring or wireless or infrared) carries the control signal over the media to the connected devices.

8. The target device receives the control signal and the device or module sets the new condition called for in the message and creates the new state or condition of the object of control.

9. The control device in two-way protocols sends back feedback if the device is capable and feedback is needed, warranted, or requested by the controller.

In later project chapters you will see examples of this process in the setup phase and at work when you follow the examples for your own projects. The control framework pieces for each technology are well defined, and all you have to do is drop your control identities, types, and unique naming information into the framework.

There is a lot more to learn about the protocols mentioned in this chapter, but luckily, for those looking to implement a home automation system, you can use these products successfully without knowing any additional information. To be successful with your project, be it your own project or a project that follows the examples in this book, you only have to keep track of some details and load them in the setup screens and application windows. Later chapters show in detail how these setups are handled. The HAL software is designed to make it as easy as possible on you, the end user, to successfully set up your system. If you can keep track of details and make accurate entries in the HAL setup screens, you can harness the power of these protocols to control any controllable object in your home.

See the author's website www.homeautomationmadeeasy.info to find sources of additional information about protocols and process information.

Chapter 4

Project 1, Installing HALbasic Software on Your PC

After you have your copy of HALbasic software, the first step is to load the software onto your Windows-based home automation computer. The home automation control platform computer ideally would be one you intend to leave on 24 hours a day, 365 days a year. Consider using a computer specifically dedicated for this purpose, because having a dedicated computer will eliminate the potential performance problems of user sharing and will minimize the potential for lockups or inadvertent reboots.

Note **Acquiring Your HALbasic Software** You can order a copy of HALbasic software from this book jacket, by downloading a copy from www.automatedliving.com, or by ordering the boxed version alone or as a part of the HALbasic Introductory Kit.

If your home has a has a high-speed Internet connection, it is best to use that connection to do a full update of the Windows software in Windows 7, as discussed in Chapter 2, "Using a Windows Computer as Your Home Automation Platform." The preparatory steps and tasks outlined in Chapter 2 will greatly help improve your overall experience with a DIY (do-it-yourself) home automation installation.

After your computer OS and chosen security software installations are fully up-to-date and patched, turn off the automatic updates for both the Windows OS and the security software. If you do not like the idea of having to pull computer update maintenance manually, at the very least set up the automated updates to run only once a week, preferably during a time window when you do not have any planned controls taking effect. Microsoft and Norton have both significantly improved the automatic update processes; however, they are not always 100 percent flawless processes. Schedule OS and security automatic updates during expected least-risk automation control periods of the week or during a time of day when no automation events are scheduled. At a later date you will also want to deploy "HAL Watch Dog" to monitor the various HAL processes, manage restarts, and oversee the computer's activities.

Starting Point

It is wise to go through a preinstall routine before installing any new software on your computer. For the purpose of this text and in this chapter and the rest of the book, we will make the supposition that you will be using a dedicated personal computer for your home automation platform to run the home automation software and perform all home automation tasks.

It is best to start with a fresh, clean install of the Windows operating system. If the computer is new and shipped with a preinstalled OS, you are all set and will not need to reinstall the basic OS; however, applying all the current patches is still highly recommended. If you are setting up an older used computer of your own or one you have purchased to run HAL, it will take some time, but it is probably worth the effort to do a fresh install of the operation system on the computer hard drive. Follow the Windows instructions or the manual that came with your computer to do the new "reinstall." In the absence of a fresh install, at least ensure that all the "Important," "Optional," and "Recommended" Windows updates have been installed successfully before you install the HALbasic or any other application software, as described in Chapter 2. It takes some effort and time, but regardless of your preliminary choice of computer, it is best to have the operating system "fully patched" before you install any new software. To do this the computer will have to be network ready with a hard-wired or wireless connection to the Internet. The steps to download Windows 7 patches from the Microsoft website are outlined in detail in Chapter 2.

Security Software

Security software is a must for Internet-connected computers. For the security software on your home automation platform, I would highly recommend that you use the latest version of Norton 360. Use your Internet connection to fully patch and update your Norton product or other security software. Over my first 12 years in working with computers, which began after Arpanet but before the first website phenomenon was launched, I learned through very bad experiences how important it is to have a quality security product loaded on any computer or server that would be accessing the Internet. It is well known in information technology security circles that those who would do harm to you with your computer data include criminals, hobbyists, hackers, organizations, and even foreign governments. They are involved in hacking, virus propagation, and Trojan horse creation—you name it. All the bad things that happen are being done by a disconnected army of people with ill intent and nothing truly productive to do. The only defense you have is a quality security product, and one that provides valuable daily updates. Over the past 15 years I have personally used and provided technical support to others for a large variety of personal computer security products. For the home user with modest to average computer skills, I would recommend using the latest version of Norton 360. Ease of use is important in a security product and Norton rates high on that scale as well. The Norton products work with very little repair intervention, updates and improvements are published nearly every day to protect you from the latest threats, and it also does more than just security by helping you manage your total computer experience. The street price is about $80, with special sale or promotional pricing often available at the big-box stores for less than list price. The technical support appears to be offshore but it is excellent; their support staff is tenacious when it comes to solving issues, and they can do most repairs by remote control over the Internet. You will need an email address to register your security software. Also, often the security software purchase includes online storage for your critical backups, and you can purchase more online storage though Norton if necessary.

When you are satisfied that you have done all that is necessary to update the computer and operating system and have Internet-level security software installed, it is time to begin the installation process with the HALbasic software. Regardless of the source of the HALbasic software—a download from the website, a disc included with this book's purchase, or a boxed version—the steps to do the install, registration, and activation are very similar.

Beginning the HALbasic Install

Figure 4.1 shows what comes in the HALbasic v5 X10 Introduction Kit. Included are the HAL X10 Power Line Adapter, a serial cable, the HALbasic software CD, and the HAL model number HAL465 X10 Lamp Module. The current list price of the intro kit is $179. That price is now added to our prototype budget.

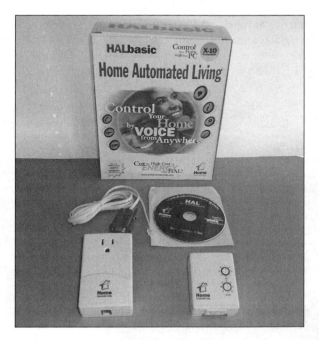

Figure 4.1   *The HALbasic v5 X10 Introduction Kit is a great home automation start for beginners.*

> **Note**   HALbasic v5 Introduction Kit cost from prototype budget: $179.
> Total prototype cost so far: $1,079.

This chapter focuses on installing the HALbasic version level 5 software. For novice users, the installation is documented step by step. Experienced computer users can use this section as a way to see what is involved in the installation process or as a checklist to verify that their installation is proceeding correctly. The exercise of working though the steps and tasks in Chapter 2 demonstrates the importance of paying attention to the details and taking actions in a pre-prescribed order. No matter the OS or software application there are important details that cannot be overlooked and steps that must be performed in a certain order. Plan to spend two to four hours for the install process. Take time to cover all the bases and record the details in a notebook as you proceed. Items worthy of note include license numbers, account usernames, and passwords. Although it might feel like overkill, taking notes is very helpful when things do not go entirely according to plan or if you need the information later.

Modify OS Security Setting

Before you begin the installation process, you need to make one modification to the security controls within the Windows operating system to facilitate the loading of the HAL application. To make this modification, follow these steps:

1. From the Start menu, open the Control Panel and select the System and Security option. This brings you to the window shown in Figure 4.2.

Figure 4.2   *The user account settings are found under this heading.*

2. Click on User Accounts and Family Safety, as shown in Figure 4.3.

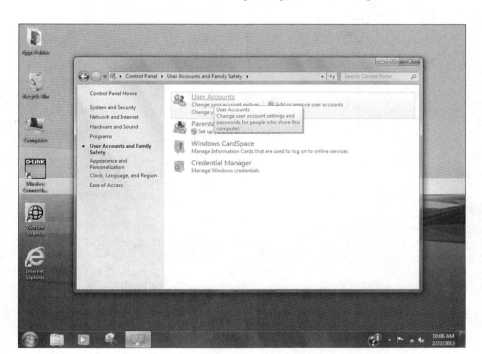

Figure 4.3   *The user account settings are found under this heading.*

3. Once you have made the selection to bring up the User Accounts window, the name of the account currently logged in is displayed, as shown in Figure 4.4. Notice that the account "Dennis" has Administrator-level privileges, which allow this named user to make modifications to settings within the Windows operating system.

4. The next step is to click on the link within the window shown in Figure 4.4 for Change User Account Control Settings. The default notify setting for Windows 7 is "Notify me only when programs try to make changes to my computer." At this level there is the potential for HALbasic to not load properly. To ensure that the software does not have trouble loading, change this setting to Never Notify, as shown in Figure 4.5. This requires a reboot, so reboot Windows and move on to installing HALbasic.

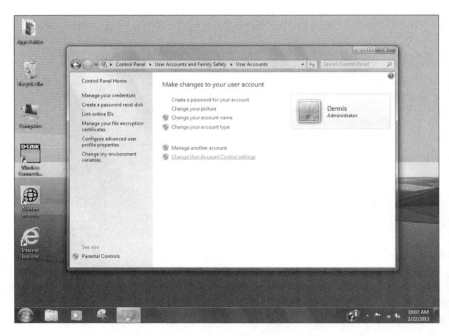

Figure 4.4   *The action links are in the main window pane.*

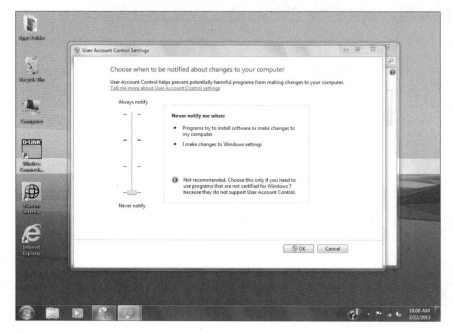

Figure 4.5   *The user account notification default is set to Never Notify.*

HALbasic Installation Steps

1. Place the HALbasic CD into the computer's optical drive and launch the HAL installer, as shown in Figure 4.6.

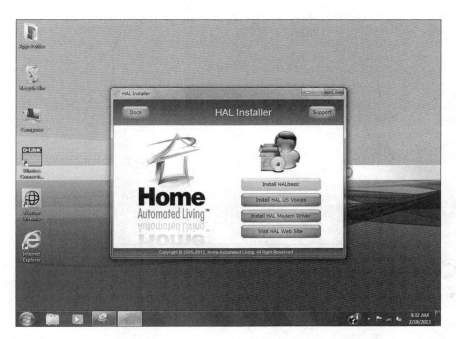

Figure 4.6   *The HALbasic installer. Notice that the Docs and Support buttons are also active options.*

2. From the launcher, click the Install HALbasic button. Click through the wizard and accept the license agreement.

3. After the software terms and conditions page, the Installation Wizard appears as shown in Figure 4.7, asking you to choose between Automatic Installation and Custom Installation. When you are doing any software application or program install for the first time or when you are unfamiliar with what choices and options might be presented, it is best to select the Automatic Installation to have the choices made for you by default. So leave the Automatic Installation option marked and click the Next button to proceed. You can customize the installation later if there is a compelling reason to do so.

4. Early into the installation, you might need to restart your PC in order to continue. If you are running applications on your PC that use the same third-party controls as HALbasic, the installation procedure will need to reboot the machine to ensure that these components are not in memory during the install. After you have rebooted your PC, start the installation procedure again as you did at the beginning of these steps.

5. Figure 4.8 shows the window indicating that the install is complete. The wizard has done its work and the next step for you is to click the Finish button.

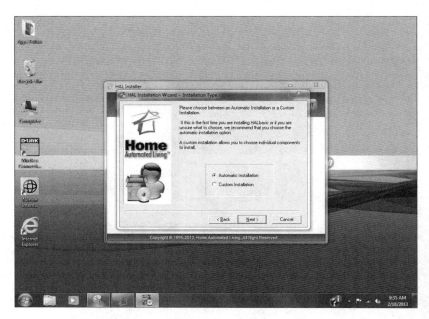

Figure 4.7   *Only two installation options are presented.*

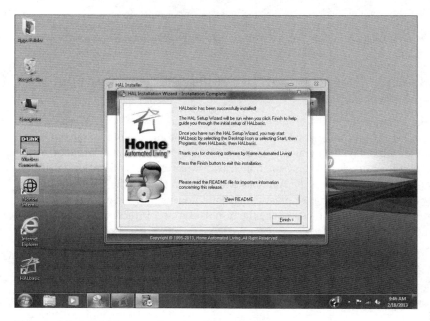

Figure 4.8   *Clicking on View Readme takes you to the software version release notes.*

6. After you've clicked the Finish button, the Welcome to HAL Setup window appears, as shown in Figure 4.9. Take note of the instructions to have a working Internet connection, to have your PC configured correctly, and to disconnect your PC from the Internet. All of these conditions are necessary to set up HAL.

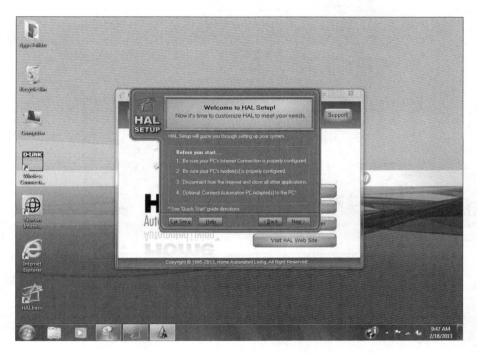

Figure 4.9   *The HAL Setup window.*

7. The window shown in Figure 4.10 presents the option to perform a Quick Setup of the HAL software or a Custom Setup. Given that this is your first time setting up HAL, keep Quick Setup selected and click the Next button.

8. In this next window you can select any Universal Powerline Bus interfaces you have in your home. Because we are working with the Introductory Kit for X10 technology, your current choice should be None for UPB Adapter; as shown in Figure 4.11. However, if you decide to pick up a UPB adapter down the line, ensure that it has a USB port so that you can connect it to your home automation PC. Click the Next button to proceed to the next setup window.

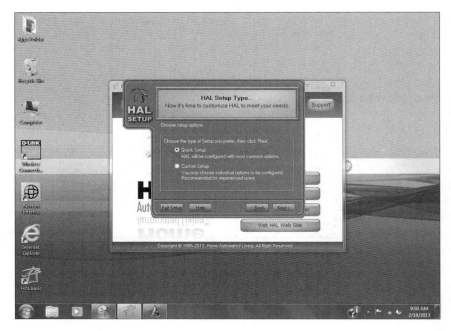

Figure 4.10 *The HAL Setup Type window.*

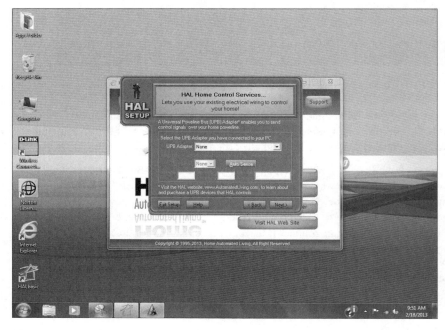

Figure 4.11 *If you have UPB adapters to connect, you can connect them and click on Auto Sense to detect them.*

9. As in the previous window, this window allows you to choose any X10 or INSTEON adapters present in your home automation system. The Intro Kit purchased for the prototype system included a HAL11 model X10 controller interface, so that selection is made from the Adapter drop-down menu shown in Figure 4.12. When using the KIT select HAL 11 from the drop down menu.

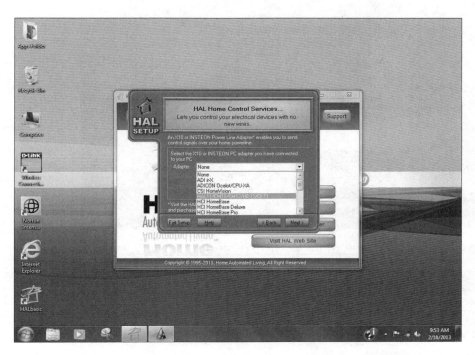

Figure 4.12 *Note the large number of compatible products available for both X10 and INSTEON adapter models.*

10. After you have selected your adapter type and model, the next step is to select which COM port to use. The prototype computer has only one COM port currently available, so COM Port 1 is selected, as shown in Figure 4.13. If you are not sure which COM port is used in your system, connect the adapter to your PC and click Auto Sense. The HAL setup automatically detects and selects the appropriate COM port. Click the Next button when you are ready to proceed.

11. The third and final choice for the Quick Setup process allows you to select any Z-Wave Adapters in the home. as shown in Figure 4.14. Don't worry if you don't have any at present, because a Z-Wave Adapter can be added to the setup later. This is covered in more detail in Chapter 10, "Project 7 Getting Green and Managing Your Home's Climate." Click the Next button to bring up the next window.

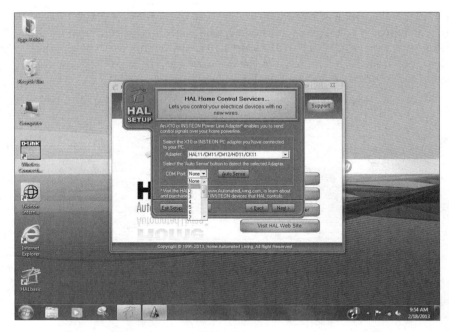

Figure 4.13   *The compatible hardware interfaces are listed in the drop-down menu.*

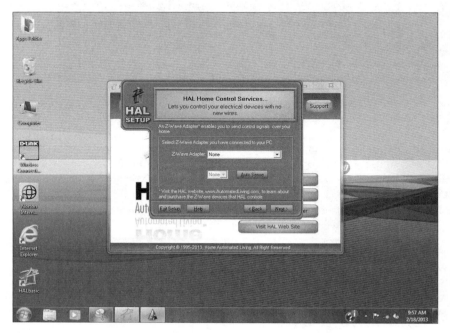

Figure 4.14   *For now the Z-Wave Adapter selection will remain at None.*

12. The Congratulations! window appears, as shown in Figure 4.15, and HAL is ready to start controlling the home automation system. Check the Run HAL Now box in the lower-right corner of the screen and click the Finish button.

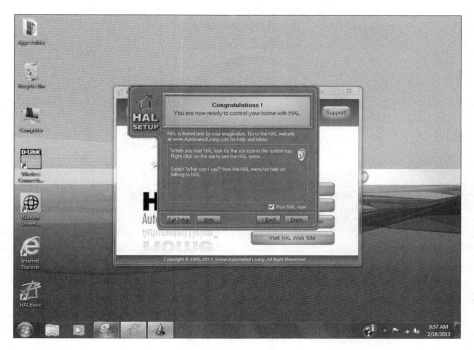

Figure 4.15 *Launching the server takes only a moment or two.*

Notice in Figure 4.16 that we are returned to the HAL Installer window. However, one thing is changed: In the lower-right corner of the Widows tray is a small telephone-like icon with an X across the icon. Also in the lower-left portion of the desktop screen is a new icon for HALbasic that we will use in a future step.

After the installation procedure is complete, it's a good idea to restart Windows to ensure a complete install. Doing so will make sure there are no Windows registry issues or other problems with the installation. Any testing during the installation and setup phase will help eliminate problems when your system is fully operational. After Windows restarts, reconnect your PC to the Internet to activate HALbasic.

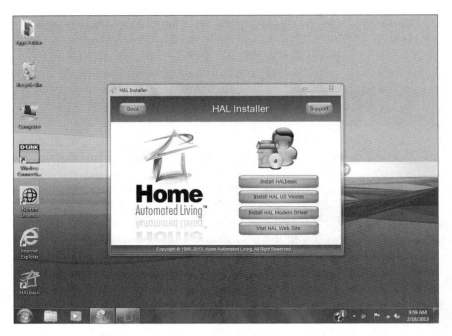

Figure 4.16   *A new icon has appeared in the system tray.*

Activation

After the system reboots, if you are using a wireless connection to the Internet, segue to the wireless icon and connect to the Internet. The advisory in the window shown earlier in Figure 4.9 advised you to be disconnected from the Internet during the install's setup process. That process will be completed when you click on the Finish button, so reconnecting to the Internet should be done now. If you used a hard wire to connect to the Internet, reconnect it now before clicking the Finish button. To complete the software activation over the Internet, your Internet connection must be operational. Alternatively, you can activate by cell phone or landline call to HAL support if your installation does not use the Internet at all. At this time click on the new HALbasic icon from the left corner of the desktop. You will again see the HALserver start window, as shown in Figure 4.17.

After the server is started, the window shown in Figure 4.17 is automatically removed from the screen; however, the desktop tray icon remains. To activate the software, we will close the application by using the up-arrow icon on the tray to reveal the HAL listening ear and right-clicking on the HAL listening ear icon to display the Shut Down HAL option and selecting it at the bottom of the menu. The HAL server is shut down in order to go through the first few install steps to get to the Run HAL License Manager option. The rerun install can be done with the HAL software disc in the drive; from your download location if you downloaded the software from the HAL website; or by using the Windows Start menu, going to All Programs, selecting the HALbasic folder on the Start menu, and expanding it to show HAL Setup Wizard. The window shown in Figure 4.18 is in the center of the desktop. Select the option Run HAL License Manager Now.

Figure 4.17 *The server launch always includes the notice "Performing Maintenance."*

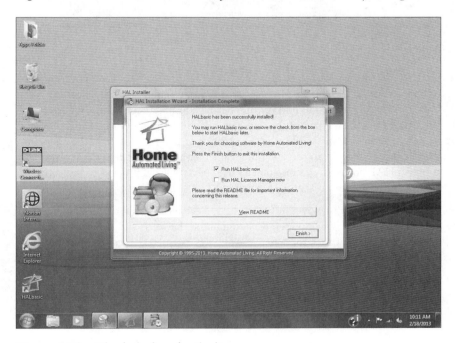

Figure 4.18 *Check the box for the license manager.*

With the correct box selected as shown in Figure 4.19, click on the Finish button.

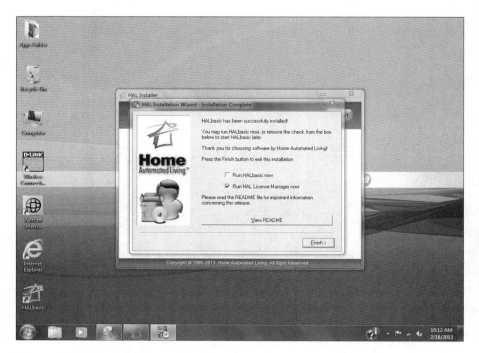

Figure 4.19   *Run HALbasic Now is not checked.*

Notice the three choices for proceeding, as shown in Figure 4.20. For those with the trial download version, selecting Try HALbasic gives you a timed version. Selecting Buy HALbasic leads you to the method for purchasing a regular license key. We have already purchased ours for the prototype and have a license key, so our choice is Activate HALbasic. After the selection is made, click the Continue button. Notice in the advisory that the user license is specific to the computer on which you are loading the software. Once you own a HAL licensed version you can use the activation process to move the software to another computer if that is ever needed.

The next window to appear is shown in Figure 4.21. Notice the string of zeros in the field next to the Activate button. Click on the box containing the zeros and enter your purchased license key without the dashes. After a valid key is entered, the Continue button becomes active. Click on the Continue button to bring up the registration window.

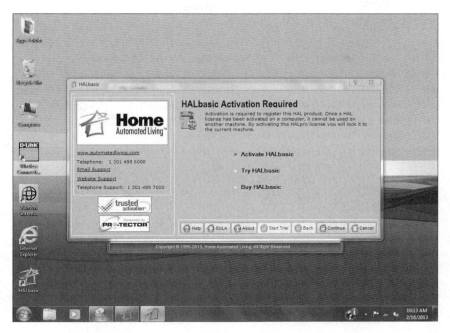

Figure 4.20 *Choose the option that best applies to your user license situation.*

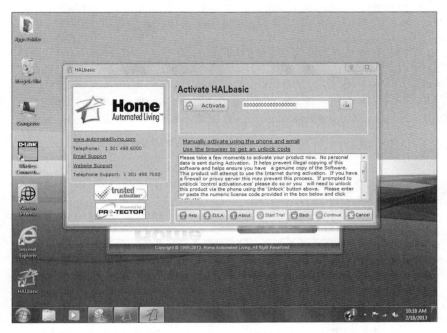

Figure 4.21 *Making a phone call to perform the activation process is an option for computers not connected to the Internet.*

Register with HAL

The final part of the installation process is to register online with HAL. Because this is a new installation, we'll assume that you have not registered with HAL. To register, complete the wizard by creating a username and password and entering all needed personal information. If you do not want to receive emails from HAL, be sure to uncheck the email communication boxes, as shown in Figure 4.22. When registration is completed, your install of HALbasic is finished.

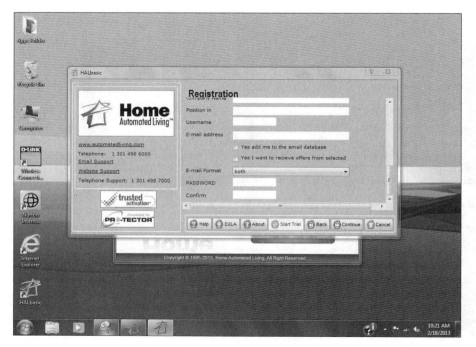

Figure 4.22   *Check or uncheck these boxes to manage HAL email communications.*

Exploring HALbasic

After your software is installed, registered, and loaded, it's a good idea to spend some time looking through the HALbasic menus. Don't worry about causing any problems; as long as nothing is saved, you won't do any harm. Not only will this give you an idea of what to expect with setting up your home automation software, but poking through the menus might give you some ideas for projects outside the scope of this book.

To access the HALbasic menus, double-click the HALbasic icon on your desktop, or launch HALbasic from the Start menu, or click on the up arrow in the desktop tray and right-click on the HAL listening ear icon to show the menu pop-up window shown in Figure 4.23. The listening ear will be present only when the HAL server is running.

Figure 4.23   *Right-clicking on the ear icon brings up the pop-up menu window.*

In Chapter 5, "Project 2, Controlling Appliances, Lights, and Devices," we will set up and control some X10 devices connected to lights and appliances using our HALbasic server install with an X10 serial interface controller.

Chapter 5

Project 2, Controlling Appliances, Lights, and Devices

Now that your HALbasic software is installed, it is time to move on to setting up some controlling actions for lamps and appliances. Imagine how many times during the course of a week you and your household members turn on and off the various lights in your home. Some of that is proximity based: You want a given light on because you walk into a room. Sometimes it is event driven: You want the porch light on because someone knocked on the door. In other cases the need to turn on a light or an appliance is time based, such as turning a light on and off at certain times so that your home appears occupied when you're on vacation.

With HAL we can perform these actions with less effort and no human interaction other than the initial setup of stored procedures.

In this section we will install and use an X10 controller and control modules. Although the X10 is an older technology, it is still a very good technology for the beginner because the sheer variety of available X10 devices, coupled with their low price, makes for a good start for home automation projects. Starting with X10 serves as a low-cost self-training opportunity for the handy person to become familiar with the installations and software control data screens and windows and data fields, and it allows users new to home automation to make sure that home automation will be beneficial to their home.

Connecting the Hardware

This project includes two lamp modules, an appliance module, and an outlet. It is straightforward and should require less than four to six hours after you have all the components, parts, and tools assembled in one place. The outlet install requires the following tools: diagonal cutting pliers, a flat-blade screwdriver, and a Phillips screwdriver. This project assumes that you are replacing an existing outlet because adding a new outlet to your home is outside the scope of this project and should be done by a licensed electrician. Along with these tools, you also need three wire nuts.

Note   **Selecting the Right Wire Nuts**   Outlets are typically run with either 12- or 14-gauge wire, so be sure to pick up wire nuts that can accommodate these sizes. Red or yellow wire nuts are appropriate here. Remember, the lower the gauge, the thicker the wire, so choose appropriately.

The other appliance and lamp control modules plug into existing outlets, making their installation much simpler. Keep in mind that the polarized plug on the control module means that it can be plugged into a polarized outlet only one way.

Connecting the Control Adapter to the PC

Figure 5.1 shows the X10 power-line interface module and lamp control module that ships with the HALbasic Introductory Kit. The serial port connector is plugged into the control module with a telephone-type RJ14. Should you have to extend the location of the power-line interface module a distance from the computer, be sure to use a telephone cable of 10 feet or less, consisting of four wires. Because some telephone cables have only two wires for connections, picking the right cable is important.

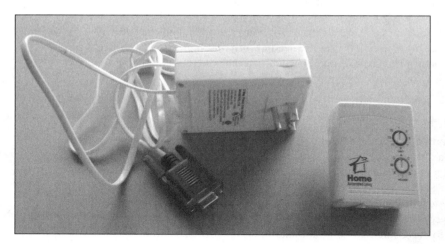

Figure 5.1   *The serial port connecter cable is connected to the control module.*

For the prototype PC, the X10 power-line interface module uses the first serial port on the computer referred to in the operating system as COM1. If your PC is already using COM1, use the next available COM port. Chapter 4, "Project 1, Installing HALbasic Software on Your PC," shows how to auto-select available COM ports during the HALbasic setup process. At the opposite end of the cable from the RJ-14 modular jack is a standard nine-pin female serial port connector, as shown in Figure 5.2. That connector will connect to the computer's nine-pin male standard serial port.

Figure 5.2   *Notice the slant on the narrow sides, ensuring it will fit the computer's connector correctly.*

The serial port connection on the computer is shown in Figure 5.3. This is the port the X10 control adapter will be connected to. Many computers have two serial ports as a standard configuration. With the prevalence of USB (universal serial bus), many new computer models do not have a standard nine-pin serial interface port available. If you do not have a serial port you could consider using a USB to Serial RS-232 DB9 Adapter Cable. Notice that the serial port is narrowed toward the bottom of the computer, allowing the connector to fit only one way.

Figure 5.3   *This serial port is labeled "A" on the back of the case.*

To connect a serial cable from the X10 controller, orient the connector so that its narrow edge is on the bottom. It fits only one way but if a pin bends and then breaks, the connector is useless; so be sure to orient it correctly before attempting a connection. The connector should fit nicely with very little force needed to slide it into place. After it's securely in place, tighten the long plastic thumbscrews to hold the connector firmly. If the thumbscrews are not turning properly, check to make sure that the connector is seated correctly.

After connecting the adapter to the computer, plug the adapter into a standard three-prong outlet. The closest outlet for the prototype was an outlet on the battery backup on the surge-protected-only side, as shown in Figure 5.4. This worked out fine in spite of the fact that surge protectors with low pass (a.k.a clamping voltage) through voltage ratings (below 500 volts) can block X10 signals on occasion. When injecting control signals into your house wiring system, it is best to use a standard outlet. You would never want a battery backup outlet to inject control signals into your house wiring system. One nice thing about the control adapter is that there is an outlet on the opposite side of the plug prongs, so you do not lose use of the outlet space.

> **Note**　**Energy Cost of the X10 Adapter**　A single X10 adapter costs less than $4 per year to operate at a utility charge of 15 cents per kWh.

Figure 5.4　*A small light or appliance can still be plugged in or another type of control can be piggybacked onto this control adapter by use of the surface outlet shown.*

Setting up the Control Modules

After you have the X10 power-line interface module plugged into an outlet in the house, you can control multiple devices though use of the HALbasic software on your computer.

Take a close look at the HAL lamp control module shown in Figure 5.5 and notice the turn dials for Unit and House selections. These turn dials will be used to identify the specific appliance or lamp that will be controlled. Each device will be set to a unique number for House and Unit.

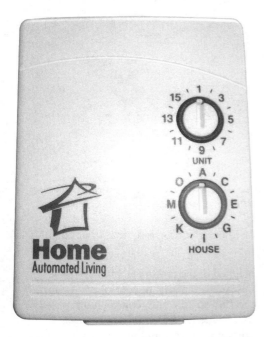

Figure 5.5   *A small flat-blade screwdriver is used to rotate the selector dials.*

Whenever you are using control modules or control devices of any kind, it is critical to not exceed the voltage, amperage, or wattage ratings of the module. The back of the HAL Model No. 465 Lamp Module, shown in Figure 5.6, shows this device's ratings. At its basic level the module is a relay/switch controlled by the X10 signal that is passed over the household wires. Internally it has a decoder that interprets the control signals by listening to a signal matched to its unique identity. After a signal is received and decoded, it takes the action specified in the rest of the coded message. The internal working electronics in this device are rated at 120 volts, so this device can be used only on 120-volt 60-cycle AC current as found in your home. Do not attempt to use this device at voltages above 120. Looking further at the ratings on the back, notice that the maximum wattage the device can control is 300 watts. The information supplied also specifies that the control can be used only on incandescent lights, which means it cannot be used with fluorescent lights or with any type of motor.

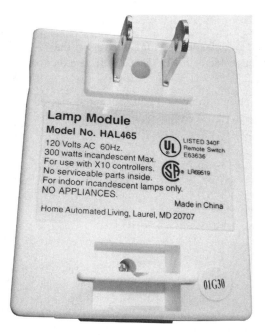

Figure 5.6   *This device is rated by Underwriter's Laboratories and CSA International for safety when used in compliance with the ratings.*

Check the ratings for every device you intend to use and be certain that what you plug in matches the safety criteria ratings on the device.

The cost of the introductory kit is already included in the prototype budget. In the prototype installation I wanted to also demonstrate using X10 to control two lamps, an appliance, and an outlet. On eBay I was able to find an appliance control module, a second lamp control module, and an X10 controlled outlet. Each of these items was about $20 and well below the suggested list price, although some components were previously used so I have added their cost to the prototype budget. Using new parts, a split outlet would list at $30.00, an appliance control would list about $25.00, and lamp modules sell for $24.00.

Note   Additional X10 controls from prototype budget: $70.
Total prototype cost so far: $1,149.

The three additional devices are shown in Figure 5.7. All of these devices are rated and approved for indoor use only. Notice that the same dials are on each one for selecting House and Unit. The Leviton outlet is a split unit with only the top outlet controlled by the X10 signals. This outlet is rated at 15 amps and 125 volts AC. The lower outlet is always on. The appliance control module is rated for control use on up to 1/3-horsepower motors, 500 watts of incandescent lighting, or a 400-watt television, and no more than a 15-amp resistive load.

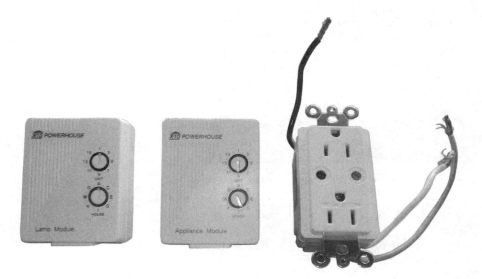

Figure 5.7   *The appliance outlet in the center can connect a two-prong appliance cord.*

Setting up Plug-in Control Modules

To set the plug-in control modules to the desired coded address, use a flat-head screwdriver to move the dials from one stop notch to the left. You will hear a light clicking sound as you rotate the dial to each letter or number.

First select a unique House setting, as shown in Figure 5.8. The House identifier can be the same letter designation for up to 16 unique and numerically identified control modules.

Next, the first lamp module is set to be Unit number 3, as shown in Figure 5.9. Each control module will have a unique Unit number identity under House K until 16 modules are used in the home.

Figure 5.8 *The letter K was chosen as the House identity.*

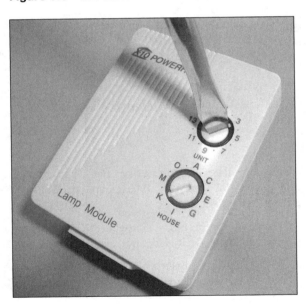

Figure 5.9 *As the dial is turned, you can hear soft clicks for each number, helping you stop at the right number, in this case 3.*

In Figure 5.10 the Appliance Module is set to K for House and 5 for Unit.

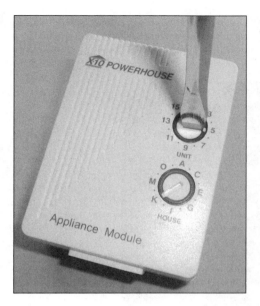

Figure 5.10 *Each Unit number will be unique until all 16 are used under House K.*

The HAL Lamp Module was set to K for House and to 9 for Unit, as shown in Figure 5.11. Notice that all the House settings are set to the letter K and the respective Unit numbers from left to right in the figure are 3, 5, and 9.

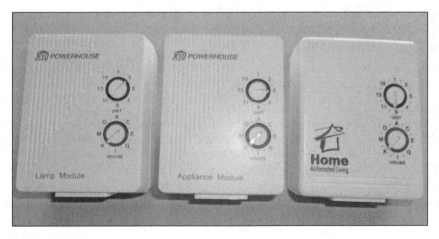

Figure 5.11 *These plug-in control modules are all ready to plug in and use.*

At this point in your project, after you have a number of control modules ready to install, it is a good time to begin a notebook to keep a record of the settings you have used, the locations where they will be used, and what you intend to control with them. These first installs are fairly simple because they do not require any electrical work beyond plugging the control module devices into an available working outlet and then plugging the lamp or appliance you intend to control into the outlet on the module, as shown in Figure 5.12.

Figure 5.12   *A lamp is plugged into the two-prong outlet on the bottom of the control.*

It is still necessary to set up the plug-in modules in HALbasic, a topic that is covered in detail in the next section. Your notebook info will be used later to make the entries into HALbasic's configuration data fields.

Setting up Hard-wired Outlet Control Modules

To set up a hard-wired outlet-style control module, the process is similar to that for the plug-in units except that some simple rewiring tasks are necessary. A smaller screwdriver is needed to fit into the much smaller slots on the outlet dial, as shown in Figure 5.13. The settings include the similar but smaller dials for Home and Unit, which have been set to House K and Unit 12. You also need a Phillips-head screwdriver, diagonal cutting pliers, and some wire nuts to connect a control module receptacle in an electrical box where a standard outlet had previously been installed.

Note   **A Note About Safety**   Never work on live/energized circuits. Always be sure the circuit breaker is switched to off or the fuse for the circuit is removed before you work on the circuit.

Figure 5.13 *The top outlet is controlled by HALbasic; the bottom outlet is always on.*

Figure 5.14 shows an "old work" PVC outlet box with shielded cable already in it, nearly ready to be pushed back into the wall for permanent mounting after the control module Leviton receptacle is connected to the wires. The white/neutral, black hot/current, and bare ground wires are stripped back and ready to connect to our Leviton receptacle.

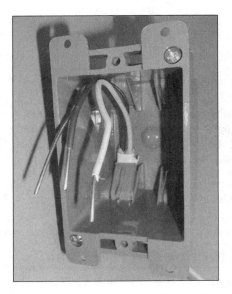

Figure 5.14 *This style of box is for old work and is easy to use as a replacement box when the original box is covered by 1/2-inch or 5/8-inch drywall board.*

As shown in Figure 5.15, the white (neutral) wire on the controlled outlet will be connected to the neutral wire in the box, the black current-carrying conductors will be connected together, and the green wire from the receptacle will be connected with the wire nuts to the bare copper (bonding) wire in the box. The wire's connections, when secured to the receptacle wires with wire nuts, are ready to carefully push back into the box.

Figure 5.15   *Match up the wires for color and use the correct size of wire nut to fasten the wires together.*

When pressing the connected wires back into the box after the box is fastened with the screw tabs to the drywall, fold and push the bonding wire to the bottom of the box first, next fold in and press in the neutral wires, and lastly fold and press in the black conductors. Then press the outlet into the box, being careful to line up the outlet mounting screws with the holes in the box. After the outlet box and the outlet are properly assembled, install the decorative outlet cover to complete the receptacle installation.

The hardware components should now all be in place. The next half of the project involves making the entries for the control modules into the setup screens in HALbasic, as detailed in the next section.

Configuring Control Modules Identities in HALbasic

This section discusses a typical setup of the four devices covered in the preceding installation section. Begin by launching the HALbasic server. After the HALbasic server is running, right-click on the HAL ear icon in the system tray and click Open Automation

Setup Screen. This brings up the HALbasic -Automation Setup Screen, as shown in Figure 5.16. No devices have been entered into the database so the setup screen is blank.

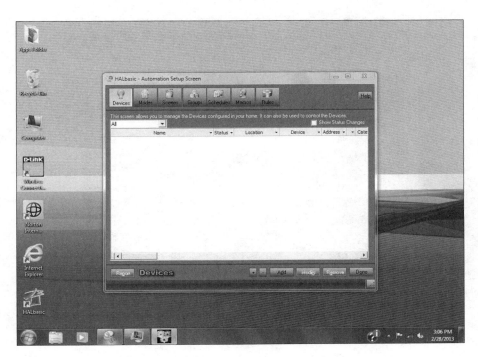

Figure 5.16 *Setup begins with this blank slate.*

In this window we will enter the four devices that were configured in the preceding section. Begin by highlighting the Devices tab at the top of the setup window. At the bottom of the window shown in Figure 5.16, click on the Add button near the lower-right part of the window.

A smaller window with four device choices appears, as shown in Figure 5.17. Begin by selecting Lighting and click on the Next button.

The next window is the Organizer section of the Device Wizard. For our prototype, I want to control a dining room light or lamp so Dining Room is entered in the Location field, as shown in Figure 5.18. Because both you and HAL will use voice commands later, be sure to spell all location words correctly. As your control database is populated with locations, the location field will turn into a drop-down list populated with your location entries. You will still be able to add locations as needed. In the next field, Device, a drop-down menu is populated with a list of popular home and office devices controlled with a home automation system. As with Location, you can add Device names as needed. For our current installation demonstration, Lights is selected in the drop-down menu. After you have selected a device, click on the Next button.

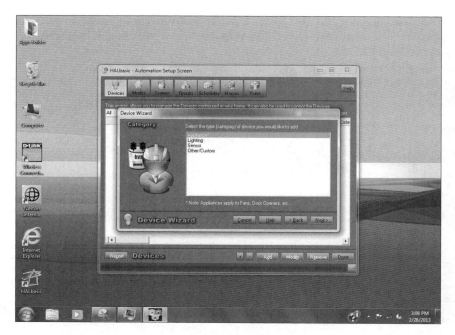

Figure 5.17 *Choose from the four items by highlighting your choice.*

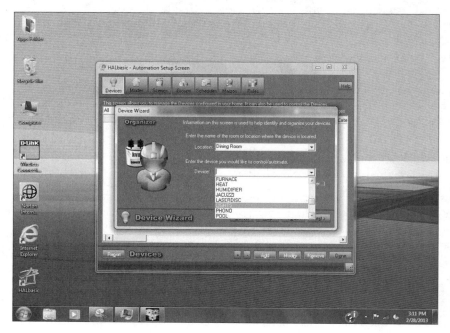

Figure 5.18 *Select Lights from the drop-down menu.*

The next window presented is shown in Figure 5.19. Notice that the application combined the location and the device name to become Dining Room Lights and made the entry in the name field. As you develop your naming convention, keep in mind that there can be only one target device named Dining Room Lights. On this screen you can enter comments in the User Comments field to help keep your devices and locations straight. I entered Near Window for my comment to illustrate this device's exact location.

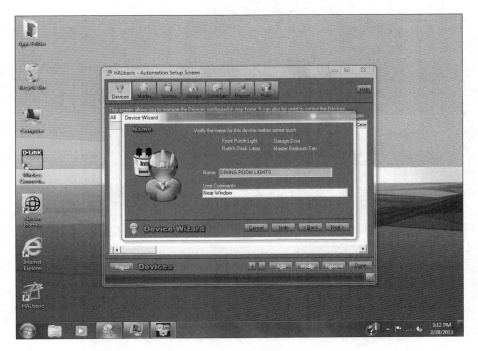

Figure 5.19   *User Comments can be any information you choose.*

After your entries are made for location and device and any comments are entered, click Next to bring up the window shown in Figure 5.20. We set the first control device from the first part of this chapter to K-9 for House and Unit. Because this device is a Home Automated Living model HAL465 module, select Home Automated Living as the manufacturer and select Lamp Module for Description and HAL465 for Model.

Click on the Next button to get to the screen shown in Figure 5.21. Notice that the dials on this screen approximate the dials on the devices shown in previous steps. This dial shown in Figure 5.21 must be set to match the device used, in this case, for Dining Room Lights. There are two ways to rotate the dials: One is to mouse over them and click (hold) and rotate the dials to the correct House and Unit settings. The other is to click in the field where A01 is shown and enter the codes. Enter the House letter first, then the Unit number.

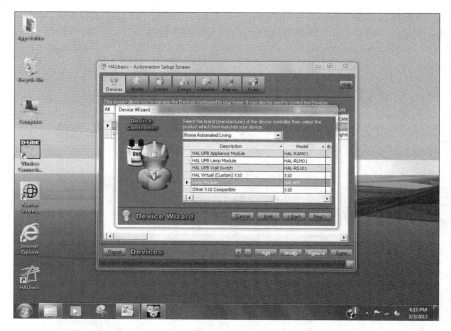

Figure 5.20 *Select the manufacturer and model in this Device Controller window.*

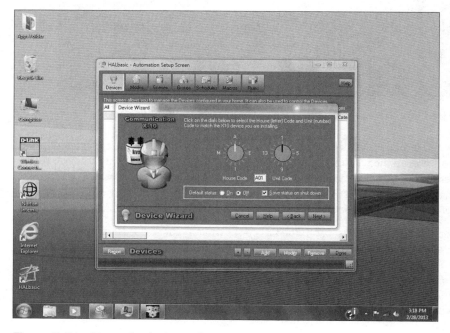

Figure 5.21 *Enter the device codes in this screen for the location being set up.*

Figure 5.22 shows the dials set to K-9, the same settings used for our Dining Room Lights controller. After all codes have been entered, click the Next button.

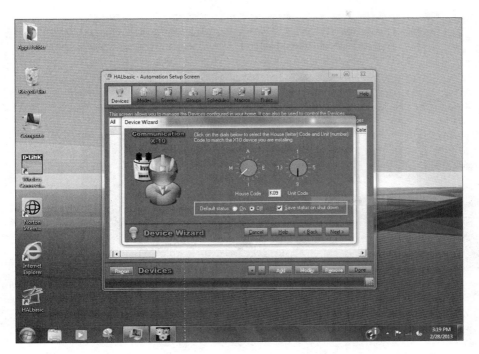

Figure 5.22   *The Dining Room Lights module, configured with the correct codes.*

You can test your control device installation in the next few steps beginning with the window shown in Figure 5.23. After you have set the control codes for your device, plug the control device into an outlet that can be seen from the home automation computer location. Plug a lamp into the lamp control module with the mechanical switch on the lamp set to on. The device that is now coded into the database can be controlled from the buttons on the screen shown in Figure 5.23. Notice in the lower third of the window three buttons under the heading You May Use This Area to Test This Device. With your device and lamp connected to an active outlet, clicking the On button turns on the lamp, and clicking the Off button turns off the lamp. In the event the lamp does not come on, make sure the light bulb in the lamp is good or go back a step in the wizard to check your device address settings. Then, retry the test.

The 465 lamp control modules support dimming, so the configuration properties also need to be set up to support the dimming feature. Click the Dimmable check box and use the scrollbar on the lower-right side to scroll to a percentage of dimming, as shown in Figure 5.24. Notice that the Dim button is no longer grayed out and has become an active button capable of taking an action. The dim Percent is set to 46 percent by the slider; you can also manually enter a percentage in the percentage box.

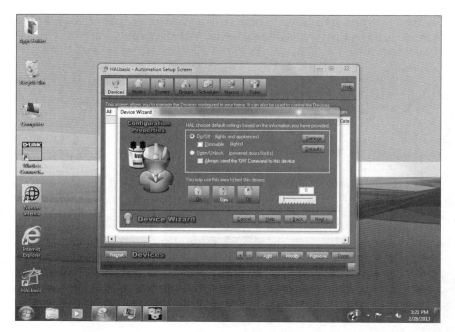

Figure 5.23   *You can test the installation and setup while you are on this screen.*

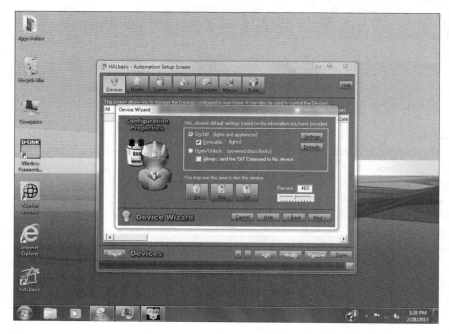

Figure 5.24   *All three control action buttons are now operational.*

Clicking on the Settings button shown in Figure 5.24 brings up the Device Settings screen, shown in Figure 5.25, where additional device settings can be modified. It is a good idea to check Enable Status Monitoring for devices that support the feature. The other selections are personal preference items and can be changed later.

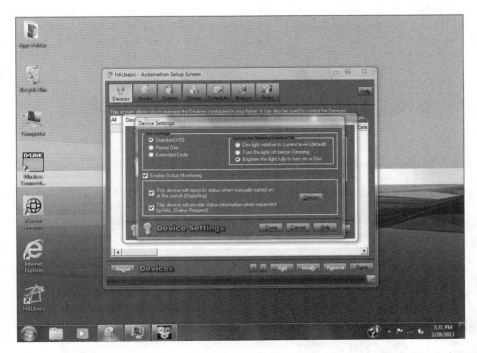

Figure 5.25 *The option to go full bright at the on command or Dim command is selected.*

After the Device options are set, click Done and then click Next. The Voice Access and Logging window appears.

For the prototype system I selected voice access, confirmation of verbal commands, and then confirmation of the action taken. This means that HALbasic will parrot back an "understanding" of any command as an implied question, and you will have to answer in the affirmative to have the action performed. When the action is completed, you will receive voice feedback as to whether the action was taken, HAL cannot perform, or the action was canceled. Over time you will learn where you want this feedback and where you can get along without it. To remove this feedback later, simply return to this screen for any device no longer requiring verbal feedback and uncheck the appropriate check box.

Click on the Finish button and all the details are written to the control database in HALbasic.

Now that we have our dining room lights set, it's time to set up the other lighting controller, this time for the living room. From the HALbasic - Automation Setup Screen, highlight the Device tab and click Add. You'll see the entries for the living room lights in our prototype system.

After you have set the device controller information, move on to the Configuration Properties window, as shown in Figure 5.26. Notice that the living room lights have been set to a different dimming level than the dining room lights. Each new set of lights or lamps can be dimmed to a specification percentage you preselect. Fifty percent is a good starting point for dimming lamps.

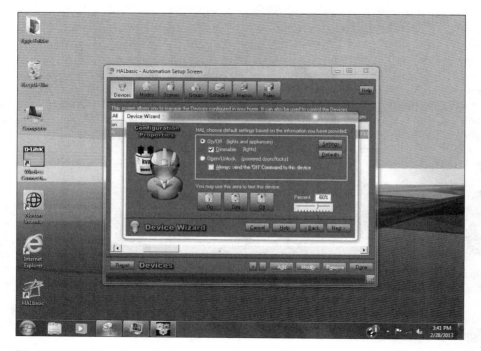

Figure 5.26   *The dimming percentage is set to 60.*

Complete the rest of the process the same as was done for the Dining Room Lights, being careful to enter the correct names and coding and conditions for the new location. After you click the 'Finish' button, you will be returned to the Automation Setup Screen, as shown in Figure 5.27. As shown also in Figure 5.27, after you've finished the steps outlined for the second time, there are now two locations and devices in the control database, one coded for K09 and one coded for K03.

This third setup is for the appliance module. This is nothing more than an on-off switch remotely controlled by the HALbasic software. The process to install an appliance control module changes on the window shown in Figure 5.28 when you select Appliance instead of Lighting.

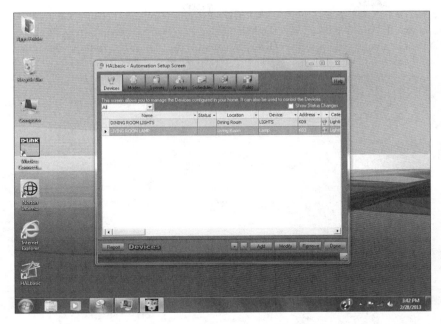

Figure 5.27 *You can add more devices or modify old devices by highlighting them and clicking on the Modify button at the bottom of the window.*

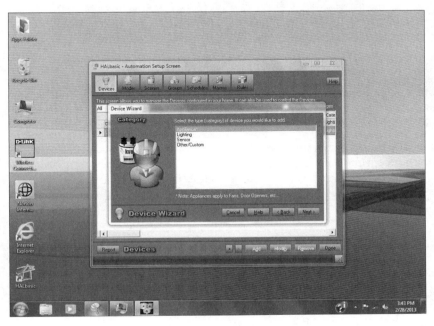

Figure 5.28 *Choosing Appliance simplifies the setup and eliminates the dimming options as you proceed though the setup screens.*

In the prototype installation the module will be used in the Kitchen to enable the coffee maker, as shown in Figure 5.29. As important as it is to have appliances remotely turned on by HALbasic, it is just as important that the software can also turn off the appliances.

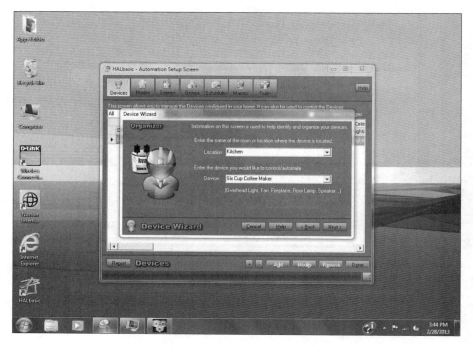

Figure 5.29   *This setup window should be familiar by now.*

Once more, it is important to make the entries here match the control module's information. In most cases you will have an exact manufacturer and model number. Notice in Figure 5.30 that the best match is the X10 model AM486 two-pin polarized module.

After the module model number and manufacturer information is entered, move on to entering the correct House and Unit codes, as shown in Figure 5.31. The control module hears all the controls but responds only to the commands coded to its identity.

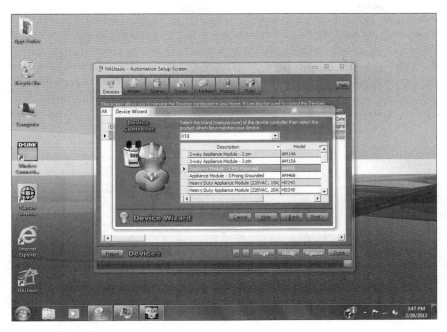

Figure 5.30   *Enter the manufacturer and scroll down until you find your best match for the control module you have.*

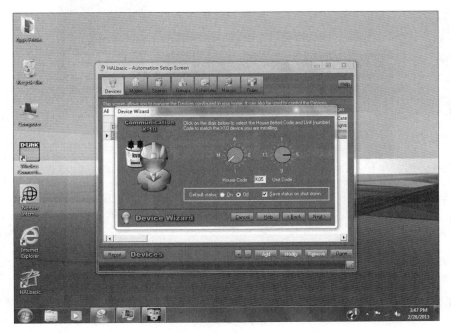

Figure 5.31   *The codes have to be unique for everything to work properly.*

After the codes are entered, move through the wizard, enabling any necessary voice feedback until you get back to the Automation Setup Screen, as shown in Figure 5.32. If you highlight and right-click the control data, you can choose to perform any of three actions: Turn On, Turn Off, or Get Status. Plug in your appliance module if you have not already done so and test the action items from this screen. The switch in the appliance module can be heard when it trips on or off. Be sure that the appliances themselves are turned on when you start using them, so they will turn on when the control module turns them on.

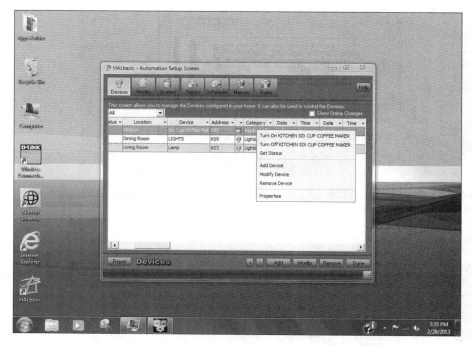

Figure 5.32 *Right-clicking on an entry brings up a menu of control options.*

Now that our lights and appliances are configured, it is time to add the outlet to our system. Return to the Category screen of the Device Wizard, as shown in Figure 5.33. Other/Custom is selected because Receptacle is not in the drop-down list.

Location entries are made next.

Move through the wizard, setting all device information and control codes as done in previous steps until you are at the Configuration Properties window, as shown in Figure 5.34. Notice that the Dim option is grayed out and On or Off become the only operable actions for testing this outlet. Click on the Next button after you have tested the device. For testing the outlet, use two lamps, one to test the always-on receptacle and the other to test the controlled outlet.

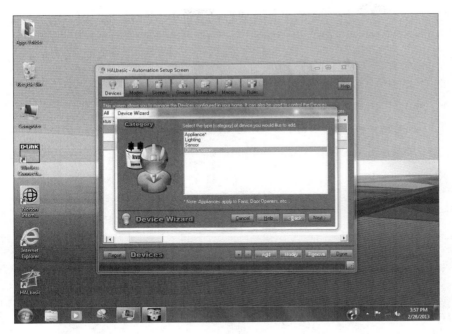

Figure 5.33 *Other/Custom is used for adapting to items not present in the drop-down lists.*

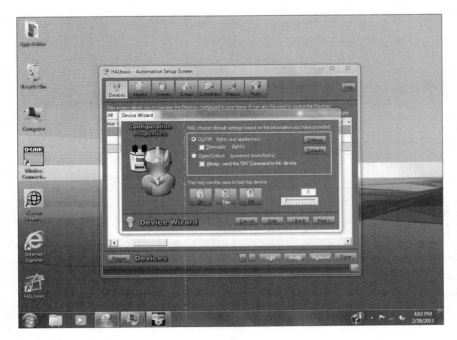

Figure 5.34 *Test your controlled outlet at this screen.*

Click the Finish button after you have made all logging and confirmation options to return to the setup screen shown in Figure 5.35, now with all four devices configured.

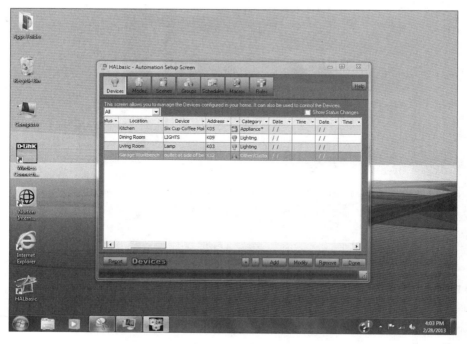

Figure 5.35   *All four devices are now visible in the setup screen.*

Note   **A Note on Troubleshooting**   If, during your device testing, your controlled light or appliance did not turn on, check to make sure that the controlled device has been turned on via the device's physical switch. After you have made sure that the device is on when plugged into a noncontrolled outlet, make sure that all control codes were entered correctly during the setup process. One wrong letter or number can be the difference between success and failure.

Figure 5.36 shows the Modes section of the setup window. The first mode for your installation is Normal. Modes allow you to shift the focus of the entire system rather than changing the focus of one particular device. As you progress with your control setup routines, some new modes you might want to build are Nighttime, where all unnecessary-for-sleeping lighting, electronics, and appliances are shut down or dimmed; Weekend, focused on energy conservation for when you've gone on a weekend trip; or Vacation mode, where the controls center on enhancing security. These topics are discussed in more detail in later chapters.

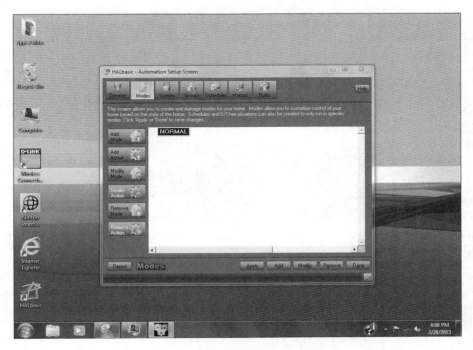

Figure 5.36   *The setup default house Mode is Normal.*

Control—Time-Based Routines

Now that our devices are installed and configured within HALbasic, it is time to put some of the power of the HALbasic application into action. In this section we will create time-based control events. To start, click on the Schedule tab, as shown in Figure 5.37.

Because we have not configured any schedules, only the Add button is available. Click Add to bring up the Schedule Wizard window, as shown in Figure 5.38.

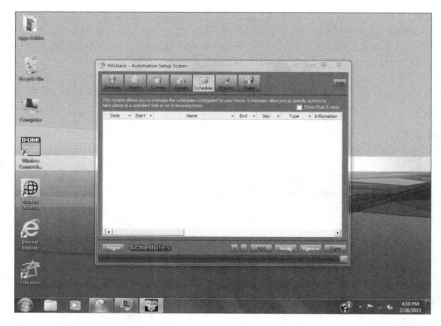

Figure 5.37 *The tabs in the setup screen show database entries and options for adding and modifying entries in the control database.*

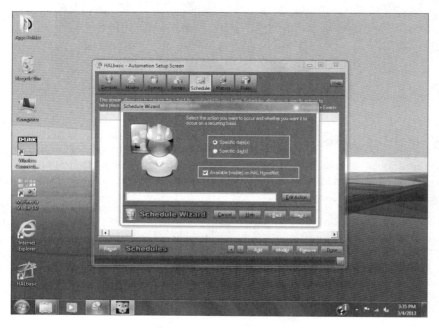

Figure 5.38 *The Schedule Wizard is where time-based events are entered for control actions to be performed by day or date and time.*

In the Schedule Wizard first select the device that will perform the action. Click Edit Action to reveal a list of available devices, as shown in Figure 5.39.

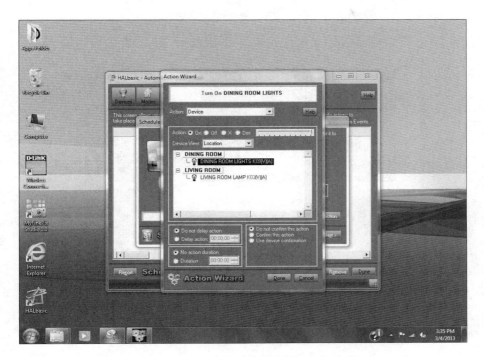

Figure 5.39 *Dining Room Lights is highlighted for scheduling.*

After a device is selected, you can select options for delaying action and confirmations. When a device and option are selected, click on Done. You are returned to the Schedule Wizard window and the action Turn on Dining Room Lights appears in the Action field, as shown in Figure 5.40.

In this instance select the Specific Day(s) radio button (the dots) and then click on the Next button to bring up the screen shown in Figure 5.41. These two buttons toggle back and forth; clicking in one deselects the other.

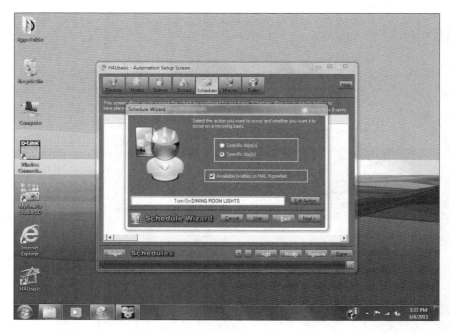

Figure 5.40   *There are options to use a date calendar or days for the next steps.*

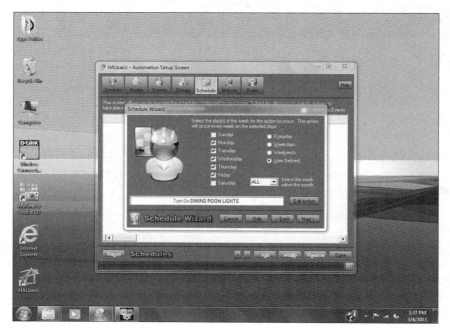

Figure 5.41   *All the day choices are displayed.*

Notice that for the prototype install each day from Monday to Friday is check-marked in the respective boxes so that the Dining Room Lights will be on at the same time Monday through Friday. Click on the Next button to display the window shown in Figure 5.42.

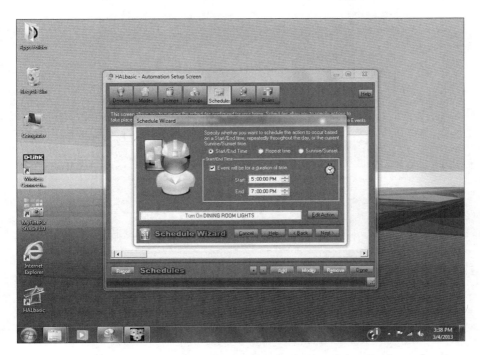

Figure 5.42 *Check the radio button for Start/End Time if that is what you want.*

Notice that the box is checked for the event to be from 5:00 p.m. to 7:00 p.m. each day. The times change as you click on the little up and down arrows next to the time field. Click on the Next button when you have finished selecting times for the light to be on, and the Schedule Wizard reveals a window for choosing a house Mode, as shown in Figure 5.43. The only mode we have available now is the Normal house Mode.

Leave this screen as is and click on Finish to be returned to the window shown in Figure 5.44.

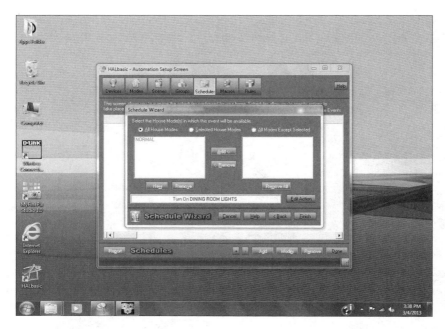

Figure 5.43   *You can create new Modes as you need them to quickly reorient actions to the unique control patterns you will design.*

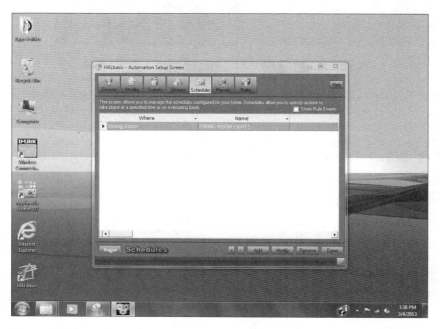

Figure 5.44   *We are shown here that a schedule now exists for HALbasic to act on when the time is right.*

Figure 5.45 has a scrollbar at the bottom of the window under the field headings. Click the horizontal scrollbar with the mouse and move it over to the right partway to reveal additional fields and the data that was just entered by using the very helpful wizards. Time to say "Thank you, wizards."

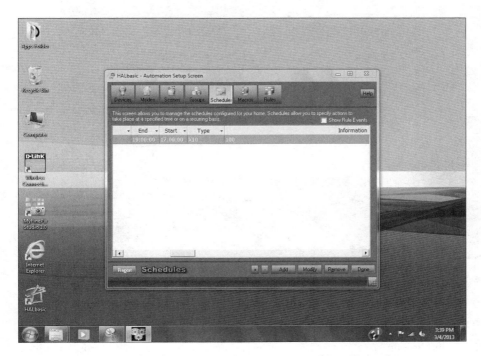

Figure 5.45   *The end and start times that were entered are shown here.*

Move the scrollbar more to the right to reveal more fields and data entries, as shown in Figure 5.46.

Click on the Done button at the bottom to return to the desktop.

Think of doing the HALbasic setups as being similar to building a jigsaw puzzle. All we are doing is putting in pieces and parts and linking them together into what becomes a very organized picture for controlling the controllable in your home. Each piece is unique going into the picture, but all the pieces can be coordinated to change the look and feel of the picture as needed by the occupants. The wizards do the heavy lifting of putting the pieces in the right places and prompt you to make the decisions that will custom build out your home automation controls to your liking and to meet your specific needs for control within your abode. HALbasic, coupled with an X10 Powerline Interface Module (PIM) and X10 control modules, shows just the beginning of what is possible in home automation, but it is a good beginning and HALbasic can introduce us to one more feature set to explore in the next section.

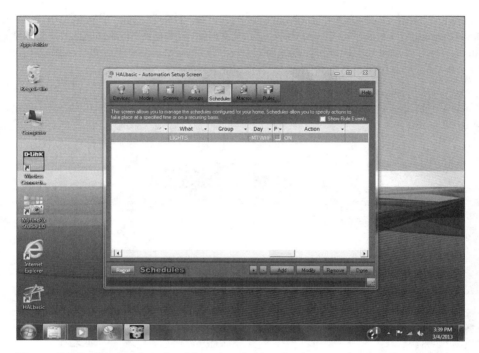

Figure 5.46   *Notice that the abbreviations for the days that were selected are shown under the field heading Day.*

Control—Voice Commands

A compatible sound card is needed on the home automation computer in order to exercise and use the voice-command option. In the prototype computer a sound card is integrated into the system board that works with the Windows operating system. Using a natural voice to control things in your house is a primary goal for many people when they begin to explore what home automation can do. At this point our prototype system will be simple and we will use inexpensive equipment to do the voice commands. To begin with, during this initial setup all that is necessary is a good computer headset such as you would use for Skype calls from the PC. I visited a local Staples store and found the headset shown in Figure 5.47 for $20. So for now the budget will show the additional expense of the headset. You can use a computer stereo speaker set for the output and a stereo microphone if you prefer or have them available.

Note   GE stereo computer headset with boom microphone: $20.
Total prototype cost so far: $1,179.

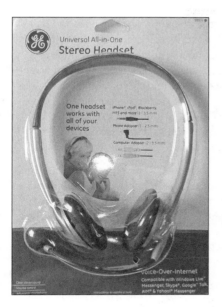

Figure 5.47   *Universal Stereo Headset in the blister pack.*

The GE headset is a versatile product; it comes with cables and jack plugs for connecting to a number of jack sockets on other devices, in addition to the computer soundcard connection such as smart phones and Apple products, as shown in Figure 5.48.

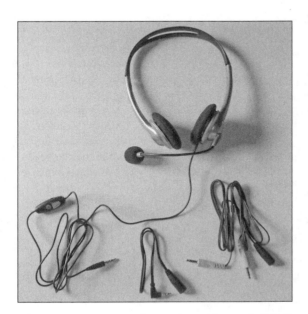

Figure 5.48   *The analog audio cables and jack plugs of various sizes and configurations match jack sockets on many types of devices.*

Make sure that your control modules are plugged in with lamps or appliances and that the power-line interface module is securely connected to its receptacle in your home. When all that is done, you are ready to try out using your natural voice to control the devices. But stop for a minute or two and think about the difficulty involved with voice commands. Each of us speaks a little differently, some have low voices, some high, some are naturally loud, some naturally soft, some have accents. The computer and HAL have to hear our voice making sound, dissect that sound digitally into patterns, match those patterns with words recognized in its command set, and then act appropriately on the control protocol and send an action command to the device.

Make sure your computer sound is turned on and let's begin. To begin an audio control session with the voice and listening ear in HALbasic, install the microphone and listening headset or speakers into the correct jack plugs from the computer's sound card. Many computers have the headset connection on the front and have symbols to represent the microphone socket and the headset socket. After you have the headset or microphone and speakers connected and turned on, launch HALbasic with the desktop icon and give it a moment or two to load.

As it is loading, you will hear a digital voice say over your speakers or headphones: "Welcome to HALbasic by Home Automated Living."

HALbasic is not actively listening to you right now, so go to the up arrow on the desktop tray, click on the ear icon, and say, "Shut off dining room lights." You will notice the icon activate with wavy sound lines in front of it.

I said, "Shut off dining room lights."

HAL said, "Shut off dining room lights?"

I said, "Yes, please."

Note **A World of Commands**   The following voice commands are just a sample of the types of voice commands that HAL can learn and understand. Play around with the software to see what is possible and how you can best get to the most natural way of issuing commands.

"Turn off dining room lights"
"Turn off the dining room lights"
"Switch dining room lights off"
"Switch the dining room lights off"
"Shut off the living room light."
"Shut dining room light off."
"Shut off family room fan."
"Turn on the living room fan for 30 minutes."
"Switch dining room light off for one hour."
"Please shut off the hallway light for two hours."
"Turn the front porch lights on for one hour please."

HAL said, "I have turned off dining room lights."

After a short pause, HAL said, "Are you still there?"

I said, "Yes, but goodbye."

HAL said, "Goodbye," and stopped listening for new commands.

To wake HALbasic back up, the default attention word in the Personal Assistant setting is "Computer." When I spoke next and said, "Computer," HAL said, "Yes," and waited for a new command. I said, "Goodbye," because I was done for now, and HAL said, "Goodbye."

The waves in front of the icon then went away again as HAL stopped listening. At this point, as an end user and successful DIYer, you should be as excited as a kid in a candy store if all that worked for you the first time.

It might or might not be necessary to tweak the audio settings in HAL, or perhaps find a better microphone, but it is very necessary to learn the command vocabulary in the HAL publications and PDFs or in the onscreen help menu. Go to the icon menu and find What Can I Say; click on it and follow the links to the command vocabulary action words.

As HAL said goodbye, is time to say goodbye to this chapter, but not necessarily time for to you say goodbye to practicing using the HAL schedules or command and setup screens, or to practicing using voice commands.

Explore HAL a bit before you move on to the next chapter. After all, a dedicated new DIYer in any craft moves from beginner (someone who wants to learn) to novice (learned some, but restricted mostly to rules or procedures) to apprentice (mostly understands how things work) to journeyman (understands how things work and how they work together) to expert (can do new and novel things with the basic knowledge) through reading and research and from practice and gained experiences.

Chapter 6

Project 3, Controlling Lighting: Indoors and Outdoors

In the preceding chapter X10 control devices were used to turn things on and off, and to dim lights and lamps. The existing house wiring played only a modest role in that chapter as to what could be done with home automation. In this chapter we move beyond one-location on/off/dim control points to installing and using UPB controls in more complex wiring situations where indoor or outdoor lighting fixtures must be controlled from more than a single location. This part of the project requires you to have an understanding of your existing home wiring. Additionally, having multiple locations to control a light or device requires a three-way or four-way switch installed in the home.

In the past using photocell (light-sensitive) controls coupled with time clocks would also have been part of the discussion on controlling outdoor lighting. With the use of automated control commands being issued from the computer to UPB controllers, these older devices become obsolete and are rarely required in a fully automated home under the control of home automation software. For example, you can use the Automation Setup Screen and the Schedule Wizard to automatically match on and off times for lighting to the local sunrise and sunset times.

In this chapter the switches and controls can utilize the older X10 technology but will include a newer, more universal technology. That technology is UPB, short for Universal Powerline Bus. A more reliable and powerful control protocol set is integrated into the UPB over line-voltage communication standards. If you have not invested in or you do not have any legacy X10 equipment, it is a good idea to begin with UPB and use it in every automation application within the home. Figure 6.1 shows, from the top left, a UPB lamp control module, a UPB appliance control module, and a UPB remote switch. In the center bottom of the figure is a plug-in UPB computer interface module with a USB cord that connects the interface module to the computer. The device control modules perform similar functions to the X10 devices covered in Chapter 5, "Project 2, Controlling Appliances, Lights, and Devices," except that they operate off the UPB standards and require the UPB interface for communication.

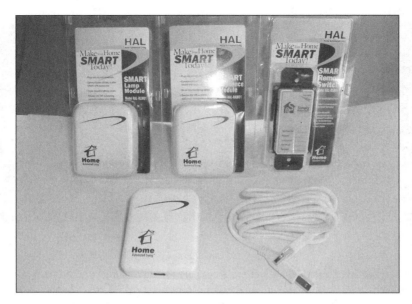

Figure 6.1   *UPB control modules, remote switch, and the UPB interface device.*

> **Note   Indoor or Outdoor?**   Products that are approved for indoor use only cannot
> be used outdoors. Only products specifically approved for outdoor use can be used
> outside and exposed to the weather. Most plug-in control modules are not approved for
> any outdoor use. Controlling outdoor lighting can still be done from the home's interior
> locations where the outdoor lighting switches are often located.

Switching for Indoor and Outdoor Lighting Circuits

Because the focus of this book is on projects for beginners, this chapter's project will
keep the degree of difficulty low while introducing UPB to the reader. It will also include
using UPB master and remote automated controls and integrating them into slightly more
complex house wiring schemes. Some of your home's lighting areas will likely already be
wired for three-way (switched at two locations) or four-way (switched at three or more
locations) fixtures, so these wiring configurations are covered in this chapter. You can
replace the existing switches with UPB-controlled switch masters and remotes in most
instances. Take time to review the information in Chapter 1, "Home Wiring and Electrical
Fundamentals," regarding multiple switch locations and current/wattage loading. A word
of warning: Existing switch locations in your home might be hampered by switch boxes
that are too shallow for installation of the UPB controls. If there is depth available in the
wall cavity, the boxes might have to be swapped out for deeper ones. In any case, pay
attention to the box depth required by the controls you purchase to be sure you can use
them.

In many homes there is more than one switch located in an electrical box, referred to as a gang box. To use multiple controls where the controls will share a space in a common gang-box location, pay attention to the current de-rating information supplied by the control's manufacturer when the control switches are collocated in a multigang box. For example, you might be using UPB controls rated for controlling 900 watts of incandescent lighting, but when collocated with others, the de-rating might reduce this controller's allowed wattage to as few as 500 watts. Violating a de-rating can both damage the devices and lead to excessive heat or even fire damage. If you find that rewiring is necessary or you will be doing a totally new installation, always follow the rules and advice in the NEC (National Electric Code) so that the work you do conforms to the latest building and wiring codes. Alternatively, you can hire a licensed electrician to perform the work.

Warning   Maintaining personal safety while doing a project and installing features correctly and to code that are safe for the end-user are the two most important objectives of any DIY project.

It is important to distinguish the types of lighting you plan on controlling because not all lighting types allow use of dimming controls. Fluorescent, metal halide, and some low-voltage light fixtures used with transformers cannot be dimmed using UBP controllers. Be sure your lighting fixtures and lamps support dimming, and keep these restrictions in mind if you find yourself upgrading a UBP-controlled lamp from incandescent to fluorescent bulbs. Some models of magnetic transformers typically used for low-voltage under-counter lighting support dimming; simply consult the transformer's data sheet supplied by the manufacturer to be sure. Always be careful to maintain loading of low-voltage lighting transformers to no more than 80 percent of the transformer's rated capacity and be sure that the transformer does not exceed the wattage rating of the control you will be using. Dimming can be disabled on the UPB master switch during setup for simple On/Off control of fluorescent lights, motors, fans, solenoids, relays, and other nondimmable loads.

Existing Multilocation Switching

Some common places in your home where three-way or four-way lighting might be in place are these:

> Entryway lights controlled by an inside switch and an outside switch
>
> Breezeways between the garage and the main house with switches located in the garage and in the house
>
> A long hallway with switches at both ends
>
> Basement lights with switches at the top and bottom of the stairs
>
> Larger rooms with multiple entryways and switches at each entryway

Before you begin this type of project, take inventory of the lighting situations you are dealing with, and then list the indoor and outdoor lights that you want to control with

UPB. Make a table similar to the sample in Table 6.1 but with at least one more column for notes. Use headings for room, number of switch locations, fixture count, total wattage, dimming capable yes/no, and control ID.

Table 6.1 *An Example of Taking an Inventory of the Control Points for Lighting*

Room	Switch Location	Fixture Count	Total Wattage On Switch	Dimming? Yes/No	Control ID #	Notes	System Name
Dining Room	2 (3-way)	3	300	Yes	(X10) House F Device 4		Dining Room
Dining Room	1	1	60	No	Not applicable	On Photo-cell	Not applicable
Living Room	1	2	150	No	(X10) House F Device 5		Living Room
Stair Case	2	1	100	No	Not applicable		Not applicable
Porch	1	2	120	No	(X10) House F Device 6		Porch Light

In an existing home the wiring for the three-way and four-way switch locations is already in place; it is just that you will be using that wiring in a slightly different fashion. Also, you will have to be able to identify the correct location to install the UPB master controller and know how to use the existing wiring to connect the new remotes. In Chapter 1, Figure 1.20 shows what an existing three-way switch would look like. You might recall that those (three-way switches) are used in both three-way (two switch locations) and four-way switch circuits. Also in Chapter 1, Figure 1.21 shows a four-way switch. which is a necessary device for lighting control from three or more locations in non-automated lighting circuits With three switch locations, two three-way switches are used along with one four-way. To go beyond three switch locations, additional four-way switches are used. This next section will help you figure out your existing home wiring situation.

A word of caution is in order here. What is being discussed in this text are conventional wiring methods that met codes at the time of installation. It is possible, even probable, that some of the circuits in your home were not properly wired to comply with the code at the time. One of the most common mistakes made by "amateur" electricians is installing a switch on a neutral wire; this type of mistake can potentially kill an unsuspecting occupant doing a routine light bulb replacement. I differentiate "amateurs" from DIYers, in that DIYers like yourself are willing to take the time to learn to do things correctly;

amateurs just think they are doing things right. If you encounter a situation where what you are seeing does not conform to current convention and codes, consult a licensed electrician in your area to help correct the discrepancies.

Deciphering Existing Home Wiring

This section will help you decipher your home's existing wiring. Knowing what you have will help you determine what you can undertake in this project and future home automation control projects.

Lighting Fixture Switched from a Single Location

The most common lighting situation is a single switch location switching one or more light fixtures. Many homes have switches connected to all or half of an outlet as well.

There are two possible wiring solutions for a single switch. Figure 6.2 is a diagram of the most common method of wiring in your home when you want to automate single switches. In Figure 6.2 the bonding wire (bare/green), neutral (white), and hot (black/colored) are brought from the fuse or breaker box to the switch box first. At this point the hot side is routed though the switch and all three wires are brought to one or more ceiling or wall fixture boxes to power the lights. This wiring method is the most convenient one for adding UPB control switches to control the lights. This configuration can also be referred to as a "standard two-way" switch even though the switching takes place in only one location.

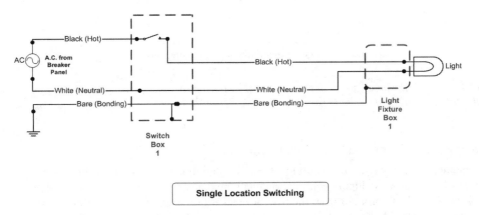

Single Location Switching

Figure 6.2 *A diagram of a single switch location with a single pole switch and the hot and neutral feeds into the switch box.*

Figure 6.3 shows the alternative method for wiring a single switch location. In this wiring method the bonding wire (bare/green), neutral (white), and hot (black/colored) are brought from the fuse or breaker box to the first or only ceiling light fixture box or first wall fixture. At this point the hot (black wire) is run with another conductor and bonding wire to the switch box on the wall. The black wire is connected to one side of the switch and the power is returned to the light fixture box on the alternate wire. When sheathed cable is used for a switch drop like this, the white wire is tape colored on each end to black or another color tape to show that it is no longer used as a neutral wire. When you encounter this situation in your home, you can still use UPB controls, but it is more expensive because you have to rewire or alternatively use a UPB master and give up on having manual control of the light(s) in that space. If your home or this type of location is wired with conduit, there might be room to pull a neutral wire to the switch location. Avoid the temptation to use the bonding wire as a neutral connection; this would be very bad practice because current returns along the bonding wire, which is dangerous for many reasons.

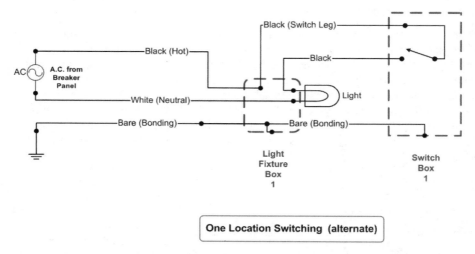

One Location Switching (alternate)

Figure 6.3 *A diagram of a single switch location with alternate wiring for a single pole switch and hot and neutral feeds to the fixture box first.*

Lighting Fixture Switched from Two Locations

Switching a light or lamp from two locations is called three-way switching. In this wiring method, shown in Figure 6.4, the bonding wire (bare/green), neutral (white), and hot (black/colored) are brought from the fuse or breaker box to the first of the three-way switches. The black (hot lead) is connected to the common screw connection on the switch. From there the bonding wire, neutral, and two traveler wires are brought to the second switch box. The two traveler wires that originate at the other two connections on the first three-way switch are carried through to the same connections on the second three-way switch. Color-coding for the traveler wires depends on the type of cable or wiring used. Usually a four-conductor cable is run between the three-way switch boxes and the wire colors are white, bare copper, black, and red, with the travelers colored red and black. From the second switch box the common screw connection on the three-way switch is brought up to the fixture box along with the neutral and bonding wire. The switch's screw terminals are also color-coded on a three-way switch. The two traveler connections have the same color screws, often brass, and the common is black or silver. The green terminal is for connecting the bonding wire.

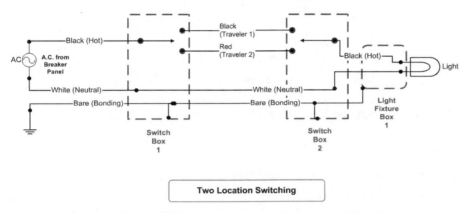

Figure 6.4 *Two switch locations using ordinary three-way switches.*

Lighting Fixture Switched from Three Locations

Figure 6.5 shows the typical wiring diagram of a single light, or interconnected set of lights, controlled from three switch locations. In this instance the wiring is partly identical to the wiring shown in Figure 6.4 except that the third switch is inserted between the travelers. The four-way switch has four contacts: two labeled "inputs" and two labeled "outputs." The main feed is to a three-way switch and the lamp load is from a three-way switch; the four-way switch is inserted along the travelers. The four-way switch in position one feeds the contacts on each side straight through with Traveler 2 in the diagram connected to Traveler 4. Likewise, in position one Traveler 1 is connected to Traveler 3. In the second position the switch crosses over the contacts, making the through circuits cross from one side to the other, connecting Traveler 1 to Traveler 4, and connecting Traveler 2 to Traveler 3. To clarify: The two travelers from one three-way switch connect to the input screw contacts on the four-way switch, and the travelers from the second three-way are connected to the output screw connections on the four-way switch. Changing the position of any of the switches alters the existing on-or-off state of the lights or lamp, and repositioning any of the other two switches restores the state to on or off.

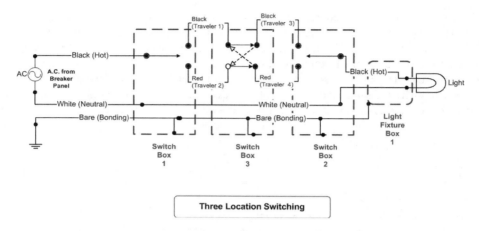

Figure 6.5 *A wiring diagram for three switch locations using three- and four-way switches.*

Lighting Fixture Switched from Four or More Locations

To go from three to more switch locations, the second, third, fourth, or whatever number of four-way switches are inserted along the travelers. They perform the same function as when compared with three switch locations, as shown in Figure 6.5. The four-way switches still either feed straight though on each side or cross the travelers over to the opposite sides as the switch position is changed.

It is possible that the electrician or installer might not have used proper cable technique and you might not have the neutral in the four-way switch locations along with the two travelers. This creates a situation where rewiring would be necessary. This situation would be identified where you have a four-way switch with only two insulated conductors entering and exiting the switch box. With only two wires the remotes can be made to operate but the feed through of the hot to the light fixture cannot be done.

Four or more switch locations would typically be handled in the manner shown in Figure 6.6.

The next set of diagrams shows the setups for removing existing switch devices and replacing them with UPB switches.

The major difference with using UPB controls is that only one point becomes the master that carries and controls the current load to the lighting fixtures. The alternate switch locations, aka remotes, simply extend the capability to control the load without carrying anything other than a modest control signal current. The other difference is that with the UPB remote switches, if the circuit's controlled conductor can be extended or is already available at the remote switch location, the remote switch can then include and display all available circuit status lights supported by the remote switch device based on signals from the master.

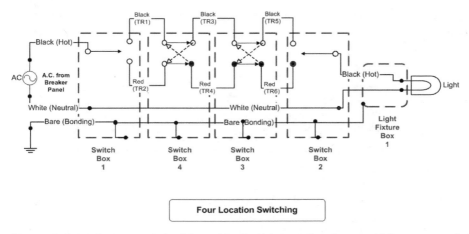

Figure 6.6 *A fixture switched from four locations using three- and four-way switches.*

Existing Home Wiring Adapted for UPB Controls

In the past, new houses were wired for automation by including a mile of control wiring in the home along with the normal current-carrying wires. The requirement for adding control wiring made it nearly impossible and at best very expensive to add controls to an existing home. The true beauty of currently available automation hardware and software is that the existing wiring system can be used with little to no change to accommodate the bulk of a homeowner's automation goals. This section demonstrates how simple it is to use an existing home wiring system to automate the control of lights, electrical appliances, electronics, and mechanical elements in a typical home.

> **Note** **Yet Another Safety Reminder**   Be sure to disconnect whatever circuit you are working on by setting the breaker to off or removing the appropriate fuse. If multiple circuits are sharing the same gang box, be sure to shut off both breakers or remove both fuses.

Single-Location UPB-Controlled Lighting Fixture

As shown in Figure 6.7, when you're installing a UPB control in a single switch location that is fed from the home's breaker box, the black lead on the switch is connected to the black wire from the circuit breaker. The white wire from the UPB master is connected to the white from the breaker box and to the white wire that continues to the fixture(s). The bonding wire/bare green is connected to the incoming ground from the breaker box, or to the box if it is metal, and is connected to the bonding wire going to the lamp fixture. The brown wire from the UPB switch is connected to the black wire going up to the light fixture. Cap off any unused wires from the UPB with a small wire nut and piece of tape.

Always be very careful to use the right wire nut for the wire sizes and number of wires you are connecting to.

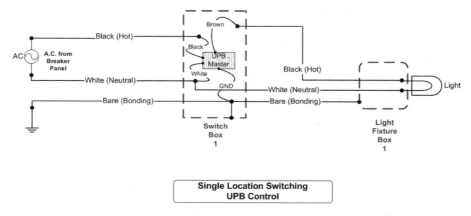

Figure 6.7 *A single UPB switch location to control a single lamp fixture.*

It is good practice to push the bonding wires into the back of the switch box first, followed by the neutrals (whites) and then the black/brown current conductors. The UPB switches will be at least 1.5 inches deep so the wires have to be firmly settled in the back of the box. Do not force the UPB switch in and never use the mounting screws to force it into the box. If the box is not deep enough, change out the box for a deeper box. Fold in and flatten the wire connections if they are in the way. One strategy is to fold the wire so that the wire-nut connections are each placed in different corners of the switch box, leaving the center of the box as space for the control. If you are doing a new work installation, begin with cutting back the sheathing to free up about four to five inches of wire for making the connections.

Figure 6.8 shows a master control switch with its five wire pigtails. Some wire nuts are also included.

The wiring situation in Figure 6.3 is not at all uncommon in existing homes' wiring. As noted in the preceding section, you can still have UPB controls but some choices have to be made: rewire, abandon manual control, or use a UPB master controller in the ceiling fixture box and install a remote switch on the end of the switch drop. The situation can be further complicated for the DIYer when the existing fixture boxes are too shallow or too small to handle the size of the UPB master control. Most ceiling cavities and wall cavities are deep enough to allow replacement of the existing ceiling box if necessary. To proceed with this situation where there is enough room in the lamp fixture box to install the UPB master, first connect the black from the fuse box to the black wire on the UPB master. The bonding wires are connected together and to the box if it is metal. The whites (neutrals) are connected together to include the source's wire, the UPB master's, the lamp's, and one lead going down to the switch box. At this point the wires that go to the single wall-switch location are located and reidentified.

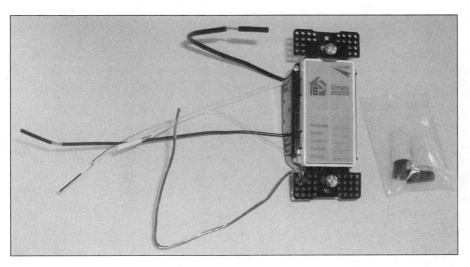

Figure 6.8 *The pigtails on the UPB master switch are color-coded white, black, bare, brown, and brown/white.*

If sheathed cable was used for the switch-box drop, the color-coding tape is removed from the white at both locations, reidentifying it as being used as a neutral. If both wires going to the switch box are colored, pick one to code white (neutral) with white tape. Do this on both ends of that same wire, in the fixture box and in the switch box. It is possible that you have wires with loads from two different breakers in the same gang box, so use an AC voltmeter to ensure that there are no other active loads. Use an ohmmeter or a continuity tester to positively identify the one you are using as the neutral when no whites are available. The other conductor wire going to the switch box will connect to the remote wire (red) on the UPB master switch to the red remote wire on the remote switch. You will end up with a neutral, a bonding wire, and a remote wire at the remote switch location. At the switch location connect the neutral to the white pigtail on the remote switch, and the incoming black (remote wire) to the remote (brown/white) pigtail on the remote switch. The bonding wire connects to the switch's ground wire and to the box if it is metal.

Figure 6.9 shows what the remote switch looks like before connection and assembly. The brown wire on the remote switch only operates the status lights on the remote switch and does not have to be used if the status lights are not needed or if you are short a wire to make them work.

In situations where you include UPB controls in an existing wiring situation with two switch locations previously controlled by three-way switches, you will likely have a neutral, two travelers, and a bonding wire connecting through to both switch-box locations. It is important to identify the box that has the feed from the panel for installation of the UBP master controller.

Let's take a look at how to reuse existing house wiring to be compatible with UPB master and remote switch installations when controlling from more than one location.

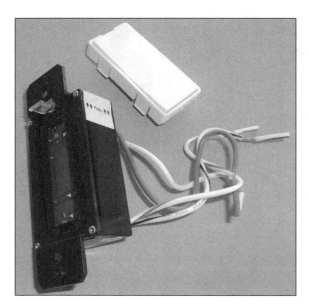

Figure 6.9 *The pigtails on this remote switch are white, brown, brown/white and red/white.*

Two-Location UPB-Controlled Lighting Fixture

Installing the UPB master control for a conventional three-way (two locations switched) switch setup starts at the switch box with the feed from the breaker box. The black wire from the breaker box is connected to the black pigtail on the UPB master control switch. The neutral (white) is connected to the white on the control module and also connected through to the next box. The bonding wire is connected through to the next box, to the box if metal, and to the bond connection on the UPB master control. One of the former travelers is used as the current carrying conductor to the light fixtures and is connected to the brown pigtail on the UPB master control. At the second box, the current-carrying conductor (connected to the brown) is connected to the black lead going to the light fixtures and to the brown pigtail on the remote switch. The alternate traveler is selected for the control wire to receive signals from the remote switch in the second box, and it is connected to the brown/white pigtail on the master control and to the brown/white on the remote. To identify this traveler wire at both ends in each box, use a wrap of red tape identifying it as a control wire. In the second box the lead designated as the current carrying wire to the light fixture is connected to the lead going to the light fixture as mentioned previously, and it can also be connected to the brown lead on the remote switch; doing so will enable all status lights on the remote switch.

This box is where the remote will be located. The neutral wires meaning the white conductors are all connected together in this box; the white pigtail from the remote switch, the neutral from box one, and the neutral to the light fixture. The control wire from box one (now coded red) will connect to the brown/white pigtail on the remote and to nothing else. So to recap: The remote switch will be connected to the control wire from box one, the neutral from box one, and can be connected to the current-carrying conductor so that the remote status lights will work. The leads going to the lamp fixture will be connected respectively to the bonding wire, the neutral wire, and the current-carrying conductor from box one. When you are finished, your adapted wiring diagram should look similar to what's shown in Figure 6.10 for two-location switching using UPB controls.

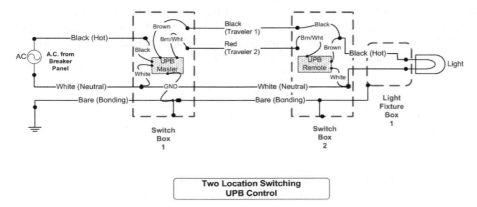

Figure 6.10   *Two UPB switch locations using one master and one remote switch.*

> **Note   A Note About Pigtails**   Each color-coded pigtail from the master and remote performs specific functions, and the color coding might not always be the same from one manufacturer to the next. Check the literature/spec sheet included with the products you are using to verify the color codes for each function on the products you are using.

Three-Location UPB-Controlled Lighting Fixture

Adapting a four-way (three switch locations) is similar to the three-way switch as long as the neutral wire is present in all three switch locations. The biggest concern is the existing four-way switch box. The two locations housing the three-way switches have to have the neutral present, but you might find a situation where only travelers are brought to the four-way switch. The four-way switches in existing homes could have been wired in with only two conductors to them going from the four-way switch to each of the three-way switch boxes. Fortunately, this method of not bringing a neutral into each switch box is disallowed with only two exceptions in the current electrical code.

In cases where only a two-conductor cable with a bonding wire is brought to the four-way switch-box location, you will have to rewire and bring the neutral from the first switch box to the four-way location. Where the neutral is present in the former four-way switch box, you would locate the master control in the first three-way switch box (Switch Box 1 in the diagram) and reconnect the travelers as shown in Figure 6.11 in the four-way switch box that will house the first remote switch (Switch Box 3 in the diagram). As shown in the diagram in Figure 6.11, Traveler 1 and Traveler 3 are connected together in what was the four-way switch box to become the current-carrying conductor to the lamp load. Traveler 2 and Traveler 4 are connected as the control wire (becoming red) to the control pigtails on the master and on the two remotes. Think of this control wire as simply a wire that carries signal pulses along its path. In the third switch box (labeled Switch Box 2 in the diagram), a lead to the lamp is connected as shown with the other end of Traveler 3 connected to the lead going to the light fixture and to the black on the remote to enable the status lights. In this diagram, in Switch Box 2 the brown wire is not connected to the current-carrying conductor, so its status lights will not work; however, the remote switch will still function properly.

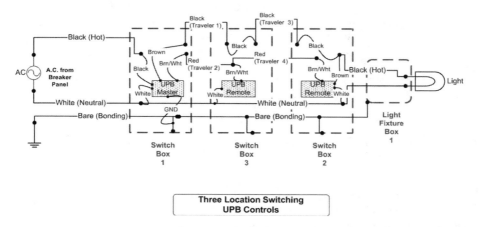

Figure 6.11   *Three UPB switch locations wired where two three-way and one four-way switches were previously used.*

> **Note   Mixing UPB and Conventional Switches**   Note that you cannot mix and match old conventional three- and four-way switches with UPB masters and remotes; it is an "either or" situation. After you decide on UPB controls for a circuit, the whole circuits and all the switches have to be changed out to UPB devices.

To use UPB beyond three switch locations, it is necessary to have the neutral present in the four-way switch boxes. Figure 6.12 shows what the wiring diagrams would look like for four-location switching using a UPB master and three remotes. The harder part of doing this is the proper identification and connection of the former traveler wires shown in the diagram from Figure 6.6. Again the (T5), (T3), and (T1) connect through and carry the current to the lamp fixture as depicted in Figure 6.12. As stated at the beginning, always be sure that the circuits are off when you do the reconnection of UPB masters and remotes. Identify the wires you will use/reuse using an ohmmeter or a low-voltage continuity tester while the circuits are not powered if they are not sufficiently color-coded for you to know with certainty which wire goes where. At no time before completion should you reenergize the circuit after you begin installing UPB devices. Partial voltages or electrical arcing of partially connected wiring can easily damage the masters and remotes, causing unnecessary damage and the expense of replacement. If you feel you need help with making these changes, you can always hire a licensed electrician to make the wiring changes.

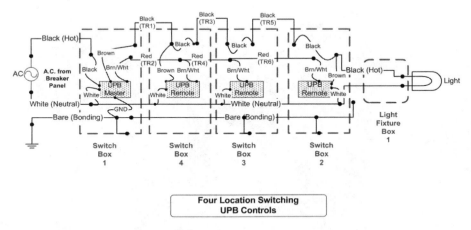

Figure 6.12 *Four UPB switch locations.*

With the explanation of wiring diagrams behind us, it is time to move forward with doing an install or two.

For our prototype UPB switched lighting installation, we will use a HAL-supplied UPB Power Line Adapter ($70), a Remote Slave Switch ($22), and a Simply Automated US1140W UPB Dimmer Switch ($56). We will add that cost to the prototype budget. The plug-in appliance/lamp control devices shown earlier in this chapter are not included in the budget here because they are an alternative choice to beginning with the X10 devices covered in Chapter 5 and their cost is similar enough to the X10 devices used in Chapter 5 for the purposes of a DIY planning budget.

Note UPB controls/modules/switches from prototype budget: $148.
Total prototype cost so far: $1,297.

Keep in mind that the UPB control devices you use are rated for far less current than a standard wiring circuit is rated for in most existing homes. Most homes have the lighting connected to a 15-amp circuit breaker, and the UPB device in our prototype is rated at only 900 watts or 7.5 amps' worth of lighting load when in a box by itself; so keep track of your wattage to maintain loading under the device maximum and heed the device's derating chart for the control devices you are using when collocating controls in a ganged box.

The UPB switch devices are equipped with color-coded stranded-wire pigtails to make the connections to the existing house wiring. As with the previous installs, connections to the wiring system will be made using wire nuts. The back of the UPB remote before installation is shown in Figure 6.13. Notice that the supplied white rocker has a groove on the top and can fit on the remote only one way. Other colors of switch rockers are available to match your home's decor.

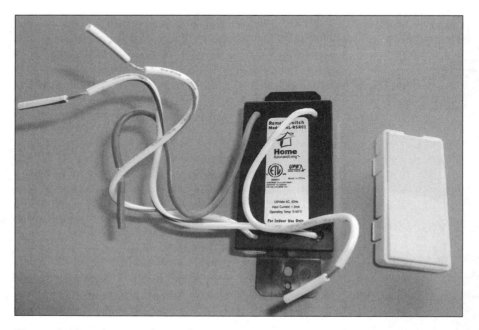

Figure 6.13   *The pigtails, insulation is partially stripped off, making for an easy connection.*

Figure 6.14 shows the back of the UPB control module before installation. Notice the screw and perforated tab to connect to the switch box. This heavy mounting bracket, used along with the perforations along both sides of the switch, helps with heat dissipation and heat transfer to the wall and box when the switch is operating in dimming mode.

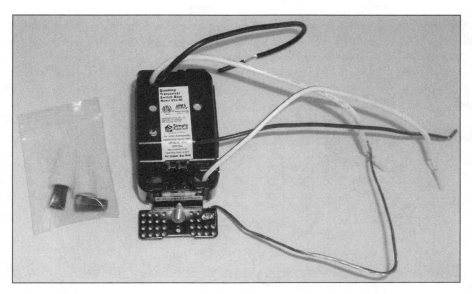

Figure 6.14 *The holes in the back and side of the UPB master switch help vent heat and help keep the switch from overheating when used in dimming mode.*

Making the Wiring Connections

Figure 6.15 shows the UPB remote partially installed in a switch box. This configuration fits situations where the UPB remote is installed in a box where feeding though is not needed or present. This switch's neutral (white), control wire (brown/white), and hot (brown) wires to the status lights are all connected in this figure.

Figure 6.16 is an example of the wire connections where the switch box formerly housed a four-way switch. The three neutral wires are connected together. The power feed though wire is connected to the wire going to the next switch and to the brown on the remote switch so that the status lights will work. The red travelers are connected together and to the brown/white control pigtail on the switch.

Figure 6.17 demonstrates the power feed entering the box and the control wires to the remote exiting to the first remote(s). The neutrals are connected together from the feed, the switch, and out to the remotes and eventually the light fixture. The bonding wires are always carried throughout the entire circuit from box to box all the way from the source panel to the load/lamp fixture. The control wire from the master is connected to one of the two travelers, in this case the red. The brown from the master is connected via one of the old travelers, in this case the black, out to the lamp load.

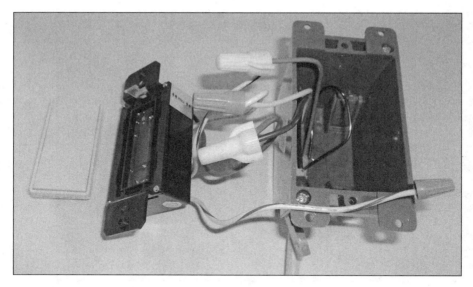

Figure 6.15   *A remote switch and its wire connections.*

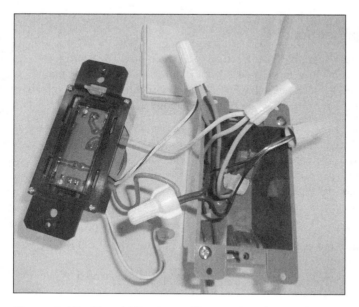

Figure 6.16   *Two 14/3 wires will enter this electrical wiring box.*

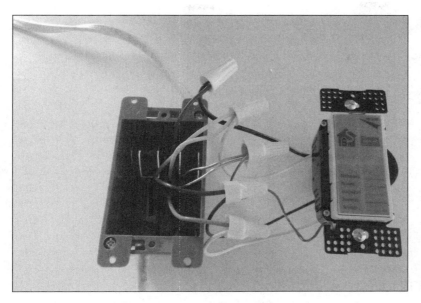

Figure 6.17 *Always be careful to use the correct size of wire nuts when making connections.*

Connecting the UPB Control Adapter to the PC

In Chapter 4, "Project 1, Installing HALbasic Software on Your PC," an X10 power-line interface module was connected to the standard nine-pin serial port on the computer so that the home automation software could communicate though it to the X10 control modules used on the project. With UPB a UPB-compatible power-line interface module is needed to communicate to all the UPB devices used to control lights, appliances, and electronics within the home. Figure 6.18 shows the HAL-supplied model RCIUSB01 ready for use. It comes with a USB cord to connect it to the control computer.

To install the UPB control adapter to the computer, with the computer booted up, plug the USB cord into the UPB adapter and into the computer and then plug the UPB adapter into an available 120-volt outlet. In a moment or two you should see the flag in the system tray, as shown in Figure 6.19. The text in the flag reads, "USB Input Device, Device driver software installed successfully." When you see this flag, you will know that the adapter has registered as available hardware to Windows.

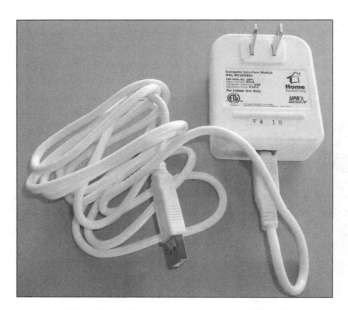

Figure 6.18   *The USB adapter uses only 83 milliamps of power.*

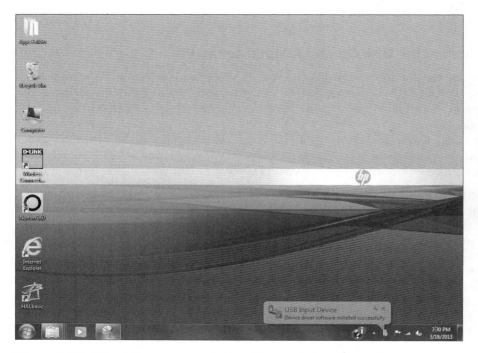

Figure 6.19   *Watch for the successful installation of the driver software.*

Setting up the UPB Control Modules

The next step is to make the HALbasic software aware of the fact that it can now communicate to UPB devices via the UPB adapter. To do this, you want the computer on and booted up but want the HAL server turned off. You can turn off the HAL server by right-clicking on the HAL icon and selecting Shut Down HAL from the menu.

With the HAL server off you can launch the HAL Setup Wizard. After the Welcome and warning window is presented, click on the Next button. In the second window choose Custom and click on the Next button to reveal the screen shown in Figure 6.20. If you followed and installed an X10 adapter in Chapter 5, your screen should already have the X10/INSTEON box checked. As you build out and customize your setup, the HAL software stores your unique setup information in a series of databases. For adding the UPB power-line interface module control adapter, check the UPB box and click Next.

Figure 6.20   *Check the appropriate boxes to choose configuration options.*

In the next window, use the drop-down menu to select the adapter. In this case the prototype project is using a HAL USB UPB adapter, as shown in Figure 6.21. UPB devices in your home have to have an identity composed of eight variables that include a Network ID, a Network Password, and a Network Name. As control devices and control modules are added to the network with the program function, they become members of this uniquely named power-line network.

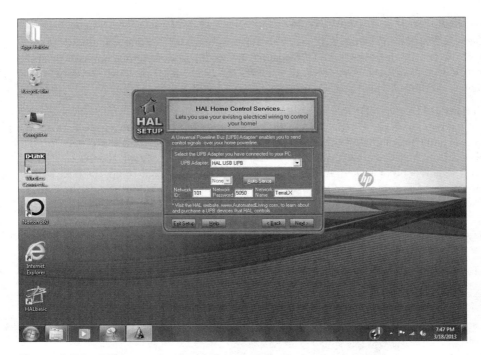

Figure 6.21   *Fill in your network data in this window.*

Enter numbers for the Network ID and Network Password fields and any combination of alphanumeric characters for the network name. The UPB protocol supports from 1 up to 255 differently identified network IDs and from 1 to 255 controlled units per network ID. Most homes can easily be controlled completely with one network and fewer than 250 controlled devices.

After you have entered your network data, move through the rest of the setup wizard and click Finish to exit.

Configuring Control Modules' Identities in HALbasic

At this point in the project, the computer should be booted up with the HALbasic server running. The UPB interface module should be set up in HAL as well as plugged into an outlet and your automation PC. The device UPB switches and control modules should be wired up or plugged in as appropriate to your project. The power should be switched on at the breaker box so that all the installed devices are powered up.

In our X10 chapter the control module's identity was dialed in on the device as Home and Unit variables. In the UPB province the devices have more information stored on rewritable memory within the device. To configure the modules, the HAL software takes care of the heavy lifting for you with its Find and Program buttons. In the setup wizard in the preceding section, you identified the network information that HALbasic will use to program the device. Some of the variables still have to be identified and entered for each device. Begin that process by entering the Automation Setup screen from the tray icon. The first window displays any currently configured devices. Click the Add button to start configuring your first UPB device control module. The Category window appears next. Select Lighting and click Next. This brings up the window shown in Figure 6.22. In this window enter the location of the lighting feature and enter a device name that fits your setup. When done, click Next.

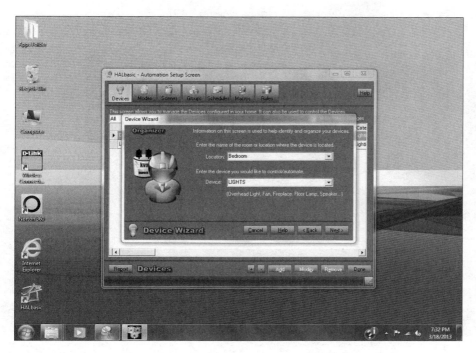

Figure 6.22   *Enter the location and device name in the blank fields.*

The window shown in Figure 6.23 appears next. Enter a comment as needed to help keep track of the device. As with the X10 setups, the software will combine the location and device names to name the object of control, in this case Bedroom Lights. After entering your comments, click Next.

In the window shown in Figure 6.24, select the manufacturer of the device from the drop-down menu to reveal a list of known devices from that manufacturer or supplier. The prototype is using a Simply Automated device model US1-40 in-wall switch, as shown in the figure. After you have made your selection, click Next. Selecting the correct device is important because each manufacturer's control device ships with some of the data fields filled in with default values for the variables. After you have made your selection, click Next.

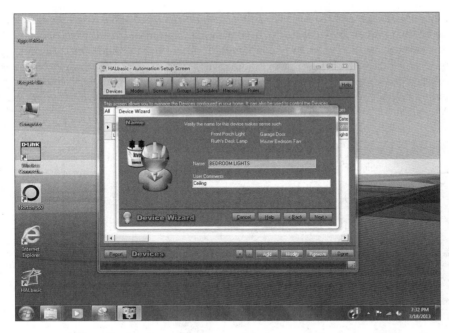

Figure 6.23 *Fill in user comments as needed.*

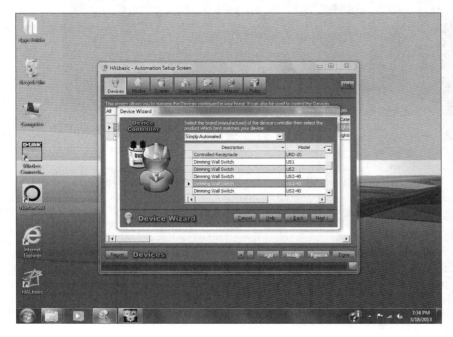

Figure 6.24 *Select your control device manufacturer and model from the drop-down menu selections.*

To make the device being programmed visible on the home wiring network, we have to identify a setup mode to have the device broadcast its presence and identify itself on the power-line network. In the case of our prototype wall switch device, the procedure is to tap the rocker bar on the switch five times in succession fairly quickly. The status lights on the installed and powered-up switch will change from a steady-state color to flashing. At this point in the project, go to the switch you are programming and tap the rocker bar as required by the manufacturer to enter into setup mode. Return to the computer and to the window shown in Figure 6.25 and click Find. In Figure 6.25 the system feedback "Unit ID 34 found" shows that the finding feature was successful. The unit you are installing will return a similar number. If a unit is not found within a moment or two, an error message will appear. If you receive an error, repeat the process and be sure that only one device is in setup mode at a time.

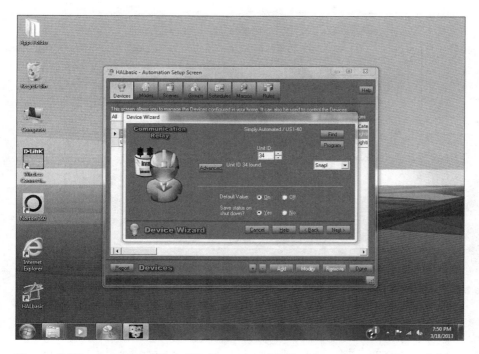

Figure 6.25   *A returned Unit ID shows that the Find function was successful.*

After the unit is found and the unit number is identified, you can accept the default Unit ID or change it in the Unit ID field. Here is where the switch and wiring locations table discussed earlier comes into play. There is a blank column for control ID where you can enter the Unit ID number.

After the Unit ID has been entered, the next step in the device module configuration is to click Program. The device now knows the network data, that it is "bedrooms lights" and its own unique unit ID number. The Find and Program features are easy to appreciate in this powerful software package. So much of the setup's heavy lifting is handled by the HALbasic program. Click Next to proceed to the next window.

Figure 6.26 shows the next screen, which you should recognize from our earlier efforts in setting up the X10 devices. Here the dimming values can be added as shown, and the device can be tested while doing the setup for on/off and dimming percentage. Uncheck the Dimmable box if you are dealing with a simple on/off control object. Click Next to move to the next window and save your setup data.

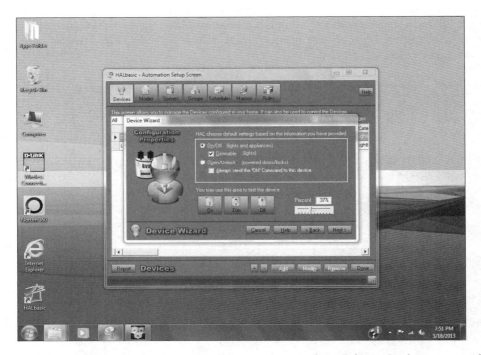

Figure 6.26 *Set the dimming percentage in this window and test the device as needed.*

Just as with the X10 devices, the next screen allows you to configure voice controls. Select the appropriate options and click Finish. You are returned to the Automation Setup Screen so that you can finish the process or add more devices. Because the prototype uses UPB plug-in modules, a plug-in module setup is discussed next.

One of the many significant benefits of UPB over X10 is in the number of devices that can be addressed and used in the home. The UPB plug-in control module is shown in Figure 6.27. Notice the two holes on the side of the device. The bottom hole shows the internal status LED. The top hole is a reset switch used to place the device into its broadcast setup mode so that it can be found on the power-line network. On the bottom is the receptacle for plugging in the lamp's cord just as with the X10 plug-in module. This device is approved for only 300 watts of lighting, and to be used in dimmable mode it must be controlling a dimmable lamp type such as ordinary incandescent light bulbs.

Figure 6.27   *A HAL-RLM01 UPB 300-watt lamp control module.*

To set up and configure this module, go to the HAL Automation Setup Screen and click Add to bring up the same series of setup screens that were used for the last UPB light switch. After you have filled in the fields to uniquely identify this device, click Next.

Just as with the UPB wall switch, the UPB device needs to be plugged into an active receptacle with the power on. To place this device into setup mode so that it will "broadcast" its presence on the power-line network, press a toothpick or plastic tool into the top hole on the side of the device. *You should feel the slight click of a button with each press.* When you are successful, the LED light in the lower hole will begin to flash as shown in Figure 6.28.

While the status light is still flashing, proceed to the Communication Relay window of the HALbasic Device Wizard, as shown in Figure 6.29. In this figure, the Find feature was used to return the Unit ID number 201. As with the wall switch, you can accept its default value or change it. The change will not take place until you click Program. Answer Yes to the confirmation question and the programming information is accepted.

This device is now a participant member of the power-line network. If the programming of the device is successful, the "Done" message will appear, as shown in Figure 6.30. Click Next to move to the dimming settings. Set your dimming settings and then your voice control options to finish the configuration of this device.

Figure 6.28 *Notice the status light and setup switch holes on the left side of the device.*

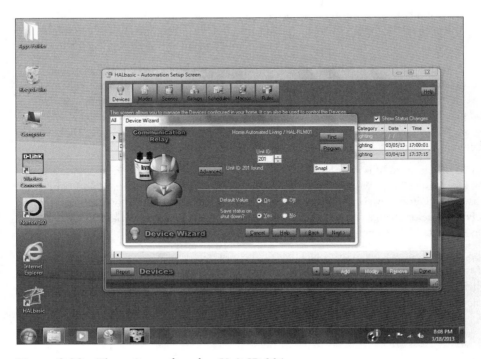

Figure 6.29 *The unit was found as Unit ID 201.*

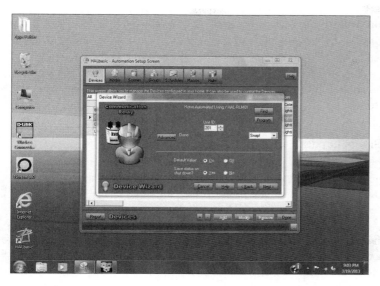

Figure 6.30   *The "Done" message shows that module 201 was properly programmed.*

When the setup and configuration of the UPB devices is completed, you are returned to the Automation Setup Screen, as shown in Figure 6.31. Take a moment to admire your work and success before clicking on the Done button. You can now use the other control features of HALbasic to program these new UPB devices and operate them in unique house modes, in schedules, or by voice in the same way as the X10s were operated in Chapter 5.

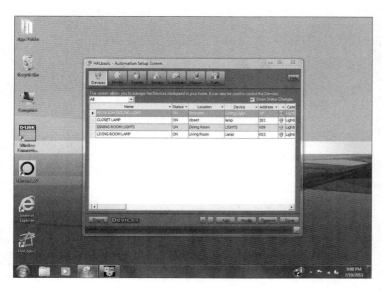

Figure 6.31   *Eventually, all of your control devices will be accessible and visible from this window.*

The Remote Wall Switches

The remote wall switches to control a UPB master do not need to be programmed or set up in any way. All that is necessary is that they be wired in correctly while the power is turned off. All they do is extend the reach/function of the rocker on the master wall switch to a second location, and the only UPB module they recognize is the one they are actually hard-wired to.

Caution on UPB Signal Limits

In some homes that are a long distance away (well over 100 feet) from the power transformer that feeds power to the home, or in homes that are fed power with many other homes that are fed from the same distribution transformer, it might be necessary to install a phase coupler. Review Chapter 1 for additional information on overhead and underground house service entrances. For single-phase houses, if you are experiencing problems with getting the signal across to the other sides of the split phase, consider using any one of the Simply Automated phase coupler models: wire-in model ZPCI-W, breaker-box model ZPCI-B, plug-in NEMA 10-30 model Plug-In 30 A, or NEMA 10-50 Plug-in 50A.

For larger homes using 208/120 (wye-connected) or in homes using 240/120 three-phase (delta-connected) service, a phase coupler is required. For three-phase applications consider using the Simply Automated model Three-Phase Repeater & Computer Interface (CIM) Model UTR.

Also in commercial applications in offices, factories, or apartments or other commercial buildings, three-phase electrical service is common so the repeaters will be necessary for using UPB controls. The repeaters will also forward the X10 signals. Those products labeled as Universal Inverting Phase Couplers pass UPB, X10, and many other higher-frequency signals. This will be important if you have a mixed control environment.

Chapter 7

Project 4, Linking Video to Your Security System

The connection between home automation and home security is probably not the first thing people think of whenever home automation is a part of the conversation. That being said, elementary home automation services have become a popular offering from many home security companies.

With a computer-based home automation system the reaction to an alarm event can go far beyond sounding an alarm and dialing an alarm monitoring company. Your imagination might be the only limit to the list of potential responses.

Integrating HALultra with your home security plan gives you greater control of the total response of your home security system regardless of which product or system is used to trigger the initial alarm. This customization is a major benefit of using the HALultra platform as a standalone or integrated "co-response" control hub of your system. Any contracted monitoring service would follow their response protocols as provided in your monitoring agreement, and HALultra would be customized to handle your localized response events in the co-response scenario. Capturing video, sounding local alarm horns, and calling a neighbor could all be a part of that response, whatever you feel is necessary based on the event trigger.

HALultra can be easily integrated with a compatible security panel, enabling you, for example, to arm or disarm your system by voice with a call to the home from your cell phone. Some of the security products that integrate well with HALultra include products by DSC, Elk, GE, HAI (www.homeauto.com), Honeywell, Napco (www.napcosecurity.com), and ON-Q at www.legrand.us. Check the HAL website's list of supported security interfaces for the most up-to-date list of manufacturers and models.

If you already own one of these systems, check the manufacturer literature for how to integrate the products with HALultra. Even if it is not called out in the literature or your system is not on the compatible equipment list, there are probably ways to get it done. It might be as simple as upgrading your current model to a newer version with an automation interface. Another method might be to use your existing sensors and swap out the security panel that does not support an automation interface for one that does.

At the core of any monitoring security system are a series of either or both of normally-on or normally-off switches. Any change in the on-off state of those switches triggers the alarm to sound and take preset actions. If an on-off sensor is placed at a door that is normally closed, the sensor is set up so that opening the door trips the sensor to on, an abnormal state for that sensor. At the most basic level all that is necessary to integrate into HALultra is for a compatible sensor, closure, or relay that is installed on the alarm system to trip-on from a normally-off state or to trip-off from a normally-on state. The compatible sensor must be linked to an interface module on your home automation system. For example, if you are using an Omni alarm system with two-way X10, your computer must have an X10 interface to receive the alarm trigger event. HALultra would then be set up to monitor for that change of state and the change would generate the execution of a predefined macro programmed into the HAL data as reaction to the alarm that triggered the event.

Some of the things you can tell HAL to do after the security alarm or any sensor is triggered include calling your cell phone, calling a neighbor, turning on all the house lights, and playing a recorded message of speakers in or outside of the house. Similar macro responses can be set up for literally any alarm condition, such as a fire alarm, a carbon monoxide alarm, ionization smoke alarms, photoelectric smoke detectors, a heat alarm, or flood alarms. It is important for you as a DIYer to be aware of all the no-cost to low-cost options that can improve your personal security and survivability and that of anyone residing in your automated home. Take inventory of the alarms in your home to begin to build your security and safety profile of needed improvements or needed interfaces. When your current situations come up short, plan and implement the necessary improvements as just another DIY project. Doing so could save your life or the life of someone you love.

When you integrate the security response with HALultra using rules and macros within HAL, your connected system can take action as a response to any number of events. NBC News recently carried a news story that smoke alarms do not always wake up otherwise healthy children, so using loud voice alarms that play recordings of parents or caregivers can increase the likelihood that children will be awakened in an emergency. Using voice-sounding smoke alarms and linking to HALultra to flash lights and play effective sound recordings is also a possibility. Because of the versatility of using a computer-based home automation platform, if you can imagine it, with enough time and budget you can do it. The rest of this chapter focuses on some of the video surveillance and monitoring aspects of home automation and security and getting a couple of camera types installed in your home.

Linking in HAL Video Capture Features

The main topic of this chapter is collecting video of what is going on at your home when an event or a potential event occurs. Who is on the premises? What cars are or were in the driveway? What is or was happening at the front door? These are all questions that can potentially be answered if you have one or more security cameras associated with your HALultra home automation implementation. To link the video streams into the

HALultra environment, it is necessary to use HAL DVC (HAL Digital Video Center), which requires an inexpensive but separate license. At this point it is a $49 software-add but well worth it because it allows you to collect, view, and record video streams in various formats from a number of camera sources and camera types. Along with the HALdvc software, you will need one or more security cameras and, to maximize the complexity of the response system, the HALultra version of the HAL software.

Surveillance Camera Selection

The first decision is selecting the kinds of video cameras you would like to use. There are several options that include what might now be considered legacy surveillance systems, but for a beginner with no investment in video surveillance systems, the two types presented in this chapter are relatively easy to set up and use.

USB Cameras

A fairly simple security camera type to set up and use with HAL is commonly referred to as a webcam, a camera that connects to a computer via a standard USB port. This is a particularly good choice if your system needs only a small number of cameras and the distances from the computer to the camera locations are small. The technical length limit spec for USB cables is 5 meters (16.4 feet). There are some specialized hubs and active extension cables that will allow you to extend out to 30 meters. If you need the distance, it is best to go ahead with the simpler wiring solution and use either a wired or wireless IP-based camera solution. Figure 7.1 shows a very inexpensive USB web camera purchased for under $30.

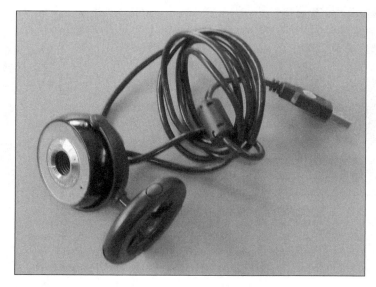

Figure 7.1   *An ordinary USB camera.*

Internet Protocol Security Cameras

For the prototype installation, I opted to use an IP-based (IP-addressable) network camera, as shown in Figure 7.2, for two main reasons. The first reason is that it would allow for easy installation using network wiring Cat6, or Cat6 shielded (for outdoor installations) Ethernet cable. The second is that using IP cameras as my camera type, I can install a good number of them if needed. Everything shown in the figure, including the mounting hardware, shipped with the camera for $90. Another great feature of IP cameras is that you can view them using a web browser on your computer, tablet, or smart phone. The easiest way to do that is using the camera's IP address, something this chapter discusses later. You can also manage your Internet router/firewall so that a select camera or group of cameras can be viewed from anywhere over the Internet. A little more on that topic is covered in Chapter 13, "Project 10, Connecting and Using the Home Automation Platform over the Internet."

Figure 7.2 *Hard-cased waterproof IP wired/wireless web camera.*

Some other reasons include that nearly all the components needed to install IP Ethernet cameras can be found at your nearest big-box home improvement center. Cat6 cable, Leviton Cat6 wall jacks, plastic staples, the 110 punch-down tool, wire cutters, crimp tool, and Cat6 jumper cables are all readily available. The only specialized tools beyond basic hand tools and a drill with a few bits needed for properly installing a cabled Ethernet network are the crimp tool and 110 punch-down tool, shown in Figure 7.3.

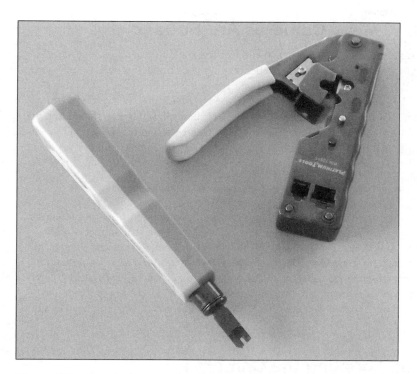

Figure 7.3   *Punch-down tool and crimp tool for terminating Cat6 Ethernet cables.*

If you do not already have these tools in your DIY toolbox, plan on spending about $50 to $60 for both tools.

IP cameras can be addressed right alongside any of your other home network devices such as computers, network attached storage, and printers. If you need to use a large number of cameras, the option is also there to install a second NIC (network interface card), making a totally separate network dedicated to the cameras and the control computer. Also, after some modest configuration effort, Wi-Fi IP cameras can be joined to a wireless network, enabling you to selectively view them on your smart phone using the phone's Wi-Fi settings. Using wireless will work well for a few cameras, but constant video streams from many cameras have a way of monopolizing available bandwidth on Wi-Fi networks. The advantage to using a Wi-Fi camera is that after it is set up, it only needs power and to be in range of the Wi-Fi network access point, making it possible to set up a hidden camera a good distance away from your residence. The advantage to hard-wiring a camera is that there is plenty of bandwidth for the video streams, allowing for more frames per second than a typical wireless stream. The hard-wired connections are also more reliable. Should you decide to build out your security camera system with wire, I would recommend using Cat6 cable and using equipment, switches, routers, computers, and printers that support gigabit Ethernet. Using gigabit speeds will also support the network traffic of a larger number of IP cameras.

Deciding How Many Cameras Are Needed

There is not a set number of cameras one could opt for; each home and its security needs are unique. A good starting point, depending on your budget, is to have one camera per home entry door; add to that one camera per home elevation (east, west, north, and south), one at the garage door, one spanning the entry sidewalk or driveway, and another in an interior hallway, porch, or entryway. For the ordinary home, that would be 10 cameras at $100 each, making the project for 360-degree protection of a small ranch-style home around $1,000 for the cameras. Having that many cameras would be atypical; common installations would be budget constrained to include one to three cameras. The HALdvc application has eight buttons for connecting to security cameras from the monitoring screen.

Should you want to install more than eight cameras and record video from more than eight IP cameras, you would need a third-party software program that supports more cameras, such as NetCamCenter Basic 3.0 (http://www.webcamsoft.com/en/netcamctr3.html), which offers a program to record from up to 36 cameras for $225. If you need to do a large number of cameras, consider a dedicated computer with a very large hard drive array to record the video streams. A computer dedicated as a video storage server can easily coexist on your separate IP network should you decide your security needs require going that route.

Installing and Locating the Cameras

One camera might be all that is desired for an apartment dweller or for a small home/condo with the doors on the same elevation. After you have decided what type of cameras to use and how many, the next step is to perform the physical installation of the cameras. Some obvious rules apply to placing security cameras: (1) Keep them out of normal human reach, (2) locate out of easy viewing by passersby or visitors whenever possible, and (3) hide and/or protect the wires in conduit. And finally aiming the camera(s) to get the view you want goes without mentioning. You can also install a fake or decoy camera where everyone can see it, as a deterrent.

The One-Web-Camera (USB) Solution

The one-USB camera solution is fairly easy. Find the place you will mount the camera and acquire a USB cable long enough to reach from the camera to the computer without exceeding the USB cable limits.

Most web cameras might not be hardened in any way or be suitable for outdoor use. Complex mounting hardware is also rarely provided. A protected porch installation or an indoor hallway should be fine for an inexpensive webcam. I would not install one where it would be exposed to the weather. These inexpensive and simple cameras might have a place in your plan, but only you can decide whether USB cameras will be up to the standard your system needs.

USB Camera Installation

You might already have a webcam installed on your computer and might only need to find a longer cord for it. The webcams are typically plug-and-play, and the drivers for the camera will load from Windows or you can use the manufacturer's supplied drivers or download the appropriate USB camera drivers.

For a USB web camera to be available to the HALdvc, it must have the Windows OS driver that matches the camera installed and be registered in Windows as an available imaging device.

When plugging in a USB camera on your computer for the first time, you are going to watch for the information flag to appear in the lower-right corner of the screen as the operating system begins to respond to the camera's presence on the USB port. Clicking on the information flag should yield the window shown in Figure 7.4, showing the install as 100 percent "ready to use" after the drivers have had time to load.

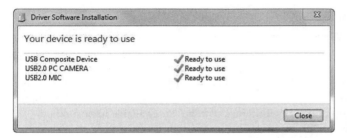

Figure 7.4 *The USB web camera's drivers are loaded and ready to use.*

The other way to check whether the USB camera is registered to the OS and ready to use is to go into Windows Control Panel under the Device Manager and click to expand the outline for Imaging Devices. At this point the camera can be "seen" by application software such as HALdvc or other applications like Skype.

> **Note**   UPB web camera: $30.
> Total prototype cost so far: $1,327.

The Multiple-Camera Solution

IP cameras like the one shown previously in Figure 7.2 are often used in large industrial, government, and commercial applications. They therefore are available with features such as hardened cases, complex mounting hardware, and night-vision capabilities, and can even include motorized control options and audio pickups along with motion detection/activation. Installing these cameras is a little more involved as a project than a simple USB webcam, but the feature sets and expansibility can make the upfront work and added expense worthwhile.

IP cameras with 640/480 resolution require you to consider how much throughput the number of cameras you will use will place on the network. For planning and design purposes, estimate that each camera will use just under 2Mbps. So putting 8 cameras on the network would use up 16Mbps, or 6Mbps too much for a 10Mbps Ethernet network, but use only about 16 percent of the bandwidth of a 100Mpbs network. This becomes important if you are adding cameras to an existing 10 or 100Mbps home or office network. If this is a new camera installation for this project and you have no investment in existing equipment, look for and install switches and components that are capable of 1000Mpbs (gigabit) speeds.

Note   IP camera: $90.

Total prototype cost so far: $1,417.

IP Ethernet Camera Installation

If you have a slower legacy home network using a separate (second) NIC (network interface card) in your computer, bringing that connection out to a separate network switch such as the one shown in Figure 7.5 solves the potential local bandwidth issue. A small Leviton 47611-5GB 10/100/1000 5-Port Gigabit Switch supports gigabit Ethernet speeds and is only about $100, providing a connection to the computer plus four ports for populating security cameras or other devices. Ethernet switches are available in port count configurations as large as you might need them. The handy little switch is a good starting point for your dedicated surveillance network.

For those readers with larger homes and properties for which it is necessary to obtain wider-ranging security views, the total wire distance limit for each Ethernet cable from device to device is 100 meters. With a single Ethernet switch located 80 meters from your computer, you can span security camera placement out to a 620-foot-diameter perimeter around your property. That should be enough for most any residential or small office security camera layout.

Note   Ethernet switch: $100.

Total prototype cost so far: $1,517.

Beyond having the cameras and at least one switch, you will need Cat6 Ethernet cable along with a few other items to make the cable runs from the switch to the camera locations. Figure 7.6 shows some of the items that will be needed, including, from the bottom to the top, a premade Cat6 jumper cable, a Leviton snap-in surface mount housing or wall plate insert, an APC Ethernet Surge protector (left), and a punch-down jack (right side) surrounded by a length of Cat6 cable.

Figure 7.5   *Small gigabit Ethernet switch by Leviton.*

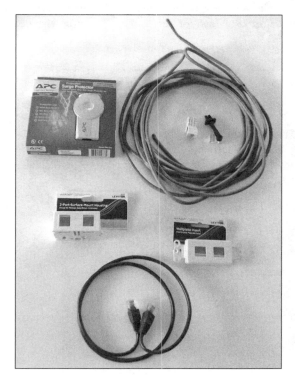

Figure 7.6   *A selection of tools and supplies necessary for installing IP cameras.*

You could wire from the switch and just use jack terminations on each end of the Cat6 cable. Terminating each end is an option, just not a particularly professional-looking one. If you are making outside runs, I would recommend that you use shielded (STP) rather than standard indoor (UTP) cable and ground your cable's shield and camera at the distant (outdoor) end or inside to the service ground; use the Leviton punch-down block in the inside and jumper over to a properly grounded APC surge protector and then over to the Ethernet switch. Jumpering from a jack at the camera locations makes good sense in the long run because the jumpers are flexible wires and the STP or UTP cable is not flexible. Use as short a jumper as possible and locate the cameras in locations where they cannot be easily accessed after they've been installed. Always be sure to use an APC Ethernet surge protector on each of your outdoor runs even if you choose not to use shielded Cat6.

When it comes to mounting the camera, use the included mounting hardware made for the camera.

The provided hardware facilitates precise aiming of the camera. When you are satisfied with the aiming angles, fully tighten the screws, bolts, and detents to spec so that the camera position is maintained.

The prototype camera can be operated as hard-wired or with Wi-Fi. Figure 7.7 shows the back of the camera and the connection point for the Wi-Fi antenna or cable, which can be run to a remote high-gain antenna location if needed for better quality or more distant reception.

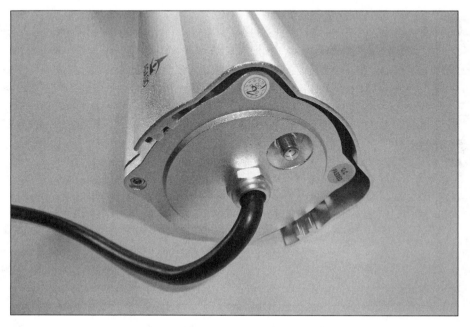

Figure 7.7   *The screw-on connection accepts the antenna or a cable connector.*

In most situations using the camera in Wi-Fi mode around most homes using a directly connected antenna is sufficient. It is screwed right on the back of the camera and can be tightened in any orientation.

The prototype camera has three additional connections, as shown in Figure 7.8. From the left in the figure are the Ethernet jack plug, the power injector connection to the power supply, and a cable with the factory reset detent switch. Read your camera's technical specification document to see whether you can use a PoE (Power over Ethernet) injector or PoE switch to power up the camera. This is often easier than locating or finding a power outlet near the camera. After the camera is installed and working, be sure to cap and/or tape over the reset detent if your camera has this feature to prevent inadvertent resets.

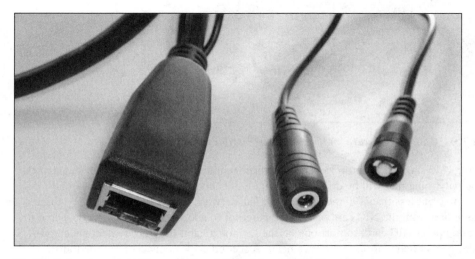

Figure 7.8 *A typical IP camera's cable and its connection tails.*

Figure 7.9 shows a close-up of the business end of the camera. When a camera is powered up and running that has IR (infrared) night vision, you can notice a faint light glow from the LED lights surrounding the camera lens.

The standard connection type for gigabit Ethernet is TIA T568A. If you are using the punch-down Leviton snap-in wall jacks for your Cat6 wiring, the color coding for both T568A and T568B is stamped on the side of the connector. It is best to use the punch-down jacks along with premade Cat6 jumper cables for your wiring because the Cat6 shielded wire is thicker, making it more difficult to use a standard RJ45 jack plug. Special shielded jacks and inserts are needed to terminate shield twisted-pair Cat6 cable. If you choose to make your own jumper connections or terminate your long cable runs with RJ45 plug jacks, there is a relatively new version of the RJ45 jack that enables you to push the wires all the way through the fitting, making it easy to get the color coding lined up correctly before you crimp the jack. The excess is cut off after crimping.

Figure 7.9   *Camera aperture and led lights are under a hardened lens.*

Figure 7.10 shows a tabletop view of the wiring required for an Ethernet camera network. The only thing that will be different in a full-blown house-size network is the length of the cable but less than 100 meters per run. The network consists of a cable (far right in the figure) from the NIC card on the computer (or to another switch that is connected to the computer NIC card) to port one on the Leviton gigabit Ethernet switch, which provides connections for one to four cameras. A second cable connects from the fourth port (far left in the figure) to the jack on the camera. This can be repeated for more cameras until you run out of ports on your switch. The installation "diagram" is that easy; running the wires and drilling and pulling them might not be so easy.

If you have never punched down a jack before, it might take a try or two to get used to doing it. With the 110 tool it is easy: Strip back the wires about an inch to an inch and a half, and line up the wire with the tabs on the jack, pulling the wires beyond the tabs to minimize the wire remaining exposed in the jack tray to half an inch. Figure 7.11 shows the white/green lined up ready to be punched down for pin one. You repeat this step for the remaining seven wires, paying attention to the color-code order for T568A as shown on the block.

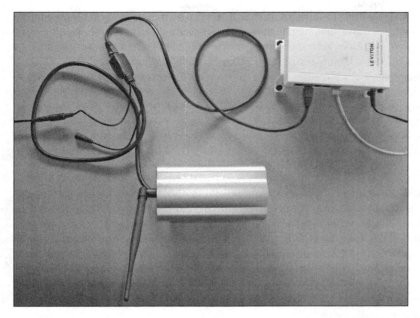

Figure 7.10 *Simplified "diagram" of Ethernet camera installations. The only variable is the length of the cable.*

Figure 7.11 *The first wire to install to pin 1 on the jack is white/green.*

Punch down the wires into the tabs with the tool so that the sharp blade on the tool cuts off the excess wire. Do the punching on a solid work surface and keep your fingers away from the punch-down blade. Repeat this process for each of the remaining seven wires. Many installers line up all the wires and punch; others punch in one wire at a time. You will need to manipulate the alignment of the cable being careful not to cut or damage the nearby wire as you punch in each wire. After the wire is punched into the jack, you can use a surface-mount housing or a standard electrical box with the decora style insert wall plate insert shown in Figure 7.6. When installing low-voltage equipment in interior walls like telephone jacks, Ethernet jacks, or TV cable, you can use a backless box in the dry-wall for ease of installation.

When doing your own cabling, it is necessary to test the installation and the pin outs to ensure continuity and correct pairing of the wires within the installed cables. The most efficient way to do that is to buy or borrow an Ethernet cable test kit similar to the one shown in Figure 7.12. When testing premise wiring, plug in a Cat6 jumper that is known to be good in the jacks on both ends of your cable run. Next plug the test terminator half of the test kit into the jack at the distant-end jumper cable and plug the tester half of the pair into the jumper at the near end. If all the pair test lights on the tester come up green in order, you are good to go and the cable connections passed. If there is a problem with the test, you might have to redo a connection pair or two. You can test jumper cables by using both jacks right on the tester half.

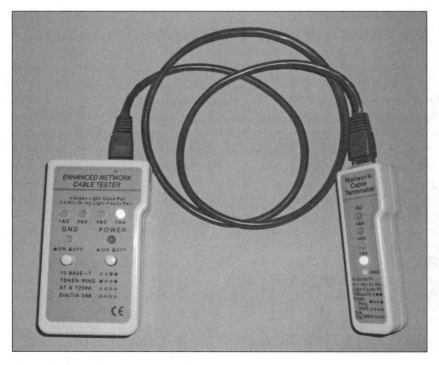

Figure 7.12   *Watch the tester for green lights as it tests each wire pair.*

After your cables are installed and tested, the next steps are to set up your camera identities, and record them in the home automation software database and for viewing in HALdvc.

Assigning IP Addresses for Cameras on Your Network

IP camera setup routines will vary somewhat based on the camera manufacturer and model and the software provided for managing and setting up the camera on your network. First, install the provided software management tools on your PC.

After the IP camera control software is installed, the next step is to set up the cameras so that they can be used on the network. The installed IP camera tool supplied by the camera manufacturer found the one camera already connected to the prototype network via the Leviton switch. The screen shown in Figure 7.13 informed me that the IP address and subnet were not a match for the network. This meant it was necessary to use the IP camera finder/wizard to set the camera IP address to match the prototype network.

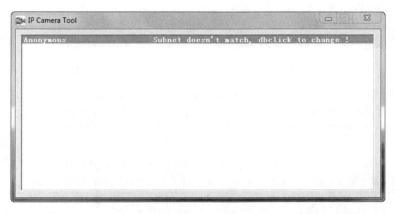

Figure 7.13   *The settings for the camera needed to be modified.*

Clicking on the IP Camera Finder tool yielded the screen shown in Figure 7.14, enabling me to make changes to the IP address to match my private network address scheme. If many of the same manufacturers' cameras were present on the network, they would have also shown up on the window shown in Figure 7.14. All that was needed was to click on the camera and change the settings for the IP address. With a full class C network the subnet mask setting will always be 255.255.255.0 to allow full visibility of all available addresses.

I wanted to use my cameras on a private network with a class C address scheme nowhere near the default network ID for most out-of-the-box equipment.

There are three defined ranges for private network address; one of those ranges is IP networks between 172.16.0.0 and 172.31.255.255. I opted to use 172.16.1.x, where the variable x would be assigned for the devices on the camera network.

Figure 7.14   *The finder tool lists all the available cameras found on the network.*

With this particular software, clicking on the IP address brings you to a setup screen where you can enter the network information and IP addresses for your wired and/or wireless network. Your camera selection will likely present a similar option within the setup software.

The new network ID IP address has to also be assigned to the computer within the Windows Network and Sharing Center; to do so, you click Change Adapter Settings and then click on the TCP/IP V4 properties, as shown in Figure 7.15. The computer's NIC card is assigned 172.16.1.10 and 172.16.1.1 is being reserved for a future network modem/router/gateway device that will be set up to view some of the cameras via the Web. The IP cameras can then be assigned any IP address on the network except the .1 and .10 addresses. Each camera must have its own unique address within the class C network range.

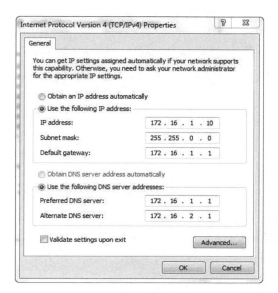

Figure 7.15 *The Ethernet IPV4 setup within the Windows OS is used to assign the NIC card with a valid IP address for the camera network.*

Registering the Cameras in HALdvc Setup

Begin this process of registering your physically installed cameras in HALdvc with the HALultra server running. Right-click on the HAL listening ear to bring up the menu to select Open Digital Video Center.

You should see the blank viewing window shown in Figure 7.16 with the Add Camera button in the middle of the window. If it does not display Add Camera, click on any of the camera number buttons at the bottom of the window. Clicking on Add Camera will begin the presentation of a series of five camera setup windows.

As shown in Figure 7.17, HALdvc keeps track of cameras with a camera number on the top of the screen. The drop-down in the center of the window enables you to enter a new location for the camera or select from rooms or spaces already included in your HALultra data for other reasons. At the bottom of the window, you assign each camera a unique Camera Name by entering a name from the keyboard. After this screen's fields are filled in with the ID information, click Next.

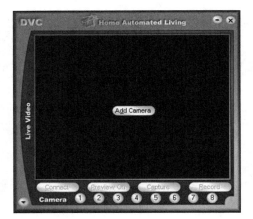

Figure 7.16   *The setup for any of the eight cameras begins here with the selection of a camera number button.*

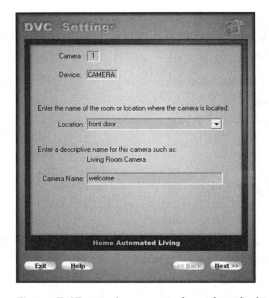

Figure 7.17   *Each camera is first identified in HALdvc with a number from 1 to 8.*

Figure 7.18 is the next setup screen presented, and your valid camera types are listed in the first drop-down menu. In this figure the IP camera setup fields are available because IP Camera was selected as the camera type. The IP address and the URL where your brand of camera will store the available video are presented. If your cameras require a username and password for HAL to connect to them, check the Require an Authentication option and enter the username and password in the blank spaces. The next two drop-down settings are for video size and frame rates per second; here you match the settings to the camera or begin with the defaults. HALdvc expects there to be a valid URL for finding the video on the camera. In this field you would fill in the correct URL directory location for your particular camera where the question marks are shown.

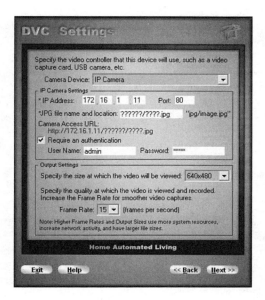

Figure 7.18   *Enter the settings for your IP network and camera details here.*

When USB is selected as the camera type, the window shown in Figure 7.19 will appear. Because the USB camera was already loaded in the Windows OS, it was present on the drop-down menu for Camera Device. Click Next after the setting button is selected for USB camera type and the camera is selected on the drop-down. If the USB camera was not previously loaded into the Windows OS, you will not see it as a valid selection.

The settings window shown in Figure 7.20 allows for setting the amount of time video is recorded from this camera. Record times can be different for each camera. This variable will depend on your security strategy. For example, if you are recording only when an event such as the pressing of the front doorbell button occurs, recording for only a few minutes might make sense. If the event trigger is a burglar alarm being tripped, recording for hours could make sense. From this screen click the Next button after you have entered your choices. The audio check box at the bottom is selected only if you have a camera that has a microphone and supports supplying audio to go with the video stream.

After you have clicked Next in the preceding step, you will have the option of changing the type of video compression; stick with the default or MPEG-4 unless you have a good reason to choose otherwise based on your camera or recording equipment specifications. Ten other video formats are supported when you click the button for Custom Video Codex (Advanced). When finished, click Next to reach the final setup window. If your camera is equipped with motion or infrared detection, check the check box to turn on detection.

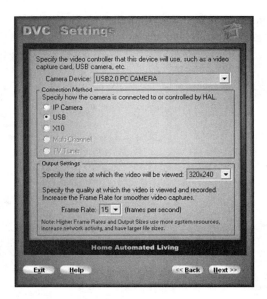

Figure 7.19 *USB camera settings.*

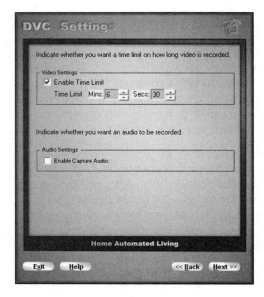

Figure 7.20 *Set the video recording time limit as needed.*

After your cameras are set up, you can view them from the first window in HALdvc by clicking on the Camera Number Button and the Connect button on the left side. When everything is properly set up, you should see the streaming video from each camera as you click on the number buttons.

Each brand and model of camera will vary somewhat in how it operates and interfaces with HALdvc and HALultra based on the camera's functions and specifications. The one I selected for the prototype example required a unique command string instead of the normal storage URL requested in the screen shown previously in Figure 7.18. HAL can accept a special command string to activate an IP camera that does not use the URL setting for the streaming video. Figure 7.21 shows the command string used with the prototype camera. Begin to look for these strings when they are needed in the camera manual, on the manufacturer's website, or on a link to your camera manufacturer from this website: http://www.ispyconnect.com/sources.aspx.

For the prototype camera the needed syntax for the entry is as follows:

http://IPaddress:port/Snapshot.cgi?user=*Username*&pwd=*Password*
&resolution=*32*

When using HAL to access the camera, HAL builds the command string from the information entered in this window, so the IP address and port number field are combined with the rest of the command string entered into the *URL field and sent to the camera. The full URL shown above can be entered from your web browser for testing the camera's response to the command.

Figure 7.21   *Special activation command strings might be necessary for your IP camera to work with HALdvc.*

Despite their added complexity, using IP cameras offers the most versatile solution. Being able to use a combination of hard-wired and wireless cameras facilitates the build-out of a substantial home security and surveillance installation. Linking into any camera with a computer, smart phone, or tablet using Wi-Fi is also a big plus, making this a very good option for a new build involving a large number of cameras.

Setting Up Camera Security Actions with HALultra

With the camera install project concluded and the links to HALdvc in place, the real fun begins. Now you can implement your security plan and take advantage of HALultra's home automation features to enhance your home's security profile. Use HALultra macros and modes to correlate your devices to orchestrate a response to your unique security triggers and events. Use the HAL documentation and the website forums to help you customize your system.

To get started with custom security-related programming, begin by opening the Automation Setup Screen, shown in Figure 7.22.

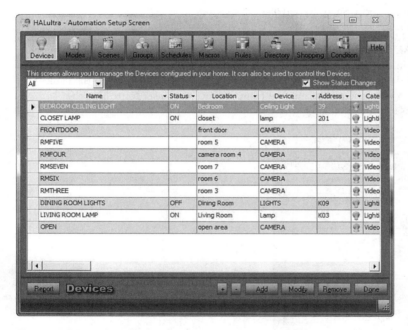

Figure 7.22 *The tabs for Macros and Rules are the starting points for customizing the response to an alarm condition.*

Click Macros and create a macro called Security. Next, add the actions you want to have executed when the macro is called up by an event, as shown in Figure 7.23.

You can add more than one action to the macro, as shown in Figure 7.24, by highlighting the named macro and clicking the Add Action button. In this case turning on the DINING ROOM LIGHTS is selected.

Notice how the programming features of HALultra can be leveraged with the aid of the "if-then" conditions to fully customize your home's response to an event.

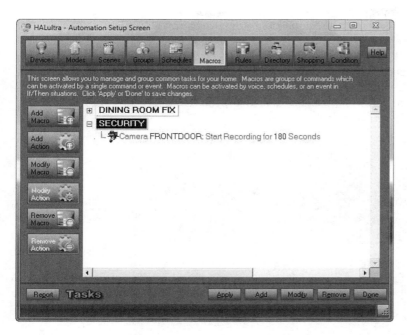

Figure 7.23   *The security macro is displayed after the macro was added with an action to record from FRONTDOOR camera.*

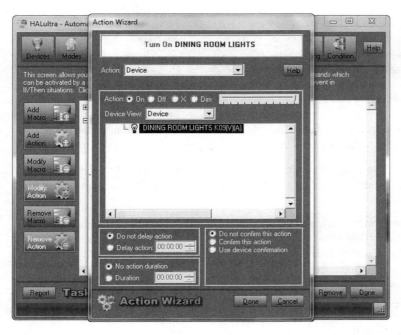

Figure 7.24   *Any actionable device available can be added to the macro.*

The Rules tab at the top of the Automation Setup Screen can be customized to build hard rules that initiate when a particular event occurs. In this case, shown in Figure 7.25, when the Front Porch Motion is activated from its motion sensor, the rule says to begin recording for 180 seconds. All responses are customizable to your needs, enabling you to leverage every device installed on the premises if needed. As long as the devices are in your system and connected with a supported interface, you can deploy them with nested rules or macros to take actions to meet your needs.

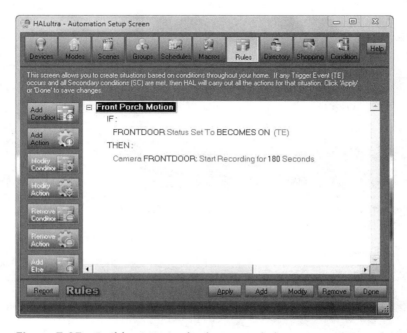

Figure 7.25　*Build customized rules as needed.*

One might have to be careful with nested macros or rules to not end up in an endless loop, but you can run a macro from Rules by adding named macros as actions.

Figure 7.26 shows the completed rule that runs the camera named FRONTDOOR to record for 180 seconds and executes the macro named SECURITY, which also turns on the dining room lights.

Your own programming with macros and rules is limited only by your imagination. The examples here are offered solely to get you started with some degree of comfort and confidence. When you are first learning the process, keep in mind that you really can't hurt anything and you can delete any entry you make or modify entries as needed. Again, check the HAL website for more information and ideas on using the programming power of HALultra. Build and test actions as you go to ensure that you are getting the results you seek. Start with small actions and uncomplicated rules and two to three event macros, and build up from there.

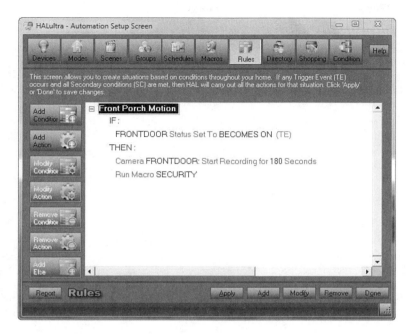

Figure 7.26 *Example of a rule used for calling up an action and a macro that calls up other actions.*

Figure 7.27 shows a snapshot of a driveway area taken with the IP camera from the Front Door location.

Figure 7.27 *Early evening snapshot of driveway taken with IP camera from a front porch location.*

Chapter 8

Project 5, Upgrading the Home Automation Platform to HALultra

After getting a taste of what's possible with HALbasic, you might want to upgrade to HALultra. HALbasic does an excellent job of controlling your home automation system, but because it is an entry-level program, it cannot handle all tasks. The added functionality of HALultra includes the direct support of HVAC controls, caller ID functions, reminders, shopping lists, home theater control, weather interfaces, digital sensors, and control of security zones. In addition, HALultra builds on voice mailboxes, address/directory information, stock lookups, devices, macros, house modes, events, and X-10 sensors.

AutomatedLiving.com will grant a credit toward the purchase of HALultra for the registered users of HALbasic. HALultra, at this writing, is list priced at $499. Going from HALbasic to HALultra is a software upgrade, not a version upgrade, and a $40 credit is offered to current HALbasic registered users. Registered HALdeluxe users are currently given a credit of $140 toward the purchase of HALultra software. Here in Project 5 we will add $450 to the prototype budget from Chapter 6, "Project 3, Controlling Lighting: Indoors and Outdoors," for the current cost of the software upgrade.

Note Software upgrade project prototype budget: $450.
Total prototype cost so far: $1,747.

Chapter 4, "Project 1, Installing HALbasic Software on Your PC," involved installing HALbasic software on your home automation platform. Some readers and end users might want to start with the additional features found in HALultra and will want to skip the installation of HALbasic altogether. If you are in this category and want to use HALultra from the start, you will still want to read and work though the tasks found in Chapter 2, "Using a Windows Computer as Your Home Automation Platform," which lays out necessary steps to prepare your PC for a successful installation. For those beginning with the HALultra version, the installation steps regarding use of X10 adapters and controllers outlined in Chapter 4 will also apply to your installation of HALultra. You can refer to the tasks as outlined in Chapter 4 to perform testing from the setup screens as you begin to set up and deploy your X-10 control modules.

Upgrading to HALultra

This chapter assumes a fully patched preinstall condition for the Windows operating system you will be using. In Chapter 4 we worked with an actual Install disc, essentially a hard copy of the software. This chapter's project demos the HAL2000 upgrade by doing an over-the-Internet software download. As an end user, you are able to make a choice for your install convention. You have two choices for proceeding with the upgrade: doing the upgrade online or ordering the CD hard copy shipped to you for the upgrade installation.

Administrative Steps

To obtain a copy of HALultra, either register at https://www.automatedliving.com/updupg_supgrade.shtml for the software to be delivered via secure download or order a physical disc to be shipped to your home.

Back Up HALbasic

Before you begin the upgrade process, use the HALbasic Backup/Restore features to store a copy of your HAL databases, settings, and other configuration files. To access the backup option, with the HALbasic server running, right-click the HAL icon in the system tray and select Open System Settings from the menu.

While in the System Settings window, double-click Backup/Restore, as shown in Figure 8.1.

The next screen offers five check boxes for selecting HAL items for backup. The most important one is Configuration Information. The more items and devices that you have configured, the more important it is to have a valid backup so that you do not have to repeat device setups. You have the option to back up your data to a local drive, a network drive, or a portable drive. Keep in mind that backing up to an external drive such as a portable drive or network drive ensures data integrity in the event of a catastrophic failure of your home automation PC. After you have checked items for backup, click Run Backup. The default backup location is the C: drive, but feel free to enter any location. After you click Run Backup, HAL will confirm that you want to create a new directory, if your backup location does not exist on the drive. Click Yes and then Yes again when HAL confirms that you want to back up your data.

After a short time, the window shown in Figure 8.2 appears, confirming that the backup has been successful. Click OK to complete the backup process.

Before proceeding with the download of the software, and after you have received your confirmation of the upgrade email from AutomatedLiving.com, turn off the HALbasic server.

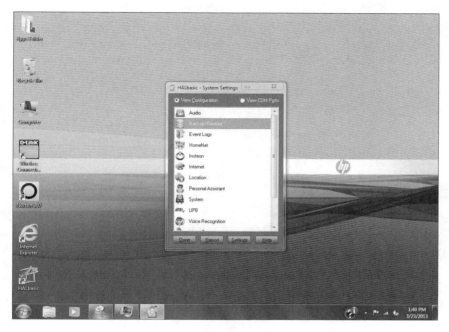

Figure 8.1   *Choose Backup/Restore from the menu.*

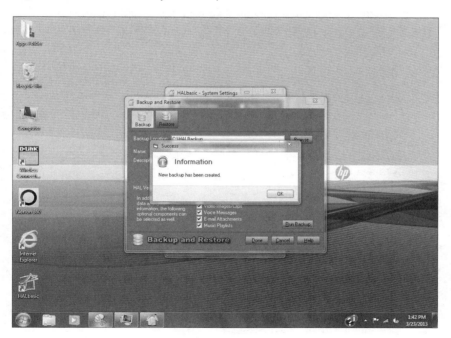

Figure 8.2   *This message shows that the backup has been created successfully.*

Installing

Whether you download the upgrade software or install the upgrade from a disc, launch the Installation Wizard, as shown in Figure 8.3. Click Next to begin the installation of HALultra.

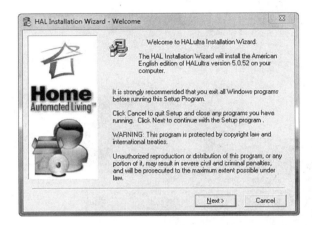

Figure 8.3   *The wizard is ready to begin the installation.*

Accept the license agreement and move through the wizard. If your installation is an upgrade, you will see a window informing you that the wizard has detected an earlier version of the HAL software. Click Yes to proceed through that window.

Move through the installation wizard until the installation is finished, as shown in Figure 8.4. At this point, it's time to activate your upgraded software. Select the check box for Run HAL License Manager Now and click Finish.

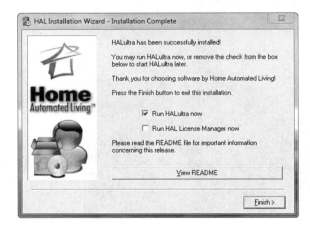

Figure 8.4   *Select the Run HAL License Manager Now option to proceed.*

Activating

After you run the license manager in the preceding step, the HAL activation window appears. In the upper-right corner of the window is a question mark. Click the question mark to bring up the next window. Connect to the Internet if you are not already connected, and click Refresh. The License Manager updates your license information to reflect any new software and add-on purchases. When the update is complete, a success message appears. If the license update is not successful, contact HAL technical support for assistance.

Testing

Congratulate yourself and the wizard for a successful installation, but test the software next to make sure that your setups are still present and that the server will launch from the Windows Start menu. There should be a new icon for HALultra on the desktop.

Now that the upgrade is complete, it's time to test the software and make sure that your setups are still present. Launch the HAL2000 server and wait for the "ear" icon to show up in the system tray. Right-click on the ear icon and select Open Automation Setup Screen, as done in previous chapters. The window on your screen should be similar to the one shown in Figure 8.5. Notice that at the top of the window it now labels the windows as the HALultra Automation Setup Screen. Any previously configured devices are listed on this screen as they were in HALbasic.

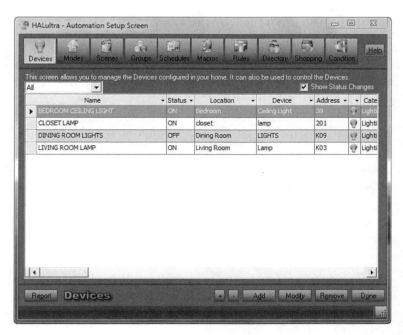

Figure 8.5 *The devices set up with HALbasic are present in the HALultra screen.*

Select a device that you know is working properly and use HAL2000 to turn the device on and off. After your testing is complete, close the setup screen. Feel free to test other devices until you are satisfied that everything is working correctly. After your system has been tested, it's time to configure the Internet settings. Close the setup screen and access the System Settings window by right-clicking the HAL icon in the system tray. Double-click Internet, as shown in Figure 8.6.

Figure 8.6 *The System Settings window.*

The next screen to appear allows you to make some adjustments to the Internet interface after you check the Internet Enabled check box, as shown in Figure 8.7. The prototype system is using high-speed Internet so Use a Dial-Up Connection is not un-selected when the "Dedicated" selection is made. After you make changes to these settings, click Apply and then click Done.

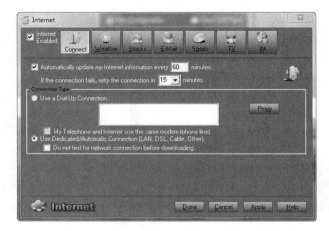

Figure 8.7 *Set up your Internet settings in this window.*

Along with having HALultra email you when stocks prices go up or down on up to 40 publicly traded stocks, you can configure HAL2000 to provide weather information for your location. Click the Weather tab to configure weather information based on your ZIP Code, as shown in Figure 8.8. Click Apply and Done to save your new settings.

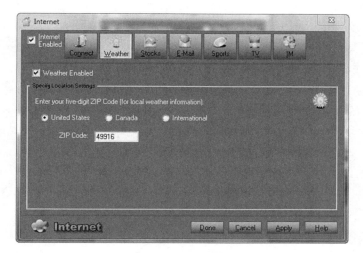

Figure 8.8   *The weather can be configured for your area by ZIP Code.*

Explore New Features

The rest of this book demonstrates projects using the HAL2000 software on the proto-type home automation system. For those readers still on the fence about performing this upgrade, there are two use cases that not only justify but recoup the cost of the upgrade. HALultra's capability to manage your home's heating, ventilation, and air conditioning allows you to control your entire HVAC system whether you are home or halfway across the globe. The potential energy savings over the course of a year or two could far exceed the cost of the software upgrade. The other case for upgrading is to increase your per-sonal efficiency. If you rate your time at $20 per hour, the things that HALultra can do for you by schedule or by voice or phone call when you are away from home can recoup the cost of the upgrade in a year. Being able to control your television with your voice is also pretty cool. Finally, HALultra can provide security and peace of mind, not just when you're on vacation and you want your home to look lived in, but day to day by monitor-ing your home so that you can see that your children got home safely.

Take some time to explore the new features of HAL2000 on your own, knowing that with the right interfaces you can control aspects of your home you never thought pos-sible. Upcoming chapters will help you build out increased functions and value for your home automation platform.

Chapter 9

Project 6, Installing a Home Automation Voice Portal Modem in Your Computer

Despite the trend of households moving away from traditional landlines for phone service, having a reliable landline to your residence extends the capability to control and manage your home via your home automation platform. Wherever you are, as long as you can receive a phone call, you can be in full control of your home.

Aside from the capability to be controlled from a distance, your home can notify you of problems as soon as they arise. Having a landline for $600 per year is significantly lower than the possible cost of an expensive cleanup or repair from any problem that HAL software could notify you about when configured properly to do so.

Voice portal hardware provides dial-in and -out phone access to all of HAL's voice control features. The HAL voice modem can work via cellular service (with additional equipment) but works best with traditional phone service or Internet-based VOIP services, such as telephone service from cable providers.

With a HAL voice portal in your computer, you can go anywhere in the world there is a working phone *or cell service* and control your home's automation features by voice commands over the phone. You can also use your home automation platform to manage custom specified voice mailboxes, caller ID announcing, custom messages to specific callers, phone call logs, voice-activated number dialing, speakerphone, and call intercepting and blocking. If your home phone's extension phones are wired correctly, you can press a specified number key on any phone in the downstream line and use voice-activated home control commands. The land line phone at home when hooked to HAL via the modem becomes a method to talk to the home and for the home to communicate to the outside world through the automation routines you design.

When the home automation computer is hooked to the Internet and a landline phone line, you can call in from anywhere in the world to hear information retrieved for you from the Internet from email, news feeds, weather, stock quotes, and more.

A HAL voice portal is an add-in to the computer and is exclusive to HAL software customers. The list price at this writing is $289, which we'll add to our prototype budget.

Note   Install HAL VP300 Voice modem project prototype budget: $289.
Total prototype cost so far: $2,033.

The HAL Internal PCI Voice Portal (VP300) modem is shown in Figure 9.1. Not all PCI slots on motherboards are created equal. This modem fits into a PCIeX1 slot.

Figure 9.1   *Side view of the HAL VP300 revision 1.50 modem showing the connection bus.*

Figure 9.2 shows the modem card on an angle to view the connections available on the card. There are four connection ports on the card, two RJ-14 connections, and two quarter-inch mono jack ports. The top RJ-14 connects to your phone or is wired to all the downstream extension phone jacks in the house for access from every phone on the line. The lower RJ-14 jack port connects to the telephone company line-in because all the downstream phones must be connected in series after the modem to provide the control feature on all house extension phones. To state it another way, the internal phones' tones and voice signal must "pass though" the HAL VP300 modem for the features to work properly. The HAL VP300 modem has an input jack that is wired to the phone company NID (network interface) and an output jack that is wired to all the house phone extensions on that line (phone number) to work properly.

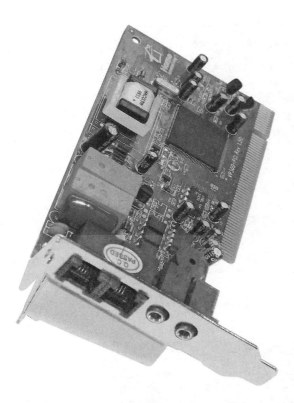

Figure 9.2 *Voice modem connection ports from top (left) are RJ14 to phone, RJ14 to line, mono microphone, and mono speaker jack ports.*

Installing the Voice Portal Modem

To start installing the voice portal modem, shut down the HAL2000 server, shut down the PC, and remove the computer's power cord to the wall outlet, as well as all the other cords connected to the computer. Find a static-electricity-free place to work on the computer (avoid rooms with carpeted floors) and use a bench, desktop, or table for a work area.

After you have your PC on your work surface, remove the back cover of the PC's case. On many computers the add-in cards and slot cover brackets are secured by a single screw in each bracket. This model of computer case is designed for quick and simple assembly and does not use screws. The semicircular metal tab shown in Figure 9.3 with the arrow is lifted up and out in an arc motion toward the back of the computer.

After the tab is rotated toward the back and bottom of the computer, the card slot fill brackets are loose in their support channels, as shown in Figure 9.4. They can simply be lifted out to make room for the new modem card and also the serial port bracket. In this case the new modem will be installed in the slot to the left so that bracket is removed.

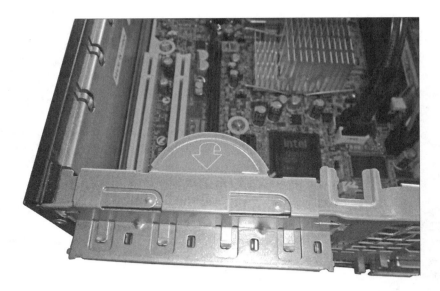

Figure 9.3   *Lifting the semicircular tab releases the tension that is holding the card slot brackets firmly in place.*

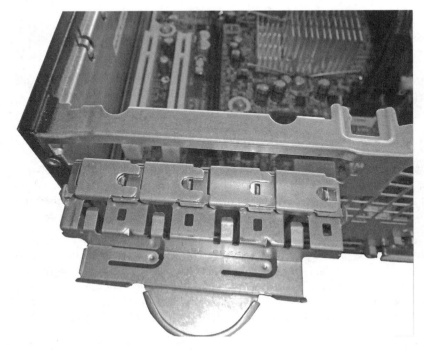

Figure 9.4   *There is a notch on the top of the brackets that slips over tabs on the case.*

A thin screwdriver blade or knife blade can be used to lift the brackets and spring brace away from the case to remove the filler brackets.

Figure 9.5 shows the card set on the motherboard slot but not seated. To install a PCI card, it must be kept parallel to the system board so that it slides straight down into the connectors in the slot. Some modest pressure with one hand on the bracket end and at the opposite end of the card will seat the card into the slot.

Figure 9.5   *The card is ready to be gently pressed into the slot.*

> **Note**   **Moderate Pressure Is the Key**   When you're installing cards into a motherboard, moderate pressure is the key to get the card seated. Do not force the card or apply excessive pressure or you run the risk of snapping the card. These cards are meant to slide in with just a little pressure, so if the card isn't snapping in, remove it, reseat it, and then apply pressure again.

Figure 9.6 shows the card properly seated into the PCI system board slot.

The card bracket is shown properly seated and aligned in Figure 9.7. Because readers might have a computer with a full-height PCI slot, it should be noted that the HAL VP300 modem comes with brackets to accommodate both low-profile and full-height slots. Installing in a full-height slot will require the removal of two screws in order to change that bracket type.

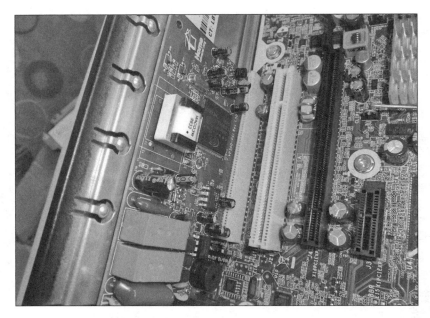

Figure 9.6   *Notice that the card is evenly seated in the card slot.*

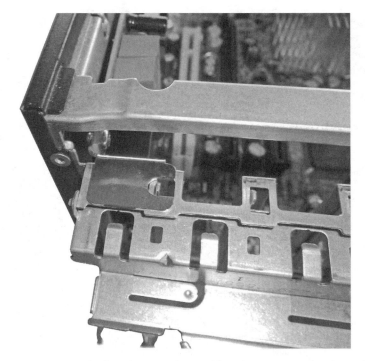

Figure 9.7   *Check to be sure the card bracket is properly aligned.*

Connecting the Voice Portal in the Operating System

At this step the cables to the computer are returned and fastened to their respective connection points on the computer case. Always connect the computer power cord last after all the other connections have been made.

Even though all the physical connections have been made, plugging in the new hardware is not the last step necessary to make the new hardware work. Now we need to get the operating system to recognize the new hardware and communicate with it successfully.

Because this modem is a "plug and play" device, the first time you power up the PC after the modem's installation, the OS will attempt to find the hardware drivers for the modem.

If a hardware conflict arises, due to either incorrect drivers or improperly loaded drivers, the conflict shows up in the Device Manager. Right-click on the Computer icon, select Properties, select Device Manager, and expand the Modem icon from the list to see a window similar to the one shown in Figure 9.8. Notice that the modem is shown as PCI Simple Communications Controller, there is a flag by the P in PCI, and the modem is not properly identified or installed at this point.

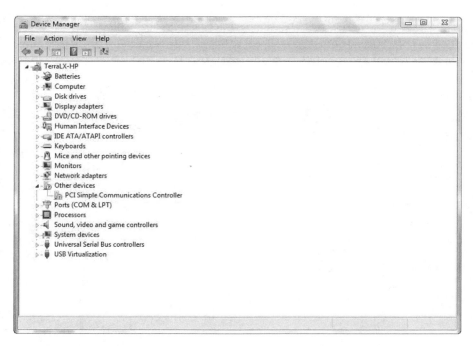

Figure 9.8 *Notice the trouble flag near the PCI indicating that there is a problem.*

If you downloaded the drivers, go straight to the directory holding the drivers on your hard drive. If you have the HAL-supplied installation disc, navigate to the Drivers directory on the disc for the HAL VP300 Windows XP Drivers. Regardless of how you obtained the drivers, double-click the HXFSetup executable to start the installation process.

After you double-click on the executable, the window shown in Figure 9.9 will display. Select the Install this Driver Software Anyway option to proceed with the driver installation.

Figure 9.9   *The Windows security settings cause this warning to appear; proceed anyway.*

After the driver has been installed, returning to the Device Manager list should show that the driver is now installed correctly, as shown in Figure 9.10. Notice that the generic information is replaced by the specifics about the HAL Voice Portal modem.

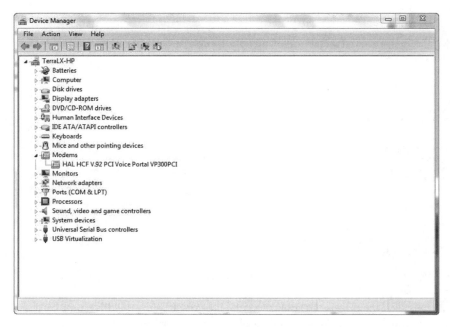

Figure 9.10   *The correct details are shown and the error flag is no longer present.*

This is a good point to shut down the HAL server, if you have it running, and reboot the computer. Carefully watch the information windows as HAL restarts; specifically, watch the information for the HAL phone port components to load.

Voice Portal Installation with the HAL Setup Wizard

Now that the OS is aware of the voice portal, the HAL software needs to be made aware of the portal's installation. To do this, simply perform a Custom install of the HAL software. Had the modem been installed in the system before HAL was installed for the first time, we could have chosen this option with our initial install. Because we have covered the HAL installation process in Chapter 8, "Project 5, Upgrading the Home Automation Platform to HALultra," we'll pick up these steps from the HAL Setup Type option window shown in Figure 9.11. Select Custom Setup and click on Next.

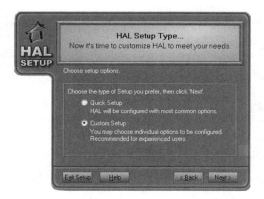

Figure 9.11   *Select the custom setup this time.*

Check the box for Modem and the sub-boxes for Remote Telephone, Digital Answering Machine, and Home Telephone, as shown in Figure 9.12. Then click Next.

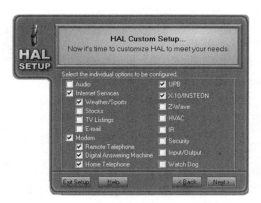

Figure 9.12   *Select which modem options you would like to install.*

The next two screens allow you to choose your type of Internet connection as well as enter your Zip Code for weather information. Keep in mind that if you are using DSL for your broadband Internet, a DSL filter is necessary to ensure that the voice modem is receiving clear signals. Enter the appropriate information and click through the wizard until you reach the HAL Telephone Services screen, as shown in Figure 9.13. The Voice Portal model information and COM port are displayed in drop-down menus. If the install has not detected the modem, click Auto Sense and the software will automatically detect the modem and COM port. In the event you are using dial-up Internet service, check My Telephone and Internet Connection Use the Same Phone Line. After you have verified that all the information is correct, click Next.

Figure 9.13 *It is critical that a COM port is associated with the voice portal modem.*

Figure 9.14 shows the HAL Remote Telephone Services configuration window. The chief benefit of installing and configuring a voice modem in our home automation platform is to be able to control this system via telephone, so select Yes on this screen. In the next two data fields enter and verify the same four-digit Personal Access Code used to control HAL. Click Next to move to the next window. This window asks whether you want to control HAL via your home telephone, so select Yes or No and click Next.

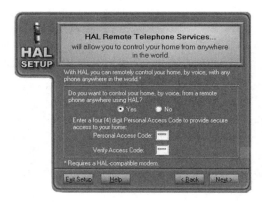

Figure 9.14 *Enter your personal pin number in this window.*

The next two windows allow you to configure HAL as a digital answering machine. If you want to make use of this feature, select Yes. Click Next and on the next window choose whether you would like to record a customized voice greeting or use the default voice greeting for now and customize later. Click Next to move to the next screen and continue clicking through until the custom install wizard is complete. Start the HAL server and bring up the System Settings window via right-clicking the HAL icon in the system tray. After the System Settings window opens, select Telephone to bring up the screen shown in Figure 9.15.

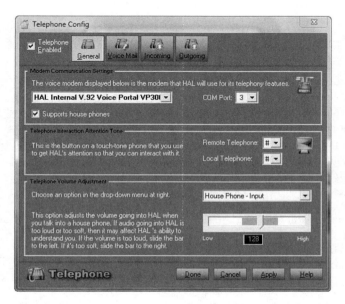

Figure 9.15   *Notice the four tabs in this window: General, Voice Mail, Incoming, and Outgoing.*

Figure 9.15 shows the General screen of the Telephone Config window. In the prototype system the Voice Portal is set to COM Port 3. In the Telephone Interaction Attention Tone panel, set your single-digit code to enter during a call into HAL from an outside line to get HAL to go into action mode and follow your commands. The second drop-down window allows you to select a single-digit number to communicate to HAL from inside extension phones. Avoid using 9 because it might interfere with 911 calls. Do not choose a code that matches the first letter in the phone number prefix you call frequently. As long as the first number you press is not the key number for HAL when you dial out from a down-line extension, the call will be placed as if the HAL voice portal modem were not present. With these codes in place, your telephone will not behave any differently when you pick up the phone. You will still hear a dial tone and will still be able to make outgoing calls as normal. The only difference is that if you enter the configured attention tone number first, HAL will effectively place the outside line on hold and listen for your commands instead.

Note   A Note on Phones   The HAL voice modem requires a touch-tone phone, not a rotary phone, so put that classic black phone back in the museum where it belongs.

In the Telephone Volume Adjustment panel you can adjust the Input and Output sound levels for any one of three telephone devices: the house phones, the remote phones, and the speaker phone imbedded in the HAL voice portal modem. You can drop down the menu to each phone device and independently adjust the incoming or outgoing sound levels by sliding the pointer with your mouse from Low to High. Start with the defaults in the blue bar range and adjust later if necessary.

After you have made your entries and settings, click Apply to save your settings. Click the Voice Mail tab to move on to configure the next section.

Figure 9.16 shows the various voice mail configuration options for HAL. The home automation computer has to be on with the HAL server running for HAL to handle incoming calls. In the Answering Machine Settings panel, check the box for Turn Answering Machine On. After this option is enabled, you can select the number of rings HAL will allow before answering the phone. If your phone service comes with voice mail, you need to know how many times your phone rings before the voice mail service answers the call. After you have this number, select a lower number after which HAL will answer. You might also be able to have your phone service provider disable voice mail for your number entirely. The second drop-down is for the circumstance in which the HAL answering service is off but the computer is still on with HAL server running; set which ring HAL will answer on in the lower drop-down. With the answering machine off, after some number of rings you still want HAL to answer the phone when you call in so you can use your access code to converse with HAL and control the devices in your home via telephone.

The rest of the panels involve selecting personal preferences for how HAL will present or save your voice messages and how frequently you will be notified by computer sounds when new messages are present. When your selections are complete, click the Incoming tab to bring up the new window.

Figure 9.17 shows options for how the voice portal will handle incoming phone calls. HAL automation software is capable of routing the incoming phone call notifications via a ringtone to your computer's speakers. In the prototype system, the Until Answered option is selected along with supplied ringtone Ring 4. Along with tones installed with the HAL software, you can use any short .wav file on your PC as your ringtone.

The next section controls how HAL works call screening and caller ID functionality. HAL can announce the caller ID information over your PC's speakers, intercept the call, or respond with a selected message. Use the variable script to configure the announcement text, being sure to spell the <NAME> and <NUMBER> variables correctly. The option to use names from the directory refers to the HAL software's internal phone directory, which most likely will not be filled in at this point in your configuration. Be sure to check the box to end the announcement after the phone is answered so that HAL won't continue to inform you while you're on the phone.

Figure 9.16 *Select the right number of rings to ensure that HAL will answer at the right time.*

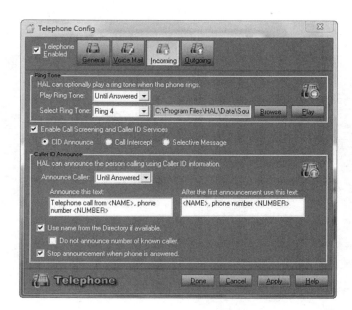

Figure 9.17 *Select and enter your preferences for handling incoming calls in this window.*

You can answer your home's incoming calls with any of the phones in your house or with HAL as long as you have a headset or a microphone and speakers connected to the sound card. As an alternative, you can switch the HAL Voice Portal over to Speakerphone mode from the telePhonePad to use the 3.5mm jacks on the lower part of the voice portal for a mono microphone and a mono speaker. When you are satisfied with your data entries and selections, click Apply to save your changes. Next, click the Outgoing tab.

Note   For International Readers   The prototype system is configured for U.S. Caller ID information. Our international readers will need to configure the modem in the Windows Control Panel so that HAL can correctly interpret caller ID information from other countries.

Figure 9.18 shows the dialing options for HAL. The first two options allow you to configure the prefix needed to dial an outside line. In most home implementations this won't be necessary so leave this option unchecked. The second part of the window allows you to enter the long-distance prefix as well as any area codes needed for local calls. Finally, from this window you can choose to log a record of calls, set the amount of time you want to keep the call logs, and configure which phone number to leave on numeric pages. After the configuration is complete, click Apply to save your data. When you have completed all four tabs, click Done. HAL will inform you that some changes will not take effect until the HAL server is restarted. Click OK and then restart the HAL server via the system tray icon.

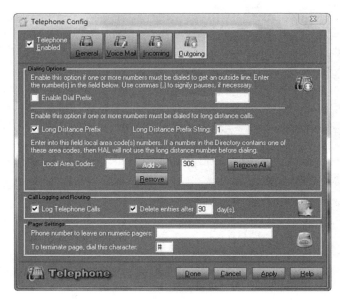

Figure 9.18   *Make the proper selections and entries for outgoing.*

Watch the desktop screen as the HAL application is started, and watch for the information banners at the top of the startup window to show "Opening Phone Port." If those banners proceed without an error message, your installation and setups were successful. You are then ready to begin testing some of your HAL voice modem features:

- **Test One**—Pick up a downstream phone handset (it's okay if you have only one at this point) and press the single-digit number on the phone's dial pad for in-house access, and then listen to the phone. If you do not speak the "Attention" word (the default "Attention" word is "computer") in a few seconds, the application will speak, "Yes?" and wait for your voice command. Issue a voice command used to turn off or on a known working device. See Chapter 5, "Project 2, Controlling Appliances, Lights, and Devices," for more information on voice commands. At this point, HAL will react with confirmations and verifications as determined by your voice commands settings. After the action has been completed, hang up and go through the testing steps again to place the device in the original state.

- **Test Two**—Using another line, call the HAL-connected line and wait the configured number of rings for HAL to answer with the custom message. Leave a message after the HAL greeting. If you cannot be present for the call, have an assistant wait in the house and listen for the caller ID and call announcement. You can retrieve the message later from the PhonePad window.

Figure 9.19 shows the HALultra PhonePad ready for use. To make a call, enter a phone number and click Dial on the PhonePad. After you dial a number, you can pick up any extension phone to talk, talk over the sound card's microphone and speakers, or click on the Speaker Phone button on the PhonePad to use the mono connected microphone and speakers. After the automation software has handled a few incoming calls, you can click on the Calls In tab (or click the Messages button) and right-click on the listed call. The menu that appears allows you to choose Call to call the person back, or you can select Add to Directory, Remove to remove that call from the list, Remove All to remove all listed calls from the list, or Add to Blocked List.

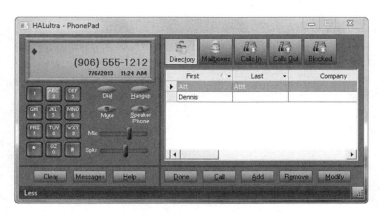

Figure 9.19   *The HAL2000 PhonePad*

■ **Test Three**—From the HAL2000 PhonePad use your mouse to enter numbers and dial out to another line to be sure your modem can make outgoing calls.

Chapter 10

Project 7, Getting Green and Managing Your Home's Climate

A very exciting feature of any full-featured home automation system is the capability to link to and control your home's energy utilization while at the same time maximizing the occupants' comfort levels. Controlling home energy use with HALultra is exciting because it offers minute-by-minute or degree-by-degree control. At the same time, HAL provides the option for automatically controlling the temperature by using monitored environmental variables or allowing dynamic management by you or a household member from anywhere you are. This chapter presents a beginner-level project toward that goal: installing a compatible thermostat and setting up a ceiling fan controller to supplement the HVAC control. The goal is to have all the components dealing with comfort in the house working together to increase comfort while maximizing efficiency. For example, if you like a lot of air moving around when an air conditioner is on in a room, having the ceiling fan on when the air kicks on is a simple task for HALultra. Another example would be automated shades or blinds; one could power them to cover the south-facing windows when the air conditioner is activated. All of this is possible with HALultra.

Getting Green

If you are inclined to use home automation temperature control features only for convenience and comfort, HAL can do that and do it very well. Alternatively, if you intend to use home automation to limit and control temperature and thereby reduce your average consumption of energy, it can do that, too. It can do both at the same time, to some degree, in amazing ways for those willing to invest some energy and effort.

Managing Temperature and Energy Consumption

Some of the considerations and bases to touch on before you plan out and deploy home automation control thermostats about your home are in the details normally left to the HVAC professionals. As with doing extensive electrical work, some jobs are best done by the pros. If you are uncomfortable with tinkering with the HVAC systems in your home, seek out your favorite "heating guy or gal" to do it or help out. As with doing extensive electrical work, in many jurisdictions it will be a state- or province-licensed profession.

As a DIYer, you might find that your involvement with an existing HVAC system doesn't need to go beyond replacing a "'dumb" thermostat or two, with units that can interface with HALultra, and adding to that a few monitoring devices to obtain more sophisticated overall control of the system in your home. These projects are all potentially within the reach of a dedicated DIYer.

Heating and Cooling System Links

As with controlling other devices with HALultra or HALbasic, the standard control model is repeated for managing heating, ventilating, and air conditioning systems. That standard control model includes the intelligence programmed into your HALultra setups, the interface modules connected to the computer, a way to communicate to the actual control device or thermostat (wire or wireless), and the control device itself. With HVAC the predominant controls will be either simple device on/off controls or multifunction thermostats that can be adjusted remotely by the automation features of HALultra.

On/Off Devices

Many of the other chapters in this book have covered installing and controlling any on/off device control modules with the various technologies. The only difference here is what they will be used to control. For example, you might have a water pump house at a remote cabin or lodge where at times the temperatures might be low enough a few days a year to cause freezing damage at the pump house. Instead of leaving an electric heater in the on mode all the time, with a thermostat set you could use an on/off control to energize the heating circuit only when the outdoor temperature falls below 34 degrees. Your unique needs will dictate how you would want to integrate simple on/off controls into your automation plans for adjusting and controlling environmental heating and cooling systems. Your home's requirements for maintaining temperatures in equipment areas of the home and to enhance or complement HVAC controls for maintaining the occupants' comfort will establish the complexity baseline for your overall project requirements to manage heating and cooling in your home. Unlike other proponents of energy conservation, I contend that you can be green without wasting a speck of energy or reducing the occupants' comfort levels. The idea is to eliminate the wasted energy consumption and use some percentage of that savings where necessary to maintain or increase comfort.

Thermostats

You can use the powers of home automation to control one or multiple home HVAC systems with HALultra. You can use one or more of the protocols or standardize on one type of thermostat. Digital thermostats often have some built-in features to handle night and weekend changes with entries made at the face of the thermostat. With HAL-enabled thermostats you can make very complex entries in the macros and rules, as well as integrate sensors into the equation on how the total system will act and respond to environmental changes.

Deploying Gauges, "Triggers," and Sensors

In the case of a Florida-bound snowbird, leaving the northern house set to 55 degrees while the occupants are gone for a few months will save money and energy. This single preset temperature will keep the house from freezing and will save money over and above leaving the thermostat set to temperatures that would keep occupants comfortable. With HALultra home automation, some if/then conditions for automated actions can further reduce heating or cooling costs regardless of where you live.

The terminology used in this area defines a "degree day" as any day in which a given structure must be heated or cooled from some energy source based on the building's or occupant's needs, when a preselected outside temperature changes by one degree. The term "HDD" (heating degree day) refers to a day in which the outside temperature is one degree, or more, lower than the level where comfort or environmental needs would be met naturally, requiring the addition of heat. A "CDD" (cooling degree day) is a day in which the outside temperature rises above the mark by one degree, or more, necessitating that energy has to be used for cooling the building to maintain inside temperature targets. If the target outside temperature was 45 degrees for a building that maintained itself at 55 degrees, then that day would account for 10 heating degree days for that building. Any time you can drive down the energy consumption to zero without risking any damage, you will save money and make a meaningful contribution toward energy conservation.

Using Time-Based Heating/Cooling Control

On days or in areas where the house is not at risk of frozen pipes and the pets left behind are not at risk of heatstroke, there might be no point in heating or cooling the house while you are at work. Having HAL monitor an outside temperature gauge using HAL's if/then logic to turn off the heating system whenever the outside air temperature is above 55 degrees might be one strategy. Another might be to turn on the heating system only when the outside temperature falls below 45 degrees. Then by using a time-based rule, the sensors would be ignored if it was two hours before you came home from work, and the house would be warmed or cooled to the programmed temperature for your comfort when you returned home.

The utility companies usually keep statistics on degree days in your area, for both heating and cooling, based on a common temperature of somewhere between 60 and 65 degrees. You can use these local area statistics for comparison and calculations for potential savings. In other areas of the country where overheating is the problem, the triggers can turn on air conditioners only when a high outside temperature is reached. The concept is the same as the heat event sensor, but it is just a reverse situation. The air conditioners can be enabled again two hours before your expected arrival back home by using time-based logic to override the energy conservation measure.

The project for this chapter discusses the sequence of actions needed to install an automated control to regulate the operation of a ceiling fan and install a thermostat to be controlled by HALultra. Within HAL's setup these can be made to operate in a complementary fashion.

For this project I elected to use INSTEON, but it could have been any of the other two-way protocols for which manufacturers offer a thermostat. Chapter 16, "Adding Future Self-Designed Home Automation Projects," lists popular protocols and many of the types of control devices available that use that protocol. You could begin your search for HVAC and environmental control devices with that list. Some of the major manufacturers of furnaces, air conditioners, and heat pumps might offer their branded thermostats compatible for use with home automation systems also. Often heat pump heating/cooling systems will need a specialized thermostat, so if your system is a heat pump, be sure to use a heat pump–compatible thermostat. If you are building a new home that you intend to automate, have the HVAC contractor install home automation HAL-compatible thermostats in the initial install. The thermostats can be manually operated before you do your automation projects and can still be manually controlled after you have automated your heating and cooling system.

Installing a HALultra-Compatible Thermostat

The first part of the project is to install a HAL-compatible thermostat. The leading challenge for many DIYers is that we are not necessarily HVAC specialists. Let's take a minute to decode some of the common wiring terms associated with a thermostat and their more typical connections to your heating and cooling system. In older homes, if the control wiring has never been upgraded or changed, you might find that the thermostat that controls the furnace has two cloth-coated wires and that the thermostat is a bimetal strip or spring coil type of switch that toggles to on or off because metal expands when hot and contracts when cold. In homes where only one thermostat controls both heating and cooling for the home or each HVAC zone, you will typically find a four-wire, five-wire, or seven-wire system. When you are hooking up a new thermostat, it is nice to know what each wire controls. For those who might find this a bit difficult, you can always have your HVAC contractor do the wiring part, leaving you with setting up the control of the device in HAL. For those who would do their own, here is a bit of information about the typical and properly installed thermostats.

Thermostat connection points aka terminal designations and wiring labels are not something most folks are familiar with. The next section presents the typical designations and labels. Your home's HVAC system might be wired and labeled quite differently. The term "HVAC" is used to describe a hybrid or combined heating and cooling unit in one shell, or a system in more than one shell that is working as one to either heat or cool your home. "Furnace" is the term used for heating only, and "air conditioner" is the term used for cooling only.

Common Connections for Standard HVAC Systems are often labeled as follows:

- **R or Common**—This lead goes to the power source (transformer in AC controlled systems).

- **C (return path)**—This lead is used when the thermostat requires a power source; commonly used with many modern digital thermostats.

- **W1 or W**—This terminal is intended for heating and turns on a relay or control circuit board on the furnace or heating unit.

- **W2**—This is for heat also but is the secondary controller to elevate a burner or system to a higher heat output. This might activate only if the temperature difference is over a preset range, for example, 5 degrees. If the furnace or heat pump needs to raise the temperature only a few degrees, the thermostat will just engage W1.

- **G**—Indoor blower fan.

- **Y1**—First stage cooling. Energizing this wire turns on the air conditioner's only compressor or only the first compressor in multicompressor cooling systems.

- **Y2**—Secondary stage cooling. Just as with heating, this is used when there is a larger temperature delta for the cooling system to overcome.

Additional Connections Encountered with Heat Pump System Thermostats and Controls are often labeled as follows:

At the most basic level, a heat pump home heating system is an air conditioner used in reverse. When cooling your home, it collects heat and moves it outside the home. When heating, it collects heat from outside and moves it inside. Controlling this mode change from heating to cooling requires a few extra control wires:

- **O & B terminals**—Used in heat pumps to change the reversing valve from heating to cooling mode. It moves a solenoid from one physical position to another so that the condenser and evaporator operate in reverse.

- **E**—Some heat pumps will use this control wire to turn on an emergency heating module such as electric coils if the heat pump unit is failing or the temperature outside is so low that the heat pump cannot operate efficiently to exchange heat.

- **X or Aux**—Some heat pumps are installed in places where it is known that the temperature will frequently fall too low for the heat pump to keep up. In those cases the Aux control will turn on the backup heat source, often electric resistance heating units, or a hot air furnace.

There are many more possibilities for wiring and connections, but the ones listed previously will apply to a majority of homes. Often heat pump controls will also be wired to an outdoor thermostat used to help the logic circuit better manage the system.

Regrettably, there is no code-enforceable color coding for wire colors in heating systems. HVAC installers will comply with a convention or past practices and will more or less follow the colors listed next. These are some frequently used wire colors for thermostat terminal connections:

R = Red wire

C = Black possible, white, blue, brown

W1 = White

W2 = Blue

G = Green

Y1 = Yellow

Y2 = Blue, pink, or alternative color

O = Orange (reversing valve)

Fortunately, most thermostats' connection points are labeled well with the letter codes shown previously. In all the ones I have encountered, there is rarely a variance in the letter codes at the terminal connections, but the wire colors are often all over the map. You can easily compensate for the lack of prior concern on standardized wire colors by carefully labeling each wire as it is removed from your existing thermostat.

When removing the wires on an existing thermostat in your abode, examine the area where the wires are connected at the thermostat for the terminal designations discussed previously. Then label each wire just before you remove it, using a labeling pad like the one shown in Figure 10.1 You could also make your own labels from stick-on address labels by wrapping them halfway around the wire and sticking the ends of the labels together.

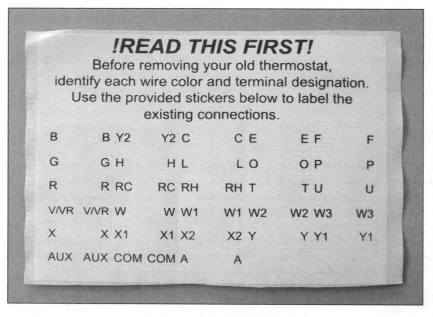

Figure 10.1   *Use labels to identify connections when disconnecting the wires on the old thermostat.*

If you are doing a new wire install on a five-wire system with new wires such as Southwire Thermostat Wire, use white, red, yellow, green, and blue wires in the cable. When installing a new digital thermostat that requires power, you can bring the common and return power up to the thermostat from the system's 24-volt AC transformer on a two-wire cable and then use the five-wire cable for connecting the control circuits.

If you are doing a new install on a system requiring more than five wires, a product such as Coleman Cable Thermostat Wire 18/8 can also be used, in which the eight wire colors encased in the jacket are black, green, brown, red, blue, white, orange, and yellow. Both products are 18-gauge low-voltage, low-current wires, so they can be used only on low-power control circuits.

For this chapter's example I found a seven-wire cable by Cerro at the local big-box store. This cable contains a red, green, blue, yellow, light brown or beige, orange, and white with a nice heavy brown PVC jacket.

In this project the replacement thermostat is a SmartLabs Model 2441 TH INSTEON Thermostat on a seven-wire system. This model is a digital thermostat and has some built-in automation features controlled from the thermostat's wall display unit, as shown in Figure 10.2. Because it is digital, it requires power from the HVAC's 24 Volt AC transformer, needing one wire each for common and return path to the power supply transformer in the HVAC unit. This model features notable ease of installation with back mounting and a swing-away control circuit board.

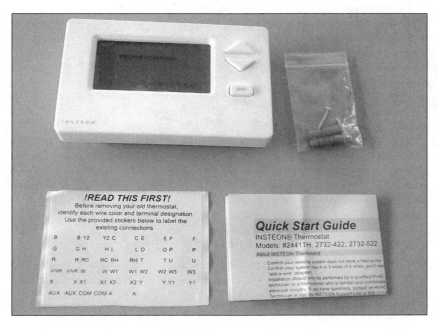

Figure 10.2 *Select a controllable thermostat that matches your HVAC system.*

To install a thermostat like this, all that is necessary is to remove the old thermostat and transfer the correct wires over to the new thermostat. When selecting a thermostat, you must know what voltage is used for the controls on your HVAC system and purchase a thermostat that is the same. Often the control voltages will be 24 Volt AC, but not always.

With the back plate mounted on the wall where the wires exit in the place of the old stat, swing the control board and cover to the side so that it will be easy to make the wire connections on the connector strip shown in Figure 10.3. If you want to move the thermostat to a new location, you can either run new control cable or carefully splice a new wire to old ones, keeping track of the connection labels. To the right of the screws is a small spring-actuated socket for receiving each connector pin.

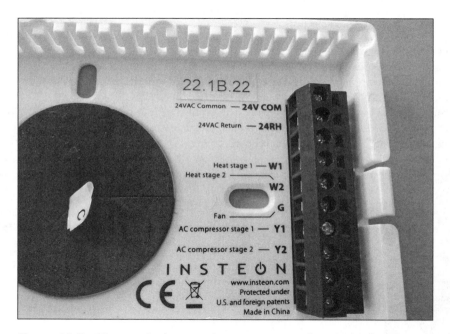

Figure 10.3 *The terminal connections are easy to identify on this thermostat's screw-down connector strip.*

The contact pins on the circuit board will contact the connector strip sockets on the right side of the connector strip when the unit is mounted and closed.

Because this thermostat is an INSTEON-compatible product, there is no need to wire any control wires to this thermostat. The INSTEON control module will communicate to the thermostat using RF (radio frequency) commands.

For older homes with just a two-wire thermostat, controlling your furnace with an advanced digital thermostat is still relatively easy to do. Even those who live on the road in motor homes, fifth wheels, and travel trailers can use digital HAL-compatible thermostats. The digital thermostats will usually run on 24 volts AC. A legacy heating system can be run on 12 volts AC control wires, and some systems (the RV ones) will use 12 volts DC to operate the furnace's start and run controller. The solution is to use a transformer to supply the digital thermostat with the required AC voltage. When the thermostat calls for heat, it will supply a voltage of 24VAC to the connection W1 (just W on some thermostats) with the common AC connection as the return path.

This control voltage from W1 would then need to be wired to the control coil on a 24 Volt AC continuous-duty on/off relay and back to the transformer common to complete the control circuit. In this case the relay (or relays) is called a NO (normally off). The relay and its switch contacts will support the current type (AC or DC) voltage and the current rating needs of the control board or relay native to the furnace. You can find the voltage and type with a volt-ohm meter, but the current would have to be found on the furnace manual or data plate. The return path for the relay activation coil is to the 24-volt common on the transformer, and the two on/off relay contacts then replace the old bimetal thermostat's contacts. This is not a particularly handsome solution but it works fine. As with all DIY projects, use the correct wire and sizes, mount the relay in an enclosure, and so on.

Note   **Checking voltages**   Whenever checking for unknown voltages with a volt-ohm meter, start with the meter's highest AC settings and work your way down. If by the time your meter range settings are in double digits, say 0–25 volts, there is still no indication of voltage, then switch to DC scales. If you start with a DC scale and the voltage type is AC, high voltage, it can fry your meter's DC circuitry. Always use caution, and use electrician's rubber gloves for safety when testing live wires, and do not ever touch the wires. The test meter probes are the only thing that should ever touch exposed wires.

A 240-volt resistance heating load could also be handled the same way, but the relay contacts must support the voltage and current required. One versatile relay that will handle 20-amp resistive loads in a nice tidy package is model number RIB2401B from Functional Devices. The datasheet for it can be found at http://www.functionaldevices.com/pdf/datasheets/RIB2401B.pdf.

This style of relay is a great product because the relay coil will operate at 120VAC/24VAC, and even on DC current.

If you are in a situation where you need multiple relays, be sure the control transformer powering the digital thermostat and the relays' contacts are of a high enough current rating to handle the loads. Never exceed the control circuit load rating of the thermostat's contacts. Instead of connecting a group of 24-volt relays to the thermostat, use down-line relays instead. For example, if you needed to control an 80-amp resistive heating circuit, the relay connected to the thermostat would be used to power up two or more 120-volt relays whose contacts would control the heating load.

In cases in which your legacy HVAC system is already powered by 24VAC, all you need to do to use the digital thermostats is to pull in three-conductor wire to replace the two-conductor bell wire to the thermostat. Because cable is less than a dollar a foot, pull in a seven- or eight-conductor cable in case you ever replace the HVAC system with a more modern one. Figure 10.4 shows the control wires correctly connected to the INSTEON thermostat with wire labels from the old thermostat.

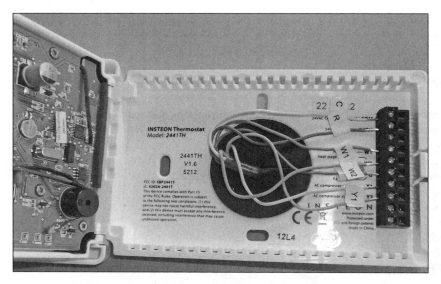

Figure 10.4 *Match the old thermostat's labeled wires to the new thermostat's labeled terminal connections.*

Note INSTEON thermostat: $150.

INSTEON PowerLinc INSTEON serial interface: $80.

INSTEON fan module: $60.

Total prototype cost so far: $2326.

Installing an In-line Fan/Light Control

After having completed the earlier projects or at least reading the previous chapters, you should find the installation of an INSTEON in-line fan controller to be fairly simple. Figure 10.5 shows an INSTEON in-line controller out of the box. It has four wires: one white for the neutral, one black for the hot, a red for the fan, and a blue for the lights. If the fan does not have lights, simply cap off the blue with a wire nut and a wrap of tape.

Figure 10.5   *INSTEON in-line fan and light controller.*

At the installation location the only potential problem would be if the ceiling box and the space in the fan cowling is not large enough to house the in-line controller and wire connections. If the ceiling fan is mounted to a very shallow box, you might have difficulty. Also, one of the install tips on the information supplied by the manufacturer is to cover the lights on the controller with black tape after the install. Here is a tip from the author: Join the in-line control module to the "network," as in, test it out by temporarily connecting the module to power and to two light bulbs before you actually permanently install the module in the ceiling box and fan cowling. One light bulb tests the lamp control and the other the fan control. It is a lot easier to see the status lights on the device as you do the setups, and this ensures that the module is working before you climb the ladder or scaffold.

Figure 10.6 shows a ceiling box and the controller wired to power. The remaining wires are connected to the fan and light with wire nuts, one wire each for connecting the neutral (white), fan (red), lamp (blue), and bonding (bare).

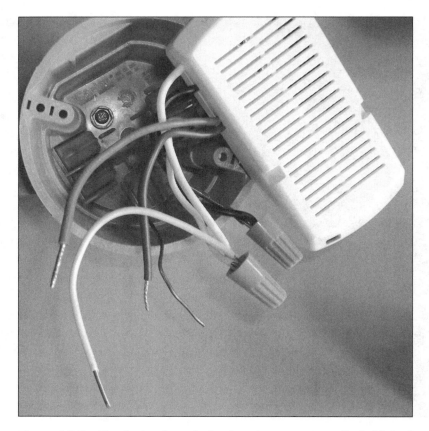

Figure 10.6   *Use the hook on the fan housing to temporarily hold the fan to the ceiling box while you connect the wires.*

Setting up the Interface in HALultra

To control INSTEON devices from HALultra, you need to set up a control interface with the HAL setup wizard. The interface chosen for the prototype is shown in Figure 10.7. It connects to the computer with a USB cable.

Plug the INSTEON control interface into a nearby power outlet as far away from the computer as the USB cord will still reach, and then connect the USB cable to the interface's USB port. The signal strength supplied from the controller will be less affected if it is not going through surge suppressors or battery backups to reach installed devices on the home's wiring. Then plug the other end of the USB cord into your computer with the computer turned on and booted up.

The Windows installer flag will show on the desktop. As with any USB device, the Windows OS must load a suitable driver to work with the control interface. Make note of the COM port that the driver finds during the install process.

Figure 10.7   *The INSTEON USB control should not be plugged into the computer's battery backup.*

After the USB drivers for the control interface have loaded, shut down the HALultra server and run the HAL Setup Wizard. After the wizard launches, click the Custom Setup button.

Begin to page through the setup windows using the Next button each time, making the new selections and checking on the existing setup selections as you have done in previous chapters. When you reach the HAL Home Control Services window, as shown in Figure 10.8, check the X10/INSTEON button and click Next.

In the window shown in Figure 10.9, select the exact make and model of your INSTEON interface device, referred to as a modem by the INSTEON conventions. In the prototype computer, this interface uses COM4, so that has to be set correctly in this window before you proceed. The right answer for your install could be any COM port between 1 and 4 depending on which COM port the INSTEON USB driver found available during installation.

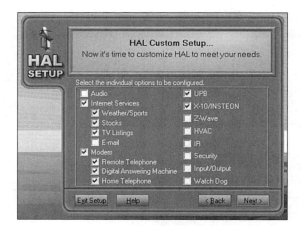

Figure 10.8 *Select INSTEON in this window, and then move to the next window.*

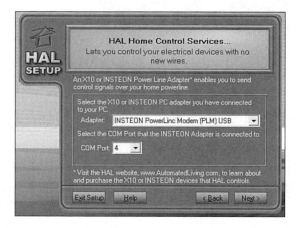

Figure 10.9 *Select the device and COM port number in this window.*

Make your way through the rest of the wizard and launch the HALultra server. With the server running, open the Automation Setup Screen, and then click the Devices tab. Click Add to select a new device, as shown in Figure 10.10, and then click Next.

In the Organizer window, shown in Figure 10.11, select the location and device information for your new interface device. Proceed using the Next button.

Figure 10.10 *Click Add to set up a thermostat device in HAL.*

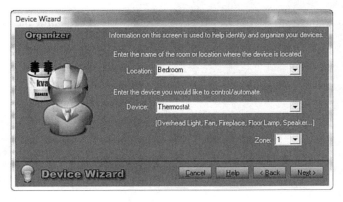

Figure 10.11 *This thermostat will control the HVAC zone for the master bedroom.*

In the Device Controller window, shown in Figure 10.12, enter the exact make and model number of the thermostat by using the drop-down menu and selecting the device from the listing of available devices. After you have made your selection, click Next.

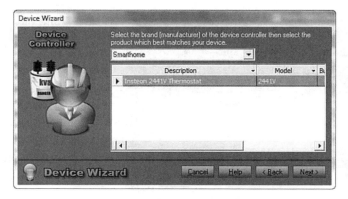

Figure 10.12　*Select your manufacturer and device model here.*

Set up the voice control and any desired logging and finish setting up the interface. When your set up is complete, the Bedroom thermostat will be visible in the Devices window, as shown in Figure 10.13.

HALultra - Automation Setup Screen

Devices | Modes | Scenes | Groups | Schedules | Macros | Rules | Directory | Shopping | Condition | Help

This screen allows you to manage the Devices configured in your home. It can also be used to control the Devices.

All　☑ Show Status Changes

Name	Status	Location	Device	Address		Cate
BEDROOM CEILING LIGHT	ON	Bedroom	Ceiling Light	39	💡	Lighti
CLOSET LAMP	ON	closet	lamp	201	💡	Lighti
BEDROOM THERMOSTAT		Bedroom	Thermostat	1		Therr
FRONTDOOR		front door	CAMERA		💡	Video
RMFIVE		room 5	CAMERA		💡	Video
RMFOUR		camera room 4	CAMERA		💡	Video
RMSEVEN		room 7	CAMERA		💡	Video
RMSIX		room 6	CAMERA		💡	Video
RMTHREE		room 3	CAMERA		💡	Video
DINING ROOM LIGHTS	OFF	Dining Room	LIGHTS	K09	💡	Lighti
LIVING ROOM LAMP	ON	Living Room	Lamp	K03	💡	Lighti
OPEN		open area	CAMERA		💡	Video

Report | Devices | + | - | Add | Modify | Remove | Done

Figure 10.13　*Controllable devices are listed here.*

The setup for the fan controller, in this case a FanLinc INSTEON Model 2475F, is nearly identical to the thermostat except for the device selection. Sometimes one has to hunt a little for the exact device. You probably expect a fan controller to be listed under "fan" controller, but because it will also control a light cluster attached to the fan, select Lighting for the control category in the Device Wizard, as shown in Figure 10.14.

Figure 10.14   *The fan controller is listed under the Lighting category.*

After selecting lighting, page forward using the Next buttons until you are shown the window in Figure 10.15. Here you will enter the manufacturer and model number of the controller. To finish the install, proceed through the wizard using the Next buttons until you can click Finish to exit the setup.

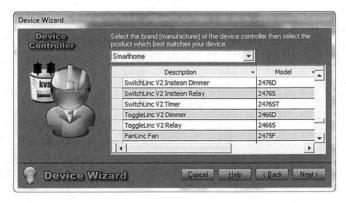

Figure 10.15   *Select the correct model number of the device in this window.*

With these devices installed and identified in HALultra, you can begin to explore and experiment with novel and innovative ways to use them to maintain occupant comfort and convenience. Try using rules and macros to control the devices, and plan out ways to use sensors to trigger the macros. Play around with HALultra to come up with a sequence of triggers and events that enable you to use the devices to best heat and cool your home.

Chapter 11

Project 8, Adding New Controllers and Interfaces: Z-Wave, INSTEON, and More

This chapter explores adding additional currently available and compatible interface devices and controllers to your HALultra computer platform. Some of the additional technologies and interfaces you might want to explore for additions to your home automation platform that are not covered in other chapters are briefly discussed in the next few sections.

Additional Interfaces for HALultra

The categories where there are interfaces and devices available in the marketplace that will work with HALultra are shown in the Hal Setup Wizard and are further defined and configured in the HALultra System Settings window shown often in previous chapters. This chapter is more informational than project-oriented and is intended to help you go beyond the basic and to migrate to more complex solutions that use multiple protocols and interfaces. Some of these interfaces are slightly more complex to set up but are still quite doable with a modest ration of patience and perseverance. The patterns established in prior chapters to add interfaces and devices with various protocols are quite similar when using these additional interfaces. Using all available HAL-compatible protocols will enable you to fully leverage this technology to nearly every home system. Fundamentally, in earlier chapters you have learned how to mix and bake the home automation cake; the only thing that is different for additional protocols is that you will be using slightly different ingredients.

ZigBee

As a DYI hobbyist, you might find that ZigBee has attracted your attention. ZigBee is a communications protocol for low-powered radio network communications. That differs from, say, UPB, which is a protocol for communicating among devices over a home's AC wiring. ZigBee might be a protocol to watch as its potential for devices serving the home automation space evolves. If you are interested in experimenting with ZigBee, one interesting ZigBee interface between the computer and the wireless RF is the ProBee, a

USB transmitter offered by Kanda.com. The link to the product info page is http://www.kanda.com/products/Sena/ZU10-01.html. One of the challenges facing the adoption of this communications standard for home automation is the limited product offerings useful to the DIY home automation hobbyist as compared to many of the other technologies. Currently there is no out-of-the-box interface between ZigBee and HAL. Until there are more home automation products available using ZigBee, I would not consider relying on ZigBee as a big part of my home automation solution.

Infrared

Figure 11.1 is a JDS infrared interface. This is a somewhat older interface type but still useful, and it has four IR expansion jacks on the back. This IR Xpander needs one COM port to control it and an infrared emitter targeted for each device. When you use a remote control for switching TV channels, you are likely using infrared. Infrared will control your home electronics, and having a HALultra-compatible interface will provide the path for controlling those electronics from HAL and by voice. For a new implementation of infrared controllers, also consider using Global Cache's model CG-100 priced under $200.00 on Amazon.com, See http://www.automatedliving.com for the up-to-date list of IR interfaces.

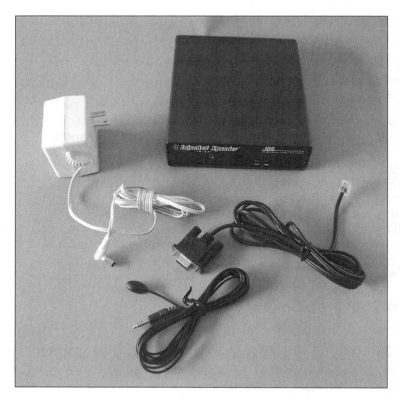

Figure 11.1 *Infrared interfaces facilitate controlling electronics by voice command.*

The corresponding setup for infrared devices in the HAL Setup window is shown in Figure 11.2. From there the device configuration is handled in the HALultra System Settings window. The target device control details are further identified in the HALultra Automation Setup Screen and are added with the Device Wizard. This same progression is true of nearly all interfaces and devices.

Figure 11.2   *HAL setup is where you identify the IR interface device.*

HVAC

When you add an HVAC device in the Setup Wizard by checking the box for it, you will be required to identify the device make and model in the window, as shown in Figure 11.3.

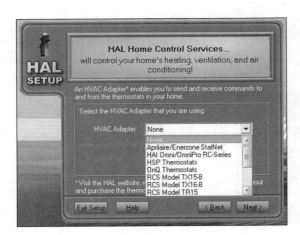

Figure 11.3   *The devices that are supported are listed in the drop-down menu.*

Security

Checking the box for Security in HALsetup will present the window shown in Figure 11.4, where the supported Security Adapters will be displayed for your selection. The drop-down shown is not the complete list of devices.

Figure 11.4　*HALultra can control and expand on security responses.*

Because HALultra can arm and disarm your security system, you will also need to make additional selections and enter the security system password in the window shown in Figure 11.5. The panel code is the one used by the security panel on your alarm system and coded into its "memory" when it was installed. The disarm code can be unique to HAL and enables you to have a completely different code than that used by your main security panel. This provides another layer of protection.

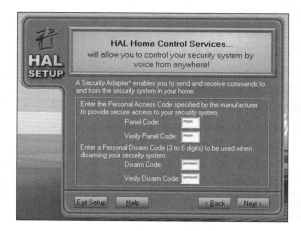

Figure 11.5　*Notice that the security codes do not display in the window.*

Input/Output

Simple devices like the garage door motors can be controlled with HALultra, and sprinkler systems and devices are available to help you make the connection between them and HAL, as shown in the Setup window in Figure 11.6. This window is presented during the setup routine only when you have checked the box for I/0 option in the earlier setup window.

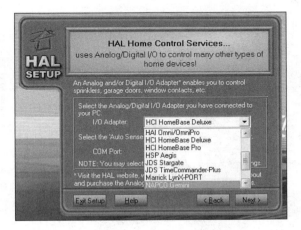

Figure 11.6   *Select I/O devices in this window.*

INSTEON

In the preceding chapter, INSTEON was used for controlling a lamp/fan module and a programmable thermostat. There is a plethora of INSTEON products that can be added to your system and controlled by HALultra. Because both Z-Wave and INSTEON are using RF (radio) signals, it is a good fit for automated electronic locks and thermostats that are *not* directly powered by a household AC voltage line. In situations where you are looking for a ready-to-go sensor, monitor, or alarm switch, start your search by looking at the INSTEON product offerings first. Refer to Chapter 10, "Project 7, Getting Green and Managing Your Home's Climate," for details on linking in your INSTEON products.

Z-Wave

The rest of the chapter examines some of the extra effort needed to set up a Z-Wave system, which is one of the more complex technologies to set up and use in HALultra. Installing Z-Wave is the detailed project for this chapter. Z-Wave products are plentiful overall, and Z-Wave, at least as far as available products go, would be considered a leader in the number of sensors, monitors, and alarm trigger devices. For a versatile interface to a broad range of product types, check out Z-Wave and opportunities for using Z-Wave in your home automation plan. I was able to purchase the Z-Wave "starter kit" shown in

Figure 11.7 on sale for only $100, which included a remote control, three lamp modules, and a thermostat; however, this low cost can be attributed to the fact that much of the starter kit's products have since been discontinued. Your individual pricing mileage will vary.

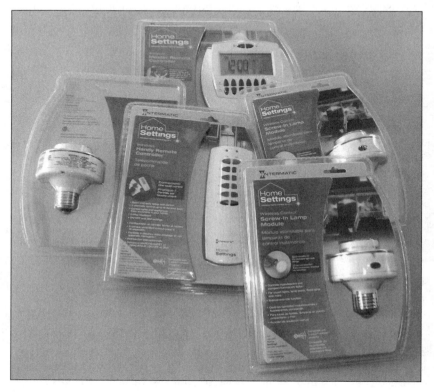

Figure 11.7 *Z-Wave starter kit included all these products.*

To control Z-Wave devices, you will need to set up a Z-Wave network. Z-Wave requires a master controller for the setup and a secondary controller for the operation of the devices. One great tool for setting up the network and including nodes is a Leviton USB Z-Wave interface/controller, as shown in Figure 11.8. This device is a radio transceiver that transmits commands to Z-Wave–enabled devices within its own identified network and receives status information from the device. The model shown here is a Leviton VRUSB-1US model marketed by Leviton as a Vizia RF + Installer Tool. To use the device, it is necessary to go to the Leviton web page (http://www.leviton.com/OA_HTML/ SectionDisplay.jsp?section=38971); to learn more about the product line and download the installer software that integrates with the controller, go to (http://emarketing.leviton. com/eMApublic/rf_installer/v1.1.1.0/Vizia%20RF+%20Installer%20Tool%20Setup.exe).

Figure 11.8   *A Leviton USB Z-Wave controller.*

In addition to having a primary controller and installer software to set up the network, it is necessary to have a secondary controller that is HAL compatible. For the prototype a Leviton VRC0P-1LW Vizia RF + Plug-In Serial Interface Module RS232 ASCII Interface, as shown in Figure 11.9, is used.

Here is the impact on the prototype budget for the project in this chapter:

Note   Z-Wave starter Kit: $100.

Leviton Z-Wave USB interface: 1 each $80.

Leviton VRCOP-1LW Z-Wave Plug in Serial Interface Module: $109.

Total prototype cost so far: $2615.

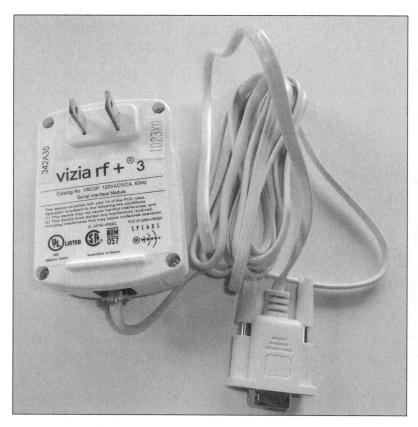

Figure 11.9   *This device connects to an available COM port and plugs into one of the home's AC outlets near the computer.*

Setting up a Z-Wave Network

Z-Wave is a great technology for home automation, but it requires a bit more effort to set up the Z-Wave network and "transfer" the control of the nodes to HALultra. Z-Wave uses what is called a primary controller. The primary controller is the only interface device allowed to add or delete control devices into the Z-Wave network. With the other technologies covered one can, for the most part, set up the interface controller in a version of HAL and proceed to add devices or delete them as needed. With Z-Wave the HAL computer that is connected via the serial port to the VRCOP-1LW Z-Wave Serial Interface has to be "admitted" to the network as a secondary controller. After it has the status as a secondary controller, it can then be set up to manage the Z-Wave devices.

Using a Laptop with the Leviton RF Installer Tool

If you plug the Z-Wave USB stick into a computer, it might not automatically load the drivers. The first challenge is that not every plug-and-play driver native to Windows might be valid for every Z-Wave device you might try to load, as shown in Figure 11.10. Do not be alarmed if this happens. It simply means that you will have to find the drivers from the device manufacturer by installing from the disc supplied with your Z-Wave primary controller or from the manufacturer's website.

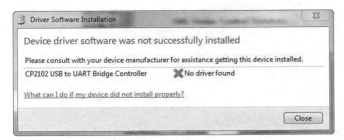

Figure 11.10   *Occasionally a plug-and-play device will not automatically be successfully loaded by the Windows OS.*

For initially setting up the prototype Z-Wave network, I used the Leviton Z-Wave USB stick shown previously plugged into the USB port on a laptop computer. To register the Vizia RF Installer tool with the operating system, it was necessary to download the Vizia RF + Installer Tool drivers and software from the Leviton website at http://www.leviton. com/OA_HTML/SectionDisplay.jsp?section=38971. Near the lower part of the web page is a link identified as "RF Installer Tool Updates"; clicking on this link will take you to the download process. Because of the relationships between the primary controller and the secondary controller, I chose to load the Vizia installer tool on a laptop or another computer and not the computer that will be used as the HAL home automation platform. If you don't have a laptop, AEON Labs offers a battery-powered USB stick (http://www. smarthome.com/75501/Aeon-Labs-DSA02203-ZWUS-Z-Stick-Series-2/p.aspx) that can be operated without a computer and placed near the automation PC. To operate the AEON Labs stick to include a nearby powered up control device, all you do is click on the button on the stick itself while the device, such as a lamp module, that is in include mode.

Using the Vizia USB stick and RF Installer tool and with the control devices nearby, click on the Include Devices button in the Vizia tool and at the same time plug in or power up the device. In the case of the Intermatic Model HAO5 Screw-in lamp module, press the program button, shown in Figure 11.11, a few times to register the device as a node on the network. The installer tool will recognize the device if it is close enough to the computer with the USB stick, and it will be reported in a pop-up window with its model number and the assigned node number. The window includes a field that enables you to identify the device with a name such as "Library Lamp." After the device is named, click OK in the installer tool window to save the device to the network. Repeat this same process for all the Z-Wave devices to be included in your network.

Figure 11.11   *Press the button on the lamp module twice to place it in program mode.*

The last device that needs to be included in the Z-Wave network is the one that HAL will use to control the devices. It must be a member node on the network in order to control its neighbor nodes. Connect the Leviton serial interface device to your PC via a COM port, press the button on the front of the module while it is plugged into a live outlet, and hold the button until the light turns from flashing green to amber. At that point click on the Include Device button on the RF+ Installer tool. When the controller is successfully linked into the network as a node, there will be a pop-up window displayed in the installer tool window that will state "Node #x, Vizia RF RS232 Interface (RZCOP/VRCOP), successfully included." There is also a field entry where the default assigned name of the device can be changed.

After you have set up all the Z-Wave devices that are to be included in your Z-Wave network, save the network to the laptop or other computer's hard drive. The file is saved the same way as in most Windows applications, using File and then Save Network File from the upper-left corner of the application window. It will be assigned a randomized number and a .vrf file extension in Windows. It is important to keep this file and a backup of it saved to a disc or jump drive in case you ever have to recover the network or make modifications by adding new devices. After you have saved the file and before closing out the application, click on All Devices on the left side and then highlight the installer tool. In the middle of the panel, click on the Get Network Information button. The node numbers and location names you have assigned will be shown. The node number and name information will be needed for the HAL setup screens later. Copy this information into a notebook to facilitate that process. Do this for each device. Each device can be highlighted in the setup window and tested using the onscreen on-off buttons.

Later in the setups you will see that the HAL controller has to listen to the primary controller to inherit control of the network nodes as a secondary controller so that control of that network can be transferred to HAL. If you are using the Leviton product line, also install the Leviton RF Installer tool on the HAL automation PC to ensure that there are Windows interface drivers loaded for the Vizia product line.

After the Z-Wave network is set up and tested sufficiently, the next step is to configure the Leviton VRC0P-1LW Vizia RF + Plug-In Serial Interface Module RS232 ASCII Interface to work with HAL. On the HAL setup side in the custom setup selection in the Hal Setup Wizard check the box for Z-Wave, as shown in Figure 11.12.

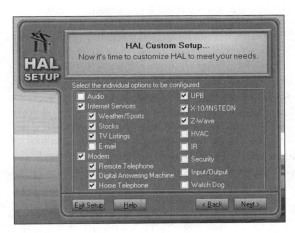

Figure 11.12   *Check the box for Z-Wave in the Custom Setup window.*

Follow through to the Finish button and launch the HAL server.

Use the listening ear to expose the HAL menu and select Open System Settings. Scroll down to the bottom of the settings listings to select Z-Wave at the bottom, and click on the Setting button to see the window shown in Figure 11.13. The Leviton Vizia software has to be loaded on the PC before Leviton Vizia RF+ will display as an available interface device. Also watch for potential conflicts with other devices sharing the same COM port number; each controller has to have its own unique COM port number. Select the COM port number you have the interface connected to if the "Auto-detect" fails to find the device.

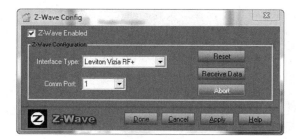

Figure 11.13   *Select your device for Interface Type and Comm Port.*

After selecting your device, in this case the Leviton interface, click on the Apply button and wait a moment or two. After this process is completed, close the remaining windows, and then shut down and restart the HAL server. As the HAL server splash screen presents onscreen, watch for the message line at the top that informs "Initializing Z-Wave Interface" without any errors.

Now it gets a bit tricky with the Z-Wave setup. Go to the device you used for your primary Z-Wave controller (other computer) and begin the process to set the controller software into the mode for enabling the transfer of network control to a secondary controller.

With the Leviton VRC0P-1LW Vizia RF + Plug-In Serial Interface Module RS232 ASCII Interface connected to the HAL computer and registered in HAL, the next step is to open the .vrf file that created the Z-Wave network on the laptop and bring the laptop with the USB stick plugged in near the HAL computer.

Note   **A Note on Controllers**   Regardless of the interface controller brand you use, there will be a "send" mode to populate the information over to the secondary controller. Even though Leviton is used and recommended in this book, other primary and secondary controllers from other manufacturers will require similar steps.

With the laptop nearby and the VRF file loaded in the Installer tool, the next step is to press and hold the button on the back of the Leviton VRC0P-1LW serial interface, while it is plugged into a wall outlet and connected to the HAL computer until the light on the back near the button changes from blinking green to amber. The amber means it is "listening" and ready to be programmed to take over control of the network. In the Vizia RF + Installer tool application, select VR Remote to expose the drop-down and select Transfer Primary Role. Then wait a few minutes until the Installer tool window reports that the transfer of control was successful. At that point the VRCOP-1LW is able to take over direct control of the devices once they are manually entered into the HAL device setup windows.

The next step is to add the devices into HALultra.

After your server is started, enter into the Automation Setup Screen window to include your new Z-Wave devices (in our case, Library Lights), as shown in Figure 11.14. The node number from the previous setup notes becomes the Address in the setup screen.

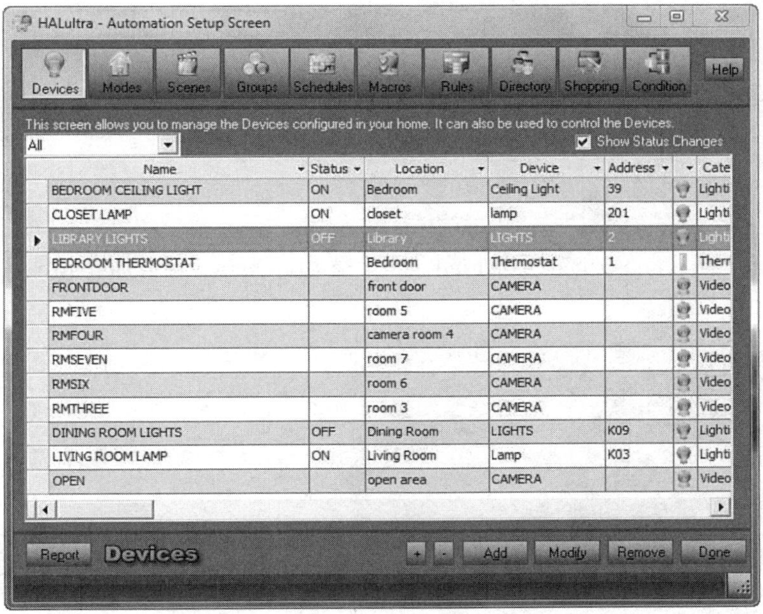

Figure 11.14   *The first Z-Wave lamp module node is shown here.*

The process to add another device is the same as with other protocol devices. From the HALultra Automation Setup Screen window, click Add. With the Devices tab highlighted, select Lighting or the appropriate device type in the Device Wizard, then click Next to fill in the location and device fields by entering information directly or using the dropdowns. In the example Office was entered and Lights was selected before the Next button was clicked. Clicking through to the Select Manufacturer field from the drop-down Intermatic was performed, revealing a drop-down allowing selection of the HomeSettings Outdoor Screw-In Lamp Recep and the model HAO5. The next setting requires the Communications Relay setting for Output, which is the node number for the lamp. In this case node "3" is entered from our notes, as shown in Figure 11.15.

The next window, as shown in Figure 11.16, is where you can set the dimming feature if the device supports that and test the communication with the device by changing the on-off state. After testing, click the Next button.

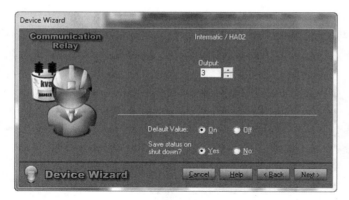

Figure 11.15   *The node number from the original network setup using the Installer tool is entered as the Output value.*

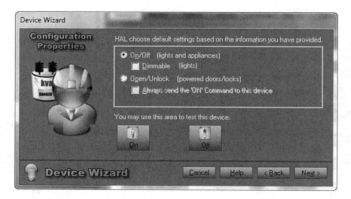

Figure 11.16   *The Configuration Properties could include selecting a dimmable device.*

Make your choices for Voice access and finish setting up the device.

In Figure 11.17 the Automation Setup Screen now reveals the Office Lights and Library Lights, both of which are now controlled by HALultra from this window or with voice commands.

The process for setting up Z-Wave devices is more complicated than other devices, but not so complicated that you should avoid them. HAL can control Z-Wave devices in the same manner as other devices. On balance, it is a little more work and many more things can go wrong when you're first learning the use of Z-Wave; however, it is an excellent control protocol and the products available using it are solid products.

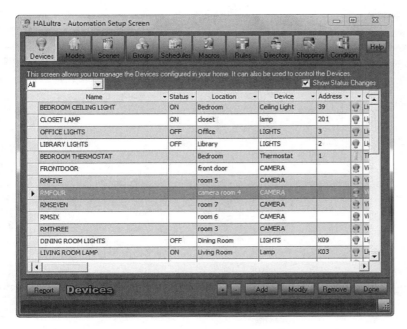

Figure 11.17   *The devices are entered and ready to use.*

Project 9, Automating the Home Entertainment Center's Music Management

We are not quite to the point yet where one electronic device will take care of all of our computing, communication, reading, education, gaming, and entertainment needs. The challenge, at least for now, is to make the best of the home electronics you already have by maximizing the value they present while minimizing the support time required to use and enjoy them. In this context this chapter explores what it takes to set up and use HALultra with the HALdmc (Digital Music Center) add-on. With this add-on, filling your home with the sounds of a custom playlist of your music is but one spoken command away, a benefit that becomes apparent the moment you use it.

The Changing Landscape of Home Electronics

It is fair to say that having a houseful of electronic devices might not be an exaggeration for many homes. The advances in technology have changed the way we live, work, and play. Adopting home automation technology presents the potential to change how we play just as it changes the way we perform household tasks. Using HALultra and DMC can simplify managing and playing your music by, for example, placing your playlists under voice command. Using static text-based playlists with conventional software locks you into using them as is or taking the time to edit them. HALultra with HALdmc allows you to create playlists on the fly, use verbal instructions, control volume with your voice, and skip songs. HALultra can't eliminate every problem or bit of tedium involved with the typical collection of home electronics; however, HAL's Digital Music Center (HALdmc) sure can make enjoying your favorite music at home far easier and might even inspire you to "retire" some playback devices.

HALdmc integrates into HALbasic, HALdeluxe, or HALultra. Using HALdmc with HALultra allows using if then logic within HAL. So for example a house mode could be associated with a particular music style. You must have one of these products on your PC in order to load and use the digital music center. The current price is $49 and is available only as a software download. Follow the instructions on the HAL software website and refer to Chapter 9, "Project 6, Installing a Home Automation Voice Portal Modem in

Your Computer," for additional instructions for installing downloaded software. The product key for the DMC is emailed to you shortly after your purchase from automatedliving.com, typically within two business days.

Note Digital Music Center software prototype budget: $49.
Total prototype cost so far: $2,182.

Select Sound Reproduction Equipment

After HALultra/dmc is installed, all you need is a good set of speakers. The sound card in the prototype computer and in most computers has at least three jack ports for sound input and output. One of these jack ports is for stereo microphone in, another is for stereo sound out to a headset or an amplified speaker system, and the third is for digital sound out to a sound processor. Although most PCs support and ship with a basic speaker system composed of a left speaker, a right speaker, and a subwoofer (a 2.1 system), high-end sound cards can support surround-sound systems with up to seven speakers and a subwoofer. Logitech, Altec Lansing, and Creative Labs all have offerings in the $50 to $250 range for computer speaker systems. If your card has a digital coaxial sound output, consider connecting this to an input on your existing AV equipment 51. or 7.1 sound processor to leverage your current electronics.

With a well-designed system incorporating other HALultra-managed controls, your music can be routed to any one room, a select few rooms, or every active living space in the house. There is not much imagination required anymore for this type of project, only some more money, time, and parts. After you have become comfortable incorporating music into your home automation platform, you can add such a task to your future projects list. For the purposes of an introductory-level project suitable for the home automation novice, an inexpensive 2.1 computer speaker system will do the trick for a cost of about $64.

Note Sound reproduction components prototype budget: $64.
Total prototype cost so far: $2,246.

Digital Sound Reproduction Quality

For the novices there are a few things you should know about digital music files before you begin. First of all, there is no way for reproduced sound to be exactly like the natural sound of human voices or musical instruments. The early popular forms of sound capture and reproduction were analog on vinyl records or magnetic tapes, each of which also had its own limitations for sound quality. Digital sound reproduction is very good and reliable, and for the most part we as consumers have come to accept the inherent quality of digitally reproduced sound on CD as plenty good enough for us to purchase and enjoy.

Digital Music File Formats

Digitally reproduced sound on CD is carried off by a number of file formats. There are a few popular music file formats that users of the HALultra and Digital Music Center should be most aware of. Because the HALdmc application only plays MP3 and WMA file types it is important to know either how to use the built in feature of HALdmc to convert music and sound CD files to one of these two file types or how to use third party software to convert to either of these two file types. Your music will likely break down into two categories; those files already stored on your home automation computer or on drives that are made accessible to it, and files that are still on CD or other media or will be downloaded over the Internet. The first goal for maximizing your music enjoyment from using HALdmc is to have all the sound and music files loaded on the home automation computer or a drive or drives accessible to it and to have those files in MP3 or WMA format. The second goal is to have them loaded into HALdmc so you can play them as needed.

Commercial Audio CDs

If you "open" a music CD in Windows, you will see a file format extension _.CDA (compact disc audio). The whole filename will be Track01.cda, for example, and will be only about 1KB in size. Copying these CDA track files to your computer will not yield music files for playback. The reason is that CDA files are not the actual music files but are references for where the OS will find the actual digital music files on the CD. The popular standard for compact disc digital audio is two channels, 16-bit values, sampled at a rate of 44100Hz, creating a quality limit of reproducing sounds up to a 22kHz-frequency sound wave, a range well within the parameter range for normal human hearing of 40Hz to 20kHz.

Music and Sound Copy to Hard Drive Utilities

Loading the files onto your computer hard drive will require using a utility application designed for managing, transferring, and converting music files. The good news is that the HALdmc application has one built in.

When you use a common product to copy a commercial music CD sound track to your Windows computer, such as the Roxio Media Import that shipped preinstalled on the prototype PC, it converts and transfers the music to the computer hard drive to a default _.wav (waveform audio file format) file. In that format a song that plays for 2 minutes and 59 seconds will take up 30.1MB of disk space. The _.wav file is not one of the formats that is directly used by the HALultra and HALdmc. If you want to play .wav files in HALdmc convert them to a HALdmc supported format; either MP3 or WMA.

That same song from the CD will take up only 2.07MB when stripped and copied using the HALdmc copy-to-disk utility that routes sound data to a _.wma (Windows Media audio) compressed file format and stores it in a designated place on your computer hard drive or attached network drive. This format also supports two channels at sampling rates of up to 48kHz for a maximum reproduction quality of a 24kHz-frequency sound. This compressed format allows you to load a larger selection of music without running out of disk space as quickly.

HALdmc will also play MP3 music and audio files, which also have the capability to reproduce sounds to 24kHz frequencies. A lot of portable music players across manufacturers and brands support playing MP3 files. By using the MP3 format it is easy to transfer a few playlists from the HALdmc computer to your "on-the road" mp3 player.

Check to see what file format your songs and audio files are in before you begin scanning any existing music into the HALultra music folder on your home automation computer or HAL home network. There is an alphabet soup of other file types for digital audio standards, most of which can be converted to one of the two file types supported directly by HALdmc. If your home automation computer already has music files loaded to the hard drive in _.wma format or _.mp3 format, the initial HALdmc scan will pick up the content and load it into the file folder you designate as your HALultra music destination folder. Sound and music files stored on your computer in other formats will not be included in the scan. If you are scanning from CD disc in the computer's optical drive, the HAL import utility will convert the files from the commercial CD's format into _.wma format for you.

Note   Load Only Legal Music on Your PC   For a clear legal reading of the current U.S. Copyright Law as it pertains to digital music and sound recordings, visit this website: http://www.copyright.gov/title17/

There are plenty of legitimate sources to instantly download your music purchases from over the Internet right to your computer hard drive. Two sources provided by the RIAA can be found here:

http://www.riaa.com/toolsforparents.php?content_selector=legal-music-services

http://www.musicunited.org/6_legalsites.aspx

Be aware of the downloaded music file format so that you will be able to work the file into a supported format for your HAL-supported music libraries and folders.

The most common method for loading music into the computer is still to copy from a CD and transfer the music files to the My Music folder under the folder for the currently logged-in user.

Before you begin, first find out what happens when you insert a music CD into your computer.

There is a Windows setting that can be altered under the heading "AutoPlay" that determines what happens automatically when you insert a music CD into your PC. To change that setting to get the best results for transferring your music files to your computer for HALdmc, check to see what your auto-play setting is defaulting to. Begin by putting a music CD into your computer's optical drive. Click on the Computer icon on the desktop. Then right-click on the optical drive (usually D: or E:). Choose Open AutoPlay, which opens the window and menu shown in Figure 12.1, where the instruction is highlighted for PlayAudio CD Using Windows Music Player.

Figure 12.1   *Many computers are set up to play the CD when it is inserted in the drive.*

The best option for using HALdmc is to set that variable load action to Ask Me Every Time. That way, if the HALultra server is running with HALdmc and you insert a newly acquired CD into the optical drive, HALdmc can be set up to be ready to copy all the tracks or the selected tracks into a folder in your HAL music library. In the window shown in Figure 12.1, on the bottom you can see the link View More Auto-Play Options in Control Panel. Clicking on this link brings up the window shown in Figure 12.2, where each media type can be matched to a default by content or disc type automatically when a new disc is put in the optical drive. Figure 12.2 also shows some of the drop-down menu options for setting this Windows variable for each new media disc type. The drop-down menus can be altered later if needed for each media type. For now, set your system to the Ask setting. Scroll down to see all the media types.

After you have altered the setting to the desired default actions, click the Save button at the bottom of the window.

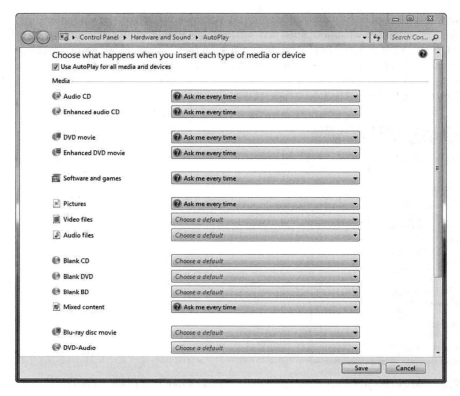

Figure 12.2   *Set default actions for media types here.*

Download and Install HALdmc

HALdmc and HALdvc can be optioned into each of the three HAL software versions, basic, deluxe, or ultra. After customers have paid for the product, they are sent an email instructing them how to use the HAL License Manager to refresh their licensed copy of HAL to enable the newly acquired HALdmc or HALdvc add-on products.

Setting Up HALdmc

Open the HAL Digital Music Center from the "ear" icon menu.

The first window to appear is the setup's welcome window, shown in Figure 12.3. Take the time to read the presented information before clicking Next near the bottom of the window.

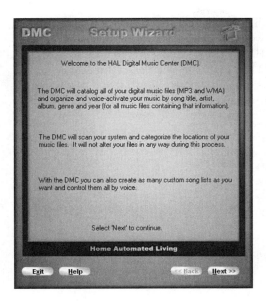

Figure 12.3   *Setup's first screen presents information about the operational potential of the DMC.*

At this stage of the setup, you are presented with a choice to have the HALdmc scan the entire inventory of the hard drive or drives or just selected folders, as shown in Figure 12.4.

Figure 12.4   *Scanning all drives will find every _.wma and _.mp3 file on the computer for addition to HAL's play library.*

On the prototype computer I used Scan All Drives to help identify any and all sound files for possible use. I did this knowing that I would be able to control all sound and music files loaded from this point on within the HALdmc application; however, choosing to find all sound files will also find any sound files associated with other installed programs. Figure 12.5 shows the window that appears during the scan process. If you have a large volume of sound files loaded, or many drives to process, this scan could take some time.

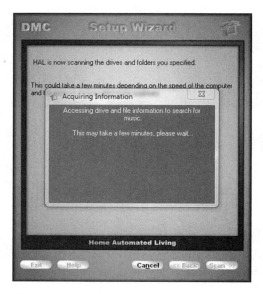

Figure 12.5 *The scanning starts when this window appears.*

After the scan process completes, click Next and you will see the setup wizard's summary window. Figure 12.6 shows the classification report of which music, songs, and sound files were found and categorized as a part of the scanning process. The application will count the number of songs, artists, albums, and genres found. Click on the Next button to proceed.

Figure 12.7 appears next, asking you to choose a location for storing music recorded from your CDs.

At this point I'd recommend sticking with Windows' default location for music (C:\ Users*User Name*\Music). Using the Windows default locations for files simplifies back-ups, helps minimize organization, helps with finding files, and keeps things simple when you or other programs are seeking files or documents.

Click Next after you have entered your music location. This step brings up the final infor-mational window, shown in Figure 12.8. The most important suggestion from this screen regards learning the voice-command "DMC syntax." A major reason for using this soft-ware is the value of using voice commands to control playing your music. Take a minute to read the information in this window, click Finish to close the wizard, and heed the advice.

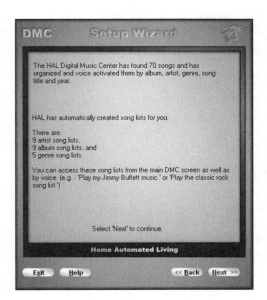

Figure 12.6   *Take a note from this window as to the drive's quantity of sound files and numbers in each category found.*

Figure 12.7   *Despite the default setting in this window, using Program Files locations for any type of end-user data is not recommended.*

Figure 12.8   *Read the advisory screen and click Finish to exit the wizard.*

As with all of our other projects, at this point it's a good idea to shut off the HAL server and reboot your machine.

Using HALdmc

You can begin using HALdmc from the ear icon right-click menu. When you first start the DMC after a scan of your drives, the resulting Master Song List that appears in DMC might look something like what is shown in Figure 12.9. In this case, the "Language Tracks" entries refer to random sound files found on the prototype system's hard drive as a result of scanning all drives for music, rather than a targeted music storage location.

If you haven't gotten around to digitizing all of your music, the next step is to add music from your CD collection to the HAL music library. With HALdmc installed and configured and the HAL server running, insert a music CD into the computer's optical drive. Even if the HALdmc is not running, inserting a music CD will bring up the window shown in Figure 12.10. The dialog box in front of the Recorder/CD Player window is showing because this CD did not contain artist and title information and this information could not be found on the Internet. If this happens, click OK to dismiss the window.

Click All to select all tracks on the CD for processing into the HALdmc music library. Figure 12.11 shows a CD with all the tracks marked and the status bar showing that the tracks are ready to copy. Click on the red Record button to capture the CD to the HAL library. While HAL is recording the CD's tracks, the record button changes color to blue to let you know that HAL is still recording.

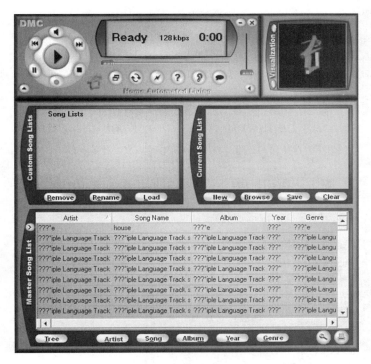

Figure 12.9 *The scan results will be entered into the song list shown in this window.*

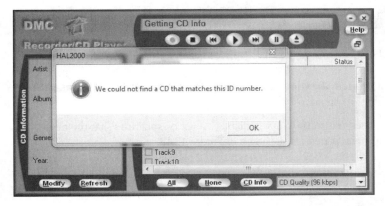

Figure 12.10 *The Automatic feature of the Record/CD Player feature shown in action.*

Figure 12.12 shows an identified CD ready to copy with all the tracks marked. This identifying information can be used later, for example, to play only music by Glenn Miller.

Figure 12.11   *All tracks are marked for transfer.*

Figure 12.12   *This CD is identified by artist, genre, album, and song name of each track.*

As the tracks are transferred, the track-by-track status moves from "copy percentage" to "processing" to "saving" to "done."

After all tracks have been transferred, DMC displays a list of song lists that the newly transferred music has been added to, as shown in Figure 12.13.

Figure 12.13   *The CD has been added successfully.*

After you have some songs loaded, you can begin to build custom playlists. Songs can be dragged and dropped into the play window and identified with a playlist title, in this case, "...Motivational Plays of the Day," as shown in Figure 12.14. Practice building a list or two but wait until we cover DMC's voice commands before you build many of them. HALdmc's voice commands allow for ad hoc playlist control that's so fun to use that you might want to forgo playlists altogether, just as I have.

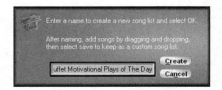

Enter a name to create a new song list and select OK.

After naming, add songs by dragging and dropping, then select save to keep as a custom song list.

uffet Motivational Plays of The Day   Create   Cancel

Figure 12.14   *Entering the name for a customized playlist.*

Figure 12.15 shows the Master Song List as it fills in after a few CDs have been identified and loaded by HALdmc. Notice that the Master Song List displays by artist.

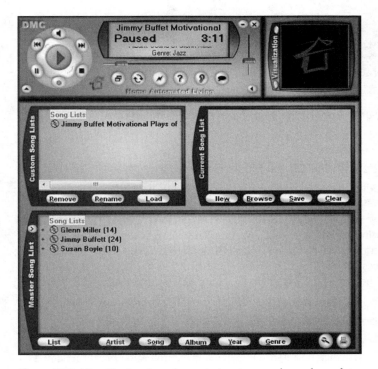

Figure 12.15   *Notice that the artist's name and number of songs are shown.*

Figure 12.16 shows the two song lists and an expanded Jimmy Buffet song list. To play a Custom Song List from this window, drag and drop the custom list into the Current Song List pane and click the Play button in the control circle.

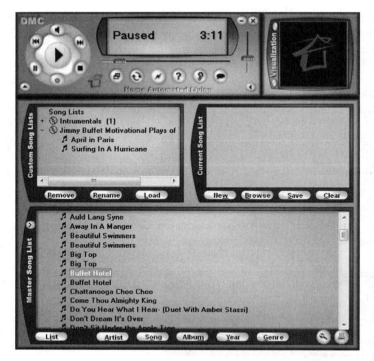

Figure 12.16 *The drag-and-drop feature of Windows is convenient for adding songs to the playlists.*

Using Voice Commands with the Digital Music Center

The power of this product is on full display when you begin using the DMC with voice controls. It is hard to show that power in a book, so for demonstration purposes, here is a transcript of a "conversation" with the prototype HAL persona "Pippa." You can follow along with this conversation with your own installation as test steps for this chapter's project. This demonstration was performed with HALultra, the HAL Model 300 Voice Portal, an inside princess phone attached to a live dial tone line, and a set of 2.1 amplified speakers attached to the prototype sound card's analog stereo output jack port.

DMC and Voice Control Test #1

Here is one way to use voice commands with the HALdmc for playing digital music with HALultra and a HAL Voice Portal installed in a home automation platform named "Pippa" (the default attention word or name is "computer" but you can rename your system's attention word from the default to a more suitable name such as Pippa as used in this example.).

Pick up any "inside HAL" portal extension phone, press your personal code key, say for example 6 if that is what you set up in HAL as your phone access code, and wait a second or two for a response:

Pippa: "How may I help you?"

You: "Open...music."

Pippa: "Music is open."

You: "Play [insert artist name here] songs." (Keeping with our previous examples, I asked Pippa to play Jimmy Buffett songs.)

At this point, songs from the requested artist should start playing.

Hang up the phone.

While the songs are playing, the DMC should look similar to what's shown in Figure 12.17. The voice command moved all the Jimmy Buffet songs into the playlist and began playing them one by one.

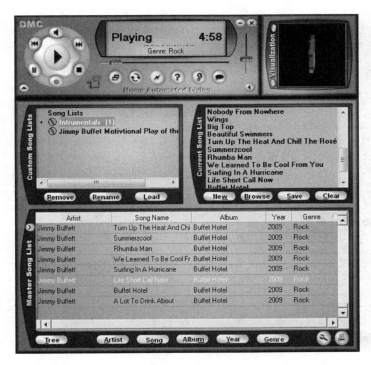

Figure 12.17   *Voice commands populated the playlist.*

After some songs have played, use the phone to enter your internal access code key, and again say the attention word (the default is "Computer;" in the example I have again used "Pippa" as the attention word).

Pippa: "How may I help you?"

You: "Stop the music."

Pippa: "I have stopped the music."

Test complete.

As you can imagine from the example, I could have used the Play command for any artist or category of music that was loaded and categorized in the HAL music library. Selecting by genre, year, album, or artist all would have worked.

There is one more interesting action you can take in the Digital Music Center that will display full-screen video shots of an oscilloscope representation of the sound track. To take this action with the DMC open, refer to Figure 12.17 and notice how the upper-right corner of the DMC displays a screen with the word "Visualization" across the left-hand frame. Click on this while HALdmc is playing a song, and it will fill the computer screen with a changing animated visual like the one shown in Figure 12.18. To return to the normal window screen, click in any area of the screen. The small buttons on the end of the word "Visualization" can also be used to find and display the album cover art, if available.

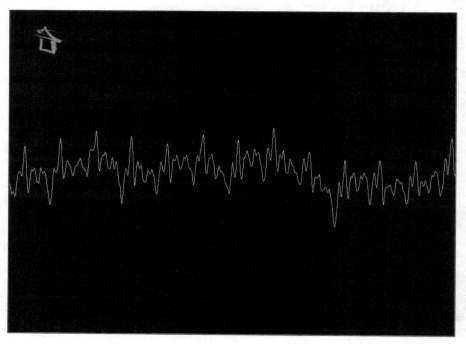

Figure 12.18   *Your songs all look different.*

There is so much that can still be done with HALdmc. Try using the time action controls in HALultra to play music as your wake-up call in the morning. Try using custom playlists to associate with room scenes or house modes. Try using voice commands to play music from a favorite time period. The more you work with this product, the greater the potential benefits. Enjoy both the hobby aspect and the results. Voice-controlled playlist manipulation is just too cool!

Chapter 13

Project 10, Connecting and Using the Home Automation Platform over the Internet

One can certainly use and benefit from computer-based home automation features without ever connecting the control platform to the Internet, but a conventional POTS line and phone service extend valuable features to wherever there is a phone available for you to call home to the HAL server. Further extending the HAL server to use and be used over the Internet increases the value of the total investment in the automation system. HAL can be programmed to act in your stead and harvest data from the Internet. Stock quotes, weather, and news are examples of the data that can be routinely collected for you. This data can then be processed using macros or rules into actions like informing you of a stock price threshold by email. On the flip side the Internet can be used for inbound control of home devices and pulling monitoring information about the state of the house to your smart phone, tablet, or office computer.

If your home automation platform is not connected to the Internet, it will have to be in order to use these features. If you have an Internet connection already, you might need to make some minor modifications or setup adjustments so that you can use the full feature set of the HAL software over the Internet. You might also want to check on the speeds available to ensure that you have enough throughput for HAL. To test an existing service's throughput, you can use a web-based test such as the one at http://www.speedtest.net/. The test will show your download and upload speeds. A respectable level of service for using the Internet features of HAL would be download speeds of 1500Kbps and uploads of 1500Kbps; however, the more Kbps you have in both directions, the better. The data throughput necessary for controlling HAL over the Internet is very small; however higher speeds facilitate efficiency.

Preparing the Internet/Intranet Connection for HALultra

Because of default security settings on the equipment that connects your home or small office network to the Internet, it is unlikely that your Internet setup will allow for the

HAL HomeNet web pages to be broadcast out to the Internet without some minor modifications. The next section explains some of the generic adjustments that will likely be needed. Considering the equipment, the default equipment settings after setup, and the ISPs and their default setups and security policies, there are too many variables to detail a one-size-fits-all set of directions.

Internet Service

Regardless of how Internet service is provided to your home you will need to make some adjustments to the default configuration to facilitate two-way communication with HAL. If your HAL computer is already connected to the Internet and you are able to use a browser with it, HAL will be able to operate one-way to get information from the Internet unless your security software is set to block if from doing so. Typically the default configuration will block incoming communication at the router or firewall. This is the area where adjustments are typically needed to allow HAL to receive commands from a device somewhere on the Internet. In generic form the next few sections will outline what must be done to facilitate that two-way communication.

Setup and Tweaks on the Modem-Router-Firewall-Switch

Regardless of how the Internet connection is brought to your home, there will be a device that translates the protocols used to communicate over the long distances to the TCP/IP Ethernet protocol suite at your network port. That device is a called a modem. The second device in the chain is a router. The router's first job is to perform network address translation between IP addresses visible on the Internet and the private IP addresses on your network. Its second important function is to provide DHCP, Dynamic Host Configuration Protocol, which randomly assigns a private IP address (192.$x.x.x$) to your internal computers, servers, laptops, and other devices. The third device or functionality is that of firewall. The firewall is used to define what traffic can pass between your home and the Internet in both directions. Think of it as a traffic cop. The fourth device, called a switch, gives you more than one Ethernet port for connections to your computers and other IP devices. Often these functionalities are combined in one box or case. A common installation would be a modem box and a router box that would combine router, firewall, and switch functionalities with some number of included connection ports.

Because there are so many different device options, rely on the manufacturer's documentation for your specific devices to make the changes discussed in this chapter.

In an ideal home control world your Internet service provider would provide your router with one or more static (meaning stays the same always) IPv4 addresses visible on the Internet. Having a static IP address facilitates reaching your home's router/firewall that same way every time. It is likened to having the same phone number to call. There are workarounds for access if you do not have a static IP address from your ISP, as discussed on the homeautomatedliving.com forums. One method to get around not having a static IP is to use the services of http://www.noip.com/. They offer a free service and also have a fee for service offering to deal with the problems associated with your router having a dynamically (changing) assigned IP address. It is worth the effort to get—and the fee to obtain—your own static IP addresses or possibly even switch to a competitive provider that routinely offers static IPs as a part of the package. For example, as a benchmark, AT&T (in their service areas where DSL is provided) offers 6Mbps download plans for about $35 per month and an additional charge of $15 per month for a static IP address.

To access HAL HomeNet from outside your firewall, a minimum necessity is to allow port forwarding for whatever port number the Hal HomeNet server uses. The default is port 80. Whatever port number the firewall/router set up has to be configured to allow connections on port 80 or an alternate port such as 8008 to and from the Internet. When you have a static IP address available that is visible on the Internet as provisioned by your ISP, you can map the visible IP address to the private IP address inside the firewall on your HAL server. When Internet services' routers/firewalls/switches are left to their defaults, your computer will get a DHCP-provided IP address from the router the first time it connects. Over time, that internal IP address could change, hence the term "dynamic." When you are using a computer on the Internet with HAL, even though it is a private internal address, it is best to configure your NIC card with a permanent (static) IP address on your internal network. The router's settings should allow you to map that relationship or allow you to reserve a block of addresses you can use for hard-coding into your computer equipment. As stated earlier, the setting screens will vary from product to product, but you should still be able to find the functionality somewhere in the setups to make these helpful and necessary adjustments.

After your Internet firewall/router devices are set up to allow port forwarding and you have mapped the IP address of the HomeNet server, you are ready to make HAL available to communicate with you over the Internet.

The other detail to pay attention to is the security software on your computer. Your operating system's firewall or the third-party software firewall setting might be blocking the type of connection and ports that HAL HomeNet needs to operate.

Setting up the HomeNet Server

The built-in HomeNet server features and the Internet services features of HAL combine to facilitate home automation features that not long ago would have seemed futuristic. Being able to display a snapshot on your smart phone of who rang the doorbell at your home a few minutes before, from a hundred miles away, is impressive to anyone. The HomeNet server is powerful yet simple enough that you will want it in your home automation solution. Much of the heavy lifting has been done and built into the server, and the learning curve for using it is a gentle one. The next step is enabling the HomeNet server and collecting some info about it.

Enabling the HomeNet Web Server

Setting up the HomeNet server is extremely easy, provided that your computer is already communicating with the Internet via your home network.

First make sure that the HAL server is running on your automation computer. The Hal listening ear should be in the system tray. To set up HAL HomeNet in HAL, right-click on the listening ear on the tray and select Open System Settings, as shown in Figure 13.1.

Figure 13.1   *Open System Settings menu item.*

The System Settings window is shown in Figure 13.2. In this chapter, we are concerned with the HomeNet settings; the Internet settings are covered in Chapter 14, "Controlling Your Home with iOS and Android," HomeNet is the way Hal presents an interface of your home automation to your internal network in your home and out to the Internet.

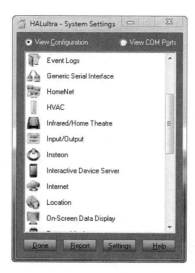

Figure 13.2   *Select HomeNet from the drop-down list.*

After selecting HomeNet from the System Settings menu, you will see the window shown in Figure 13.3. This window is what is seen the very first time HomeNet is selected. To enable the HomeNet features, check the box next to HomeNet Enabled.

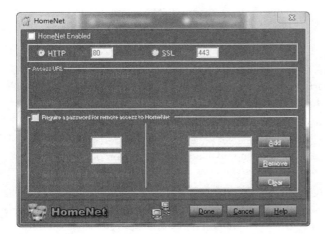

Figure 13.3 *To enable the HomeNet feature, check HomeNet Enabled to start the built-in HAL web server the next time the HAL server restarts.*

Figure 13.4 shows what happens if the computer is already connected to the Internet. All the settings will be populated with default values. Note that in the center panel the information includes the computer name TerraLX-HP translated to a URL of http://TerraLX-HP and the current private IP address assigned to the computer (192.168.1.235), also presented as a URL. Both addresses are going to be different for your computer unless your home automation PC has the same private IP address.

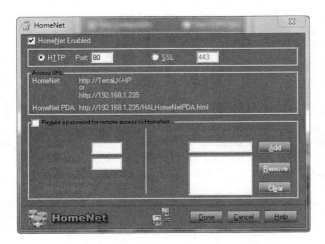

Figure 13.4 *The defaults for HomeNet are displayed in this window.*

Click on the Require a Password box shown in Figure 13.4 to begin assigning usernames and passwords to family members for remote access. My habit is to test everything without security and then add passwords and other security measures later. I rely heavily on my Norton 360 to protect my systems when I first set up and begin to use new applications. I add the complication of usernames and passwords after the systems and features are known to be working.

Logging In to HomeNet

The HAL server should be restarted or the computer should be rebooted to restart HAL. Restart the Hal server if it is not set up to automatically run when the computer boots up.

Logging in to HomeNet from inside the firewall is as easy as bringing up a web browser and navigating to your personal HomeNet page. Use the IP address version http://*x.x.x.x*/HALHomeNetPDA.html to bring up a larger print version of the control page with a condensed format for use on smart phones and tablets.

To use these same pages from outside your firewall, you will have to work through the port-forwarding issues as discussed earlier in this chapter. The key to success with that is enabling port forwarding of the port number default (80) in your firewall/router from the setup screen shown in Figure 13.4 or selecting another port number to use, commonly 80 or 8008 for HTTP.

Note **Internet Ports and Security** For the complete listing of common Internet ports and their typical uses, visit http://www.iana.org/assignments/service-names-port-numbers/service-names-port-numbers.xhtml. Enter "HTTP" in the search field to see all the HTTP port number assignments if you are interested in learning more about them.

For those rigidly concerned about security, you will want to use the SSL settings; everyone should at least use a username and password for access to the HomeNet from the Internet. You would hate to have someone else turning off your lights or viewing your security videos.

Using HAL on the Internet

HAL provides services over the Internet in dealing with data in both directions. One way of using HAL as your personal assistant is to have HAL periodically collect data from Internet data sources. Think of this feature as sending out an assistant to the library to collect some information. If you are a TV fan, be sure to set up your five favorite networks for voice access to "...what's on TV at 7:00 PM?"

Collecting Internet Data

To use HAL to collect data, you must already have the HAL computer connected to the Internet. A dial-up service can be used but it is not recommended because of dial-up's slow speeds. Begin setting up the HAL server by right-clicking on the HAL listening ear and selecting Open System Settings; then scroll down on the menu to find and select Internet. The window shown in Figure 13.5 will be presented.

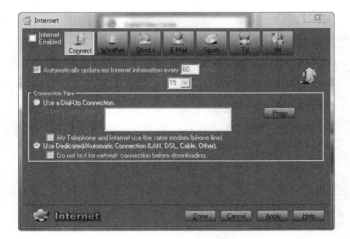

Figure 13.5   *Internet data collection features are set from the tabs on this screen.*

Check the Internet Enabled check box and then click the Connect tab shown in Figure 13.6. In this window you will select the frequency with which the server will reach out to the Internet to collect information, emails, sports, and news. In the figure the selection is to collect information once an hour, providing a good balance between timeliness and bandwidth utilization. The second setting is the frequency of reconnection attempts should your Internet connection fail.

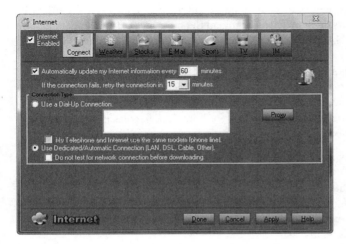

Figure 13.6   *Make your selections here for timeliness of information collection and retry attempts.*

The next feature to enable is the weather collection. As shown in Figure 13.7, check the box for Weather Enabled and the button for your country, and then enter your Zip Code in the Zip Code field. Click on Apply to save your settings when you finish entering data in each tab.

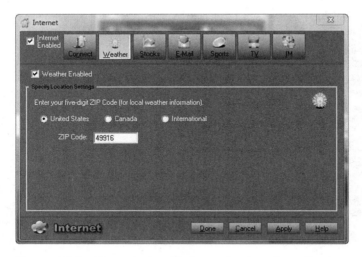

Figure 13.7 *Enter the local information here for collecting weather data for your hometown.*

Skip over the Stocks tab for now and proceed to the E-Mail tab, as shown in Figure 13.8. There are two types of email accounts: web-based and POP3. Yahoo Mail and Gmail are both web-based, meaning that along with accessing your email via the Web, all of your email messages are stored on the hosting company's servers until you either delete them or take steps to get the messages onto your computer. POP3 accounts, typically offered by Internet service providers, allow you to download the messages off of the company's servers onto your PC. For HAL to download email for you, you must have the POP3 server information for your email account. If you rely primarily on web-based email, you might be able to upgrade your service to a POP3-based account, typically after paying a one-time upgrade fee or paying a monthly subscription fee. Enter your POP3 account information as well as any authentication information in the E-Mail Server Settings screen. Click Advanced to see additional options for how HAL handles email attachments, as well as other options.

While on the window shown in Figure 13.8, click on the E-mail Notification button to bring up the window shown in Figure 13.9. You can program HAL to send you email notifications based on events. HAL uses your POP3 account to send email to you or anyone else. Note in the figure that the first account will be the one HAL uses to send the email notifications, in this example myaccount@yahoo.com. The rest of the list is email addresses that notifications will be sent to.

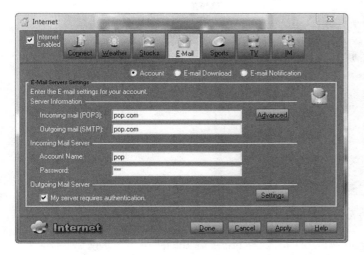

Figure 13.8   *Enter POP3 mail server information here from the data provided by your ISP or email service.*

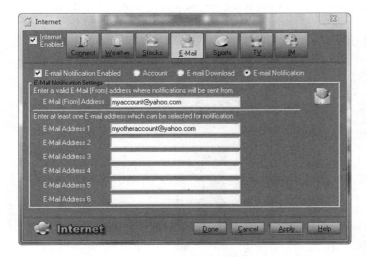

Figure 13.9   *Enter your notifications email addresses here.*

With the email setting applied you can now move to the Stocks tab and enter stock information for HAL to monitor. You can also configure HAL to notify you if there are stock price fluctuations outside of the range selected, as shown in Figure 13.10. Enable the stock notifications by checking the Notify Me When check box and filling in the parameters for each stock symbol you want monitored.

Figure 13.10   *Fill in data for tracking stock prices here.*

Figure 13.11 shows the Sports tab. Check the boxes for the teams you want to follow. You can also change the spoken reference for the team. For example, instead of using "Baltimore Orioles," you can edit the team to be referred to as "Orioles" or "O's". Then when speaking to HAL, you can use the reference you have designated for that team.

Figure 13.11   *Check your favorite teams and select sports areas from the drop-down.*

The TV tab, as shown in Figure 13.12, enables you to get TV schedules from the Internet and view them all in one place. Checking the boxes for your five favorite networks will facilitate voice commands with HAL. You can then ask for shows that are on at a particular time.

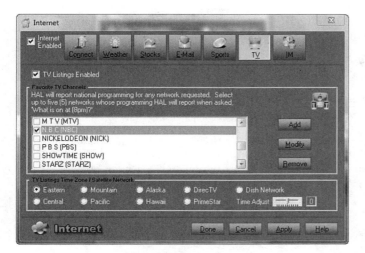

Figure 13.12   *Enable the TV schedules and select your five favorite networks to view.*

On the IM tab, shown in Figure 13.13, you can enter the instant-message account information for your IM service of choice. This enables you to not only receive notifications from HAL via IM but also issue commands via IM.

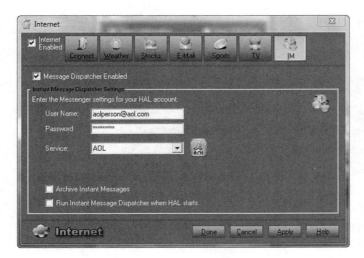

Figure 13.13   *Instant messaging account information is entered here.*

Using home automation features over the Internet is the direction the entire home automation industry is headed. Although a lot of lesser control models provide some similar features, HAL is already positioned and proven as the one-stop solution for leveraging the power of the available communications technologies to control devices in the home. The option to make your life easier and better by leveraging the power of a PC and a good

Internet connection brings HAL to the forefront as a wise choice for automating your home today and in the future.

Viewing Internet Data Collected by HAL

Now that HAL has reached out to the Internet to gather all this data on a scheduled interval, it is time to explore what you can do with the data. This section covers a few of the basics for that collected information.

Each tab covered in the preceding section relates to a tab you access by right-clicking on the HAL listening ear and selecting View Internet Information. Click the Monitor tab to see a window similar to the one shown in Figure 13.14. In this screen HAL logs its successes and failures in collecting the information it has been configured to collect.

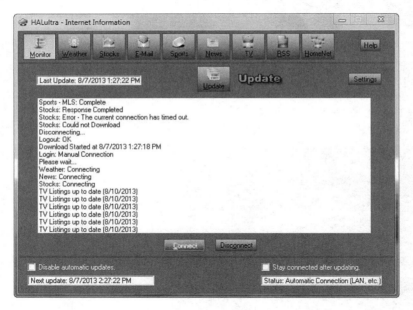

Figure 13.14   *Under the Monitor tab you can view the log entries for pulling data.*

Clicking on the Stocks tab will bring up a window similar to the one shown in Figure 13.15. Notice that the price changed for Ford and its change percentage is highlighted.

Figure 13.16 shows the TV tab, a feature I found quite useful because the compilation by time is there for every satellite channel I want to view. Reading it here is easier and faster for me than using the satellite box's view of this data, where only a few channels are displayed at a time. I can also use HAL's speech recognition interface to simply ask, "What is on NBC at 9 PM?"

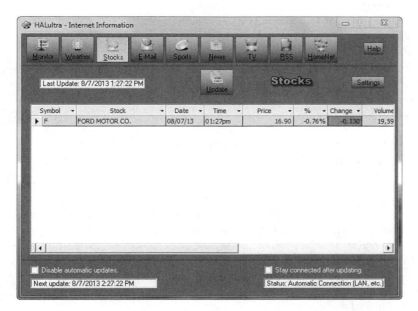

Figure 13.15 *Stock prices are monitored and reported in this screen; you can program HAL to email you notices on changes in price.*

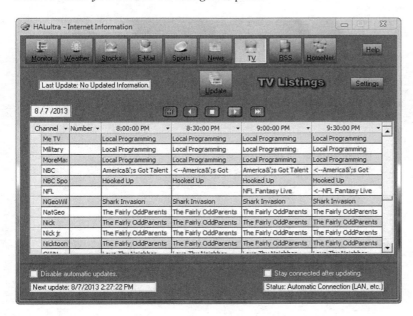

Figure 13.16 *TV prime time schedule downloaded by HAL.*

The last few examples provide a basic insight into how this harvesting of data can save you time and effort. After your system is set up, take the time to view the data you have selected for downloading by exploring every tab on the Internet Information screen. Then take a few moments to look at or review the HAL scripts for more examples of the data that can be summoned to your ears by voice command.

Controlling HAL over the Web

No small effort has gone into your getting the two Internet components of HAL set up in your system. At this point we will briefly explore using a connection from anywhere on the Internet with HAL HomeNet.

Entering the domain name or URL of your HAL HomeNet server in your remote browser will bring up a window as shown in Figure 13.17. This is the summary screen where you get a bird's-eye view of what is happening at home with HAL. In this example there are no sensor events to report or device events, making it a quiet day on the home front. A computer is being used to provide this example; however, just about any Internet browser will bring up this screen, making all manner of Internet-capable devices a solution for monitoring HAL via the Internet. There are special apps for Apple devices and one in development for Android devices.

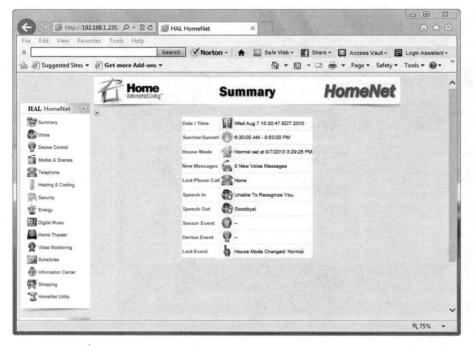

Figure 13.17   *The summary web screen for HAL Internet control using HomeNet.*

Figure 13.18 shows the window displayed after the Device Control is selected. From here you can issue change commands using the buttons and drop-downs. Selecting Dim, for example, brings up a Percentage of Dim drop-down. This is a great feature because you can control lights, stats, locks, essentially anything you have set up with an interface to HAL and a control module at the device.

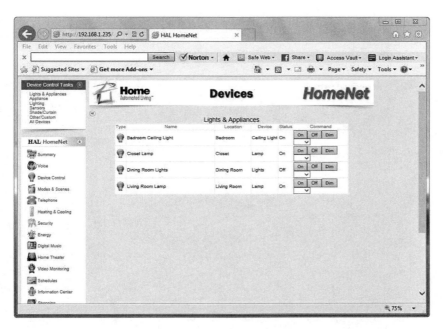

Figure 13.18   *The Device Control screen, one of many available control screens in HomeNet.*

These few examples demonstrate the potential and value of setting up the HAL HomeNet service and making it available on the Internet. This project is a low- to no-cost project that can take up a weekend or two but one that will pay dividends and provide value long after its installation.

Chapter 14

Controlling Your Home with iOS and Android

In the preceding chapter we touched on using HAL's HomeNet features to enable control of features in HAL and devices in your home from over the Internet. When you are remotely connecting to your HAL HomeNet server from over the Internet, a web browser on a computer is all that is needed to connect to HAL HomeNet. In this chapter the text explains how to connect to and control HAL from your home network or over the Internet with its built-in HALids (Interactive Device Server). The Interactive Device Server is a feature designed to interface with your Apple or Android smart phone or tablet.

Interactive Device Server Applications

Two applications, or apps as they are commonly called, are available that are intended to improve end users' experience while they are using an Apple or Android smart phone or tablet to interact with HAL's Interactive Device Server. The smart phone and tablet categories include operating systems such as iOS, Blackberry, Android, Windows 8, and Symbian. Your smart phone or tablet will likely be running one of these operating systems. Check your device, or check with your device's manufacturer or your cell phone carrier, to find out which OS your device runs. The iOS HALids app is available for download from the Apple store at a modest price. The Android application is free for owners of the HALultra software.

To use the Android application, you will have to have an Android smart phone or tablet. To use the Apple iOS application, you will need an iPhone, iPad or iPod touch. Currently there is no support for other mobile operating systems; however, you can always connect to HAL HomeNet via your device's web browser.

Apple App

To find out more about the iPhone iOS app that complements interaction with the HALids server, visit the Apple iTunes store at this address:

https://itunes.apple.com/us/app/hal-ihomenet/id387552020?mt=8

or:

https://itunes.apple.com/us/app/id387552020?mt=8&ign-mpt=uo%3D4

The app will work with an iPhone, iPod touch, and iPad, and requires iOS version 4.1 or later.

Android App

The Android HALids, a HomeNet app, is currently available in multiple places in the greater Android marketplace and is available to registered users of HAL as a free download from the www.homeautomatedliving.com website, under Downloads.

The Droid app is available in two levels: one that supports voice commands and another that is generic without voice. The Android OSes required to support voice command are Android OS versions above 4.0. Download the correct one for your phone's level of the OS or see if you phone can be upgraded to a 4.0 or newer OS.

Using Smart Phones and Tablets to Control HAL

Cell phones have progressed to the point where most of us now carry a miniature computer to make phone calls. In all probability you are already carrying a cell phone that can be used for home automation. Even if you are not using a smart phone, Chapter 9, "Project 6, Installing a Home Automation Voice Portal Modem in Your Computer," describes what is needed for interfacing with HAL over any phone, including a simple "legacy" cell phone, a landline, or those nearly obsolete pay phones. If you choose to connect to HAL via smart phone or tablet, feel free to connect using your device's data plan or over Wi-Fi, if a Wi-Fi signal is available. Both offer more than enough bandwidth to communicate with HAL; however, Wi-Fi has the benefit of not dipping into your plan's data allotment should you have one. A Wi-Fi enabled tablet or phone also allows you to connect over a home Wi-Fi network when you are at home if you know the IP address of the HAL server.

Enabling the "Interactive Device Server"

To use a smart phone or tablet with the HALids app, you will need to make one setting active in the HALultra System Settings menu. You will also need to make a few selections for how your phone or tablet will connect to the IDS server. Start with right-clicking the HAL listening ear, and from the menu select System Settings and then Interactive Device Server from the menu. From the window that displays, you can choose your connection method, choose whether to require a password, and choose to make HALids start automatically. If you elect to require a password, enter that password here as well. The first time you set these settings, you will need to reboot the computer to restart HALultra to enable the IDS service. HALids is an independent service that has to be turned on to use and left on. After the restart of the HALultra server, there will be a small phone icon in the system tray.

Clicking on the new icon will bring up the server, as shown in Figure 14.1.

Figure 14.1   *Settings for using IDS with HTTP port 10080 on the house's Wi-Fi network.*

With the HAL server running and the IDS feature enabled, the next task is to connect to the server with the smart phone or tablet. Remember that the HALids application is started from the phone icon; it must be loaded from the System settings and the service must be started from the Interactive Device Server window. You can also check the Automatic Start option in HALids so that the application will start automatically.

After HALids is running, download the correct app and install it on your device.

With the Android phones you can download directly to the phone or use a computer to download the application and then link the phone by USB cable and move the downloaded application from the /downloads directory on the computer to a /download folder on the phone. From the phone's Folders icon, touch it and navigate to the /downloads folder containing the application. Highlight the HomeNet.apk file to begin the application load. The HALids.exe file must be in the same /downloads folder. Your phone might have security set to not load new applications; if this is the case, change the security setting to allow the application to load. Change the security setting back after the load is complete.

Using HALids with iOS

On your iOS device, tap the app's icon and scroll to the Settings menu item for the page, shown in Figure 14.2. In this Settings page tap the first field to enter the IP address of the computer running the HALids server and enter the port number. Refer to Figure 14.1 for the port number. After these settings are correct and saved, tap on the Connect item's right arrow to reveal the next screen. It might take a moment or two to make the Wi-Fi connection to the server.

Figure 14.2   *Settings for connecting to the server and IP address are entered here.*

The menu's top entries should display on the next page, as shown in Figure 14.3. If the Summary page displays first, do not be alarmed; just tap the Menu icon at the top of the page to the left of Summary to bring the main menu into view.

The pages on the phone are very similar to the HomeNet web pages; however, they are a scaled version with font sizes more suitable for the smaller device screens.

A tap on the Summary arrow will bring up a page similar to the one shown in Figure 14.4.

Figure 14.3 *The top portion of the main menu page is displayed here.*

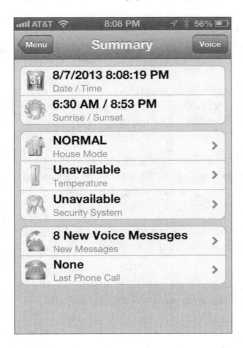

Figure 14.4 *The Summary page is the quick look at a few important home statuses.*

Tapping Menu again and then tapping on the right arrow for Devices will give you a listing of all the all of the rooms and locations where there are devices you can control, as shown in Figure 14.5.

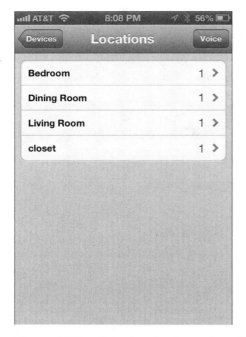

Figure 14.5   *This page displays a list of the home's available devices by room location.*

Selecting Dining Room or any other room or location will give you a new page, as shown in Figure 14.6, where you can turn the light or other listed devices on or off or use the sliding scale at the bottom of the page if it is a dimmable light. On this sample page I turned the light to Off.

The IDS feature is intended to be used remotely from somewhere on the Internet and at home on a local home Wi-Fi network. In the next few examples some of the controlling you might want to accomplish while at home is presented, beginning with controlling the Digital Music Center.

Figure 14.7 shows what is displayed when the arrow for Digital Music is tapped from the main HAL iHomeNet menu. From here you can make selections for what to play based on the filter categories listed on the page.

Tapping on the arrow by Artists displays the artists who are identified in the HAL Digital Music Center, as shown in Figure 14.8. Pressing the arrow next to one of the artists will bring up the individual songs to play.

Figure 14.6   *A tap on this page's On button turns the light to Off, as shown here.*

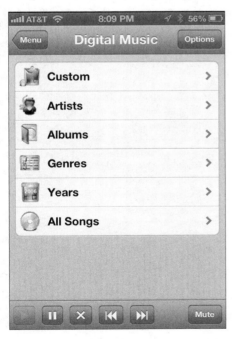

Figure 14.7   *The page provides control of the Digital Music Center from the iPhone.*

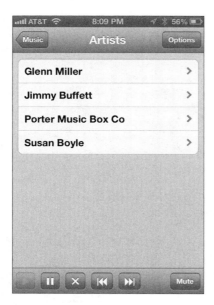

Figure 14.8 *Any of the other music filter categories could have been used.*

If you have ever forgotten to pick something up on the way home from work, you will appreciate the screen shown in Figure 14.9, which comes up when you select Shopping from the main menu screen. Scroll to the bottom of the screen to see this option.

Figure 14.9 *The shopping list could have been made by any household member with access to HALultra.*

Using HALids with Android

The next section of the text briefly explores the HALids experience on Android devices.

Beginning with Figure 14.10, the Android OS displays the icons for apps installed on the phone.

Figure 14.10   *The Android phone screen will look something like this one.*

After downloading and placing the application in any known folder on the phone, install the HAL app by tapping the HomeNet.apk file as mentioned in the first part of this chapter. After a moment or two, you should see a screen similar to the one shown in Figure 14.11. Tap the Install button at the bottom of the screen to proceed with the install.

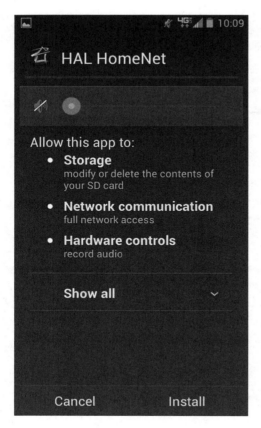

Figure 14.11 *The application's requirements are shown before you tap Install.*

When the install is complete, the option to launch the application will be offered in a screen, and selecting that option will bring up the screen shown in Figure 14.12. The screen will present with default information that might or might not match your system.

Enter your connection information and connect to the HALids server. After the HAL HomeNet splash screen is displayed, you will see the Summary screen shown in Figure 14.13.

Figure 14.12   *The application default settings will need to be changed.*

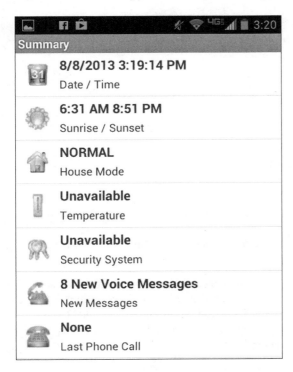

Figure 14.13   *The summary is a quick view of the state of the house.*

Use your Android phone's back button to move back from the summary screen to the main menu, and begin to explore items listed on the main menu screen. The same list found on the HomeNet screen with a PC, and that displays on the iPhone/Pad, will display. From there, for example, you can go to Devices and control the lights as shown in Figure 14.14.

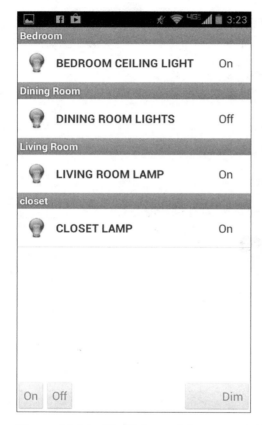

Figure 14.14   *The lights and device available for control actions are presented here.*

From the menu you can check on or change the Current House Mode, as shown in Figure 14.15.

Having just read Chapter 13, "Project 10, Connecting and Using the Home Automation Platform over the Internet," you will recognize that many of the control options available via a web browser and HALultra are also available via your mobile device and HALids. Pick the option that best works with you when you're out and about, and rest easy knowing that control of your home is just one tap or click away.

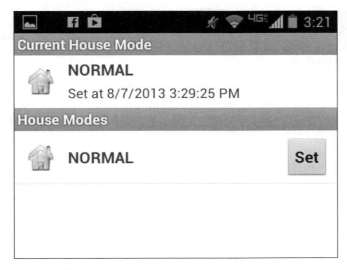

Figure 14.15   *There is only one house mode shown here but you can create as many modes as you need such as "vacation mode" or "day mode."*

Checking the IDS Log

Figure 4.16 shows the server window after it was loaded and started. Notice from the figure that change events and actions are logged. This would be helpful when you're checking on things or if troubleshooting the commands is ever necessary.

Figure 14.16   *The log of events processed by the IDS server.*

These examples show the full power of full-featured home automation. We're not quite to the point where you can think it and the change will happen magically in the automated home, but these useful control interfaces are really only one step back from that: think–touch–done. It does not get much better than that.

Chapter 15

Evaluating Broadband and Telecom Home Automation Offerings

Doing your own home automation system without outside assistance is admirable, but it might not be for everyone who wants to benefit from the technology. There are many companies poised and ready to help you with achieving part or all of your home automation management and monitoring needs. The major telcos here in the United States plus some in Canada see the opportunity for profit by helping the ordinary homeowner with monitoring and/or management of home automation systems. The nature of this "outsourced to others" service might be particularly attractive to the tech-averse personality. Having a home automation system installed, supported, and monitored by others will not be the route a typical DIYer would travel first, but over time the idea of having a second pair of trusted eyes and ears on duty 24 hours a day, particularly for alarm monitoring, might appeal even to those individuals who would insist on building their own home automation platform from the ground up. A broad range of options are available in the marketplace for monitoring and managing a home automation system. Those options for monitoring can begin for as little as just under $10 per month, on up to just under $100 for various services. Systems can be installed on a lease-purchase option in which there is no upfront fee for the hardware and the cost is rolled into the monthly contract payments. For example, as of the publishing of this book, AT&T's new Digital Life Service costs $70 per month with an upfront charge of $3,919 for hardware. This doesn't include applicable taxes and fees for installation. Given the wide range of offerings, it is a good idea to have some comparison criteria in mind before you pick up the phone and negotiate a contract. In any case, as a consumer, you'll find that it is best to have your personal criteria thought out and your specific needs written down on paper before you compare the options from the various companies and vendors offering HA management or monitoring services.

The buzzword for marketing contracts to consumers is "bundled" services. You are probably familiar with bundled Internet, phone, and cable or satellite services. Alarm monitoring companies also have had a small segmented presence in the home automation space by providing monitored and managed services of home security systems, but rarely offered any other off-script services along with simple security monitoring. It took a while but cable providers and telecoms are looking to add additional services to provide managed home automation. There is a barrier to entry based on a perception that home automation is only for dedicated hobbyists and the wealthy and that managed home automation and monitoring services are not a top priority for every home dweller. Combining quality and affordability in their offering, along with customized value-added-services and raising the awareness of compelling value propositions such as security, energy management, and lifestyle, certainly has the potential to pique consumer interest and increase demand for and use of this type of service.

Selection Criteria for Monitoring and Managed Service Providers

It is important to know what you are getting into when signing any installation or service contract. The more informed you are about what is available, the greater the likelihood you will be satisfied with your decision. In the next few sections the text briefly discusses criteria you can use to help determine a choice among the potential providers of alarm monitoring on up to full-blown combined HA managing and monitoring service.

Market Service Area

From the service providers' point of view, they would like to be able to offer products and services across the globe. Certain business, economic, and regulatory realities, however, get in the way. There are many factors that could prevent a company from offering home automation services in your neighborhood, so prepare yourself to hear "not at this time" from some providers in your area. Your first question when you call to inquire about services from the simple monitoring to complex HA management will be, "Do you offer monitoring/management services in 'my town'?" You might need to call a few potential providers to build the list of possible providers for your area. If you live in a very rural area with little population, your list of potential providers could be small. Although you can certainly research in the white pages or yellow pages, Internet research might be a more efficient means to discover the providers in your area that warrant consideration.

Proprietary Technology

The collective message carried as a theme throughout this book is to avoid locking yourself and your home automation system into only one proprietary technology. True proprietary technology and systems means that only products made by or offered by a single vendor will work with your system. That in itself is not a bad thing, but it is a substantial limiter when you desire to do something with home automation but the proprietary vendor does not have a product to offer you to solve the automation problem you are trying to solve. The same can happen with technology that, for lack of a better term, could be called "semi-proprietary." Semi-proprietary would be a technology that is licensed to be manufactured by others, so there might be many vendors making and offering the products; but again the whole group of manufacturers still might not offer sufficient product types to meet your wants and needs. Another problem with proprietary technology is that the interface to other devices might be nil or limited to a select few, taking away choices you might otherwise like to make. It is okay to get locked into a proprietary product line as long as you completely understand and can live with the limitations of the products and service offerings available. To evaluate, simply ask whether the vendor's offering is proprietary. If the answer you receive seems evasive, ask whether the HA system they are proposing will work with X10, UPB, INSTEON, and so forth, and the conversation might lead to getting the answers you need. Beware if you are bombarded with buzzwords and acronyms that seem confusing. Don't be intimidated. Simply take good notes and do your research. Generally, service providers have done a lot of the homework for you and have determined the best technology to base their offering on. This is in both your and their best interests because it means the offering is generally stable, easy to install, cost-effective, and future-proof.

You could also evaluate a potential provider with a solutions-based set of questions, such as, "Do you have a widget that will manage my house temperature, video record an intruder, and allow me to change an action response with my cell phone?" Use questions that support whatever your unique requirements might be. If you are getting locked into a propriety solution by a service provider, at least do it with your eyes wide open to the potential limitations and consequences right along with the upside and good qualities that vendor is offering. Just keep in mind that just because a provider uses an industry-standard technology doesn't mean their resulting version of the product will work with others. A good example of an open-industry standard is ZigBee. There are providers that use this technology, but the resulting product is a proprietary flavor that works only with their other products.

PC or Controller Based

You will want to know whether the solution being offered is computer based like the one covered in this book or whether it is based on a controller with limited programmability. Offerings by third-party HA service providers could include commercial versions of HAL running on a PC or another competitive home automation software running on a PC or Linux/Unix computer. Alternatively, their control and service settings could be done with a feature-limited controller box or gateway. As a DIY hobbyist, you could utilize a controller-based solution and build out a hybrid system as long as the controller was using a HAL-compatible protocol at the device level as discussed in earlier chapters. This approach would allow you to take control or maintain control for certain features such as house modes. For some HA enthusiasts this hybrid option might provide a sort of "best of both worlds" solution in which the service and security monitoring are outsourced and the management and control of features are left up to the home dweller.

Initial Installation Cost

I think it is fair to say that the scope of the projects covered in this book goes beyond what is being offered as typical entry-level equipment or kits from most telcos or cable companies.

As of the writing of this book, there are four popular cost models that are offered in the home monitoring/management marketplace today that more or less fit these four sample plans. Use these for cost comparison to get you started with a third-party home automation management or monitoring service should you decide to look for help managing your system.

Cost Model 1

Let's say, for a first example, that your Internet service provider offers an initial home automation gateway and a few pieces of equipment such as a web camera and light control or two, priced under $150 from the vendor if purchased with the connectivity to the Internet component for about $10 per month for some minimum period of time. Any further customization of the system could be left to you. In this scenario the provider could already be getting a revenue stream as the provider of your Internet service, and the value-add for you is an easy-to-use gateway in which the "monitoring and management" task is left for you to do. The vendor might be responsible for simply keeping your HA gateway up and running.

Cost Model 2

In a second scenario the initial cost might be replaced by a contract term and a cost of between $40 and $60 per month. However, it might include buying a value-added equipment package approaching $1,000 or more and perhaps getting a discounted price on the installation of control modules and the equipment you have purchased.

Cost Model 3

In a third alternative scenario your initial equipment cost might be rolled into a three- to five-year contract in which there is a lowered initial outlay and the equipment is chosen by the homeowner a la carte with an increasing cost per month based on the equipment. The plan's monthly charges might be as low as $22 per month and as high as $70 or more due to the equipment rental/amortization fees. With plans such as this the equipment might become the property of the homeowner after the three- or five-year mark. This cost model also typically has an early termination clause that accelerates the total amount that would have been paid over the term of the agreement to become due immediately.

Cost Model 4

The fourth example involves a cost model in which you have the equipment and you simply need the 24-hour, 365-day monitoring of your alarm events and want notification given to you, a security company, or the police should an alarm go off. As little as $10 per month can get you hooked into a simple monitoring service in which a landline call or cell phone call is triggered by an event and the call is made to the monitoring company. As a DIY future project with HALultra, you can customize such a response to events and program your system to call the police, your cell phone, 911, the monitoring company, and a neighbor. For the economy-conscious DIY person this "alarm monitoring only" model could present the most affordable option.

Monthly Service Fees

The question that needs to be answered regarding fees is how much money over the lowest cost of a simple alarm monitoring service is managed home automation services worth to a typical home dweller or homeowner. It is easy to do comparison shopping of HA monitoring services or management services just based on price. The reality is that the price difference will usually reflect at least a modest difference in real or perceived value. Price, however, should not be your only consideration when you are making the comparisons. Build your list of required features and contrast that with the nice-to-have features to help determine which vendors have the best value options based on your needs. Then decide whom you would contract with. You can also use a provider to help you learn more about HA and refine your needs. The very best time to collect information about competing plans is during the presale discussions. Experience teaches that the sales force answers the phone at a better rate than the help desk at most companies.

Commitment Term

Contract commitment terms will vary from provider to provider. When you are comparison shopping this duration issue, it is helpful to get the fine print and find out, for example, whether there is an "out clause" if you move or your circumstances change. Take the time and energy to know what the commitment clauses are before you initiate the contract. A two- to five-year contract would not be atypical, generally speaking, if the initial hardware is provided without a large upfront cost.

Level of Ongoing Service Support

Service levels will vary quite a bit from vendor to vendor. Part of the issue is the availability of HA-trained service personnel. Do they link in remotely to service your system? Can they make a house call to fix a broken component? How far away are their service personnel stationed? What are the hours for technical support? You can add your own items to a list of service-related questions. Are there fees for service when the HA system fails, or is the cost of service covered by the monthly service fees?

Installer Competence and Tech Support Quality

The standard to which your installation is done should be a primary concern, particularly if the home security features of your HA installation will become something you intend to rely on. The ordinary cable-guy subcontractor might be able to install and configure a phone and phone modem, but you might not want to rely on him or her to properly wire in an alarm system. Then on the wiring side there is a level where the devices might be wired in well enough to work but not well enough to meet electrical and building codes.

Some of the key things to ask about include who would be doing the install: you as a do-it-yourselfer, the company your service is with, or a third-party contractor? After that is determined, the next questions relate to individual qualifications: Are the installers licensed and/or do they have appropriate trade certifications? The skills needed to install and maintain an HA system cross a number of what we consider typical trades and skill sets that include electrician, network tech, computer technician, telephone tech, alarm installer, and you could even include programmer in the mix. Take the time to base your expectations for installation and tech support by asking the hard questions upfront.

The true value of the tech support will be determined with the first call. Is the support technician knowledgeable about the equipment installed in your home regarding its proper operation? Does the technician have the skill and experience he needs with troubleshooting when something is failing and presenting an out-of-the-ordinary condition? When you can tell that the tech is reading from a script, it might not seem as though the service is of great value to you. It will be difficult to get information about the qualitative aspects of the technical support for comparison, but one should ask anyway.

Monitoring/Management Center Location

Before contracting with a monitoring company, the first thing I would want to know is where the monitoring is going to happen and what the primary language spoken there is. Companies that use the Internet as a communications media for monitoring and a provider across the pond are doing so to reduce costs, but you should consider whether that approach also could put you at risk from an Internet outage or put a loved one at risk from lack of understanding in a communication. I would award extra points in a comparison to any company that is more local to me while still offering national coverage. Having state-by-state or province-by-province monitoring centers would be graded more valuable to me than having one central location anywhere in the world. The providers won't likely tell you but some redundancy in locations and communication paths to the monitoring centers would be nice to have and to know about as a potential consumer of these services.

What Is Being Monitored?

When using a partner for monitoring of a system they install or a situation where you are partnering with them in a hybrid fashion, the most important factors are to know what event types are being monitored and what spaces or rooms are protected through monitoring. Here is a list of important event triggers well worth having monitored in some way in every home:

Smoke

Carbon monoxide

Temperature

Break-in/burglary

Moisture

Glass breakage

Medical event

Low battery

Response to an alarm

Response to a malfunctioning alarm

Some companies offer broad alarm response that can include all the trigger events listed, with a customized response to each alarm type. Other companies are specialized and focus on a small subset or only one type of event, such as medical event monitoring.

What Is Being Managed Versus Offered?

Along the same lines, one must evaluate within the company's offering what they offer in the way of control and what they manage. It is also important to consider what you can manage using their Internet gateway solution. For example, if your home has multiple HVAC zones and the temperature management offering is for a single thermostat device, it might not be a very helpful solution for you. Popular HA management offerings typically include the following:

Thermostat(s)

Door, window, or motion alarms

A security camera or baby/nanny camera

A single or small group of lighting or appliance controls

Full-blown security alarm systems

A full-blown managed HA system typically comes with everything. So all the installation, programming, personal instruction, maintenance, and even additions or revisions to the automation settings are all included in your monthly fee. With a managed system you should expect the provider to not only monitor your security system for alarm conditions, but also monitor every aspect of the HA system. This is done to ensure that it is operating flawlessly based on the various installed automation hardware and the customized settings such as schedules, rules, and macros. The provider of a managed HA system will be generally more proactive than reactive to potential issues with your system. This is because their system will have embedded routines to provide a constant report on the heath and state of your HA system. It is far more cost-effective for the provider to provide remote management to attempt to resolve an issue than it is to roll a service truck each time there is a reported issue. Typically, managed HA offerings provide the following:

Installation of selected automation equipment

Programming of equipment and custom settings

Monitoring of the security system

Off-site backup of HA configuration and other various logs

Remote modifications or additions to the programming

Remote updates of the HA system and other related software

Remote diagnostics of and issues identified by monitoring

24/7 customer support

Miscellaneous Concerns

You might have a few or many more items of your own to add to the list to evaluate which company you are going to invite into your home to provide HA management and monitoring services. The list presented here is not exhaustive of the concerns and considerations one should have before partnering with a managed HA service provider or a monitoring company; however, it does hit on the minimal list of important comparisons to make.

Expected Future Offerings

This marketplace of full-featured HA management and monitoring offerings is in its early stages and is nowhere near a mature commodity market such as the one for Internet service. Expect that in a five-year time frame many new and familiar providers will enter this HA services arena with ever more complex and complete HA offerings.

Mainstream Companies with HA and Monitoring Systems or Services

The advantage that you have as a DIY person is that you can build out a system that rivals and exceeds those being offered today by others as entry-level or intermediate systems. Building a valuable home automation system is not something you have to wait for or rely on others to do entirely for you; however, if you are looking for a big-name giant to do a system for you or are just looking for a partner to help with monitoring, here is a list to begin your search for prospective partners. The list in this chapter is not fully inclusive of companies with offerings in this market, nor are the companies endorsed by the author or publisher in any way. They are presented to provide you with the first few steps in your search for a trusted partner. Their sales literature and presentations found on the websites will provide an opportunity for you to learn the latest information about current offerings. This information about their services will help you to compare and contrast the offerings with your unique needs. Use the list in the previous section and the additional concerns you might have to evaluate which company can best meet your needs.

ADT

http://www.adt.com

Alarm Relay

http://www.alarmrelay.com/

AT&T Digital Life

https://my-digitallife.att.com/support/digitallife

Bright House

http://support.brighthouse.com/Article/Home-Security-And-Automation-10217/

Comcast Xfinity

http://xfinity.comcast.net

GE Home Security

http://www.gehomealarmsystems.com/

Protect America

http://www.protectamerica.com/

SecurTek—SaskTel

http://securtek.com/

Time Warner Cable

http://www.timewarnercable.com/en/residential-home/intelligenthome/overview.html

Verizon Home Monitoring and Control

https://shop.verizon.com/buy/Monitoring-Energy-Saving/Home-Control/Verizon-Home-Monitoring-and-Control/cat30006

Looking for an HA management and monitor partner can take some time because you have to sort out the details of the various options offered and evaluate the companies making the offers. Dedicate the time the purchase deserves to ensure that your needs are met for the term of the contract.

Chapter 16

Adding Future Self-Designed Home Automation Projects

If you can picture yourself living in an advanced automated home, it can be yours if you take on one additional DIY project at a time. After working though the first 15 chapters, you have gained a lot of the knowledge needed to design, plan, and implement your own home automation projects. When you can visualize your automation control needs, the the building blocks can be easily acquired from off-the-shelf components and assembled into your system to make your unique HA project visions a reality. The basic building block is HALultra, which will provide the logic, data storage, and action platform to achieve the desired control results. The next piece is using this control platform with one or more of the available protocols transmitted to the desired interface module and then to the target control module, activating the device to achieve your desired results. The process is the same with all the technologies currently available and is likely to be similar with any new and improved products or with new communication technologies.

Design Steps

To add new automation actions to your existing system, there are a number of steps to take. After you know your control objective, you need to find, install, and set up the pieces and parts needed to make the control action happen.

Here is the Design and Do eight-step list:

1. Define the desired result.

Begin working on your project with the desired automation result in mind. What process or event do you want to automate? Perhaps you have a manual rolling gate at the entryway to your property that you would like to close every night at 8 PM but it also needs to open automatically for driveway traffic. If the gate is now manually closed, the first part of the project is to set up an electric power-driven motor to open and close the gate. After the motor is in place, you will connect the control of that gate motor to your system using the available or best protocol. If there are control modules that fit your application with the control interfaces you already have, use that unless there is an overwhelming reason to add a new interface type.

Out-of-the-box solutions are available to interface with semi-automated items such as garage door openers and sprinkler systems, so a little less design and planning is needed when all you have to do is assemble the parts.

2. Determine the initiating event or time.

In the next step you define the action-initiating events or times. Having the gate roll closed at 8 PM and roll open at 8 AM would be an example. Perhaps you are looking to do a backup system for your sump pump to pump water if the level of water in the sump bowl is getting too high. Whatever it might be, this event will be the trigger for setting the automation in motion to achieve the new result. In the sump pump example, you would need to have a water or moisture sensor or a float switch that is monitored by the automation computer. Some piece of sensing hardware has to be a part of the system unless the actions are to occur by the computer's clock. When the sensing device triggers the software into action, the computer has to send out the action signal to a control device. In the gate example, the arrival of a preset time would activate the control process for times when the gate would be powered to operate.

3. Select the protocol and interface module(s).

Next up is to determine the desired protocol and control interface module. Will it be UPB or a wireless protocol such as Z-Wave? Do you already have the interface module as a part of your system? Unless there is a strong technical or performance reason to add another device and protocol to your system, levering existing modules is always the best bet. The time to add new types of controllers is when your existing system cannot control the modules needed for your new action. It is necessary to know which control devices are available for a given protocol. You might want to use Z-Wave for your project, but if no Z-Wave device is available, you will have to choose from devices and protocols that are currently manufactured for your application.

4. Select the actual control device(s).

After the protocol and interface module is selected, the next step is finding the control module or modules that are best suited for your specific application. Often there will be many brands or styles of control modules to choose from. If your project is checking for rising water in the basement, there are a number of vendors with modules that can fit this need. Your project might need to include two components: an event-sensing device followed by a call to an action device such as a switch module for turning on a sump pump. You might want or need to use one protocol for the sensing half of the project and another protocol for the take-action portion. This is one of the areas where the HAL control platform pays dividends because it is not tied tightly to any one protocol, product, manufacturer, or set of products.

5. **Define the action logic.**

The next step is sketching out the logical sequence of events to take place after the trigger occurs. The action steps will have to be entered into the HAL Automation Setup as stored if-then conditions. Think of the process as knocking over dominoes: one sensing event, then an action event, followed by feedback, followed by more additional actions as needed.

6. **Acquire and install the control devices.**

Follow building, electrical, and safety codes appropriate to the project when installing your control devices. If you are not sure, do the necessary research or consult with a trade professional. Many tradesmen are willing to help with advice to a motivated DIYer. If you're still not comfortable doing the work, pay a licensed professional to install the control devices.

Maintaining safety is your single-most-important action item for any project or task covered in this text or in your home automation future.

7. **Implement by doing the data setups in HAL.**

This same pattern of design and implementation can be followed for nearly every future automation project that can be controlled in HALultra. These data setups include steps covered in previous chapters.

Linking any new control interfaces is first followed by identifying in the control database the particular device you will control. Often you will then use the Open Automation Setup Screen to set the control parameters for that device.

8. **Test the actions.**

The last step is testing the process. In the basement flood-protection example, you might have the system turn off the main sump pump and let the water rise enough to dampen your sensor that would activate a backup sump pump and notify you by phone or email that the trigger event happened. Whatever logic you designed into the setups should be tested so that you can rely on the actions to happen in your absence. Testing will also reveal any problems in your if-then logic.

Popular Home Automation System Add-ons

This section presents a few of the more popular devices that can be interfaced into your home automation control system. This list is not exhaustive; it represents many of the readily available and popular add-ons.

Growing Your Automation System with Additional UPB Devices

In Chapter 6, "Project 3, Controlling Lighting: Indoors and Outdoors," the targets of control were lamps, lights, and appliances. UPB is an excellent and easy-to-use protocol and technology to expand the reach of your automation control platform. It does not take much imagination to envision using the UPB controls for any items that are of a simple on-or-off nature.

Commonly available UPB control devices for expanding your automation control reach include these:

> Light switches—Control on/off/dim.
>
> Lamp control modules—Control on/off/dim.
>
> Appliance modules—Control on/off only.
>
> Thermostats—Give granular control.
>
> Inline dimmers—Control dimmers for all lights in a room.
>
> Scene controllers—Remotely control other modules.
>
> Split duplex receptacles—Provide on/off control only.
>
> In-line relays—Enable you to use 120-volt circuits to control higher-voltage, higher-amperage, or more-distant loads.
>
> UPB/X10 wireless remote hubs—Enable you to map X10 wireless devices such as key fobs to a porch light, for example.
>
> Slave switches—Provide basic on/off/dim controls for multiswitch-controlled loads.
>
> Low-voltage I/O modules—Allow for sensing of or controlling low-voltage circuits. They can be used to sense an alarm such as a burglar alarm on a window or door, or to monitor a doorbell line and report to the home automation system that someone has pressed the doorbell button.

Some of the advantages of using UPB in future projects include simplicity without sacrifice of command, reliability, or low device cost, and it can be leveraged by adding additional devices to handle most automation chores in the ordinary home.

Expanding the Reach of Your Control with INSTEON Controls and Kits

INSTEON-compatible devices are a good choice for increasing the number of household devices you can control with your home automation platform. One of the advantages of INSTEON is that kits are offered in which all the parts you need for a particular type of project are included.

INSTEON devices you might consider adding to your system in the future may include the following:

> Light switches
>
> On-off appliance switches
>
> Fan and light controls
>
> Garage door controls and status kit
>
> RF/wireless sensor receiver
>
> Window alarm sensor kit

Chime alert kit

Low-voltage relay controller

Photo beam entry alert

Door strike kit

Programmable thermostats

Proximity RF key reader

High-low temperature alert kit

Ethernet on-off control switch

Rain sensor

Freeze sensor

Flood or leak sensor

Bluetooth control interface

Enlarging the Control Zone with Additional Z-Wave Devices

Z-Wave is supported by one of the major suppliers in the home-wiring industry. Device types offered by Leviton include these:

Wall switches

Lamp dimming modules

Wi-Fi interface controller

Deadbolt locks

Pool/spa controls

Thermostats

Duplex receptacles

Appliance controls

Wall dimmer switches

Motion/light/temperature sensors

Outdoor lighting controls

Indoor siren

Window sensor

Key-chain remote

Electrical energy use monitor

Water valve

Temperature and humidity sensor

Dimmer remotes

Fan speed controls

Combination controllers

Remoting with IR

Various infrared interfaces are available to control electronic devices. One model to consider for future projects is a network IP addressable interface from Global Cache. Global Cache's GC 100 family of IR network adapters is available with three or six IR sensor/output ports.

Improving Security Reactions with Interfaces to Home Automation

One suitable security alarm kit that is available at a modest cost and could make for an interesting project is the GE Concord Hardwire/Wireless kit.

The ELK Products M1 family and many other security systems can be installed by authorized distributors and resellers or by the security monitoring companies themselves. Many will offer the capability to interface with your home automation system for an additional setup fee.

By connecting security controls, you can substantially improve the range of responses after an alarm is tripped. You can be emailed or phoned, or a neighbor or neighborhood watch captain can be called to look out to see what's happening at your house when an alarm triggers. A barking-dog sound file can be played while the alarm system monitor company is contacting the first responders. All these options are low-cost and have the potential for a high positive impact on the potential security deterrent value.

Setup Correlations

As you grow your home automation system configuration to increase your span of control, you might on occasion need to set up new interface modules depending on the configuration of the existing system. The Setup Wizard is the starting point for adding a new interface. If you have been following along chapter by chapter, you might have noticed that one screen in the HAL Setup Wizard plays an integral role in what devices' interfaces are included within the control options. After the new control modules are registered in the HAL software, you can begin to use and control the downstream devices using that new protocol to communicate to them. In this chapter we focused on X10, UPB, INSTEON, and Z-Wave as control protocols. There are proven products available for each of these control protocols that can be used in both routine and novel ways in your home automation setups. By using a computer platform and HAL software, you are, at least to some degree, future-proofing your investment in home automation. With the computer as the central controller, it is far easier to add new protocols, new modules, and new devices because you are not limited to any one protocol.

Summation

The device list and the few recommendations in this chapter are intended to get you thinking about maintaining DIY home automation as an ongoing hobby. By using the versatile HAL software platform that can be expanded to new uses as time and project funding permits, becoming a full-fledged home automation hobbyist could maintain an interesting and rewarding hobby for many months or years to come. Doing expansion projects on your own substantially reduces the cost and gives you a home automation system that you know and understand completely. Knowing the wide range of possibilities presented by home automation technology and having some sense of the current product offerings available also put you in the great position of being able to offer a helping hand and advice to others who could benefit from the technology in their living spaces. I wish you every success as you begin to automate your tomorrow today.

Index

A

AC (alternating current), 11-12
  delta-connected three-phase transformers, 14
  household AC wiring and devices, 19
  single-phase AC circuits, 12
  three-phase AC circuits, 12-13
  transformer connections, 13
  wye-connected three-phase transformers, 14-15
acquiring HALbasic software, 69
action logic, defining, 299
actions
  automation processes, 67-68
  testing, 299
activating
  HALbasic software, 82-84
  HALultra, 187
adding new automation actions to existing systems, 297-299
ADT, 294
aHomeNet app, 274

air conditioners, 210. *See also* heating and cooling systems
Alarm Relay, 294
all-in-one computers, 38
alternating current. *See* AC (alternating current)
alternative power sources, 30
aluminum, 10
amperage, 16
amps, 16
Android apps, HALids (Interactive Device Server), 274
Android devices, controlling HAL, 281-284
APC battery backup, 56
Apple apps, HALids (Interactive Device Server), 274
appliance modules, configuring, 108
apps
  aHomeNet app, 274
  Droid app, 274
  iOS app, HALids (Interactive Device Server), 274
arc fault breakers, 24
assigning IP addresses for cameras, 171-181

AT&T, Digital Life Service, 287, 295

audio CDs, 243

automated control, 60

communication based events and actions, 61

event-based actions, 61

need-based events, 60

time-based actions, 60

AutomatedLiving.com, 37

automatic updates, installing HALbasic, 69

automation actions, adding to your existing system, 297-299

automation processes

actions, 67-68

events, 67

Automation Setup Screen, 101

Aux, 211

B

backing up HALbasic, 184

backup generators, 30

backup power sources, 30

Backup/Restore, 184

battery backup, 56-57

power supplies, 30

benefits of home automation, 2-3

bonding wire, 20-21

Bright House, 295

bundled services, 288

C

C (return path), 211

cable TV/satellite, 25

call screening, 202

caller ID, 202

cameras

deciding how many are needed, 162]

installing, 162

IP Ethernet cameras, 164-171

multiple-cameras, 163-164

one-USB-camera solution, 162

USB cameras, 163

IP addresses, assigning, 171-181

IP cameras, 164

registering in HALdvc setup, 173

security actions, 178

surveillance cameras. *See* surveillance cameras

card brackets, 195

CDD (cooling degree day), 209

CDs

copying, 251

sound reproduction quality, 243

Check for Updates button, 48

checking

IDS logs, 285-286

voltage, 215

checksum, 63

children, smoke alarms, 158

choosing computers, 2

dedicated computer option, 35-36

having home automation systems professionally installed, 37

networked computer options, 36

purchasing new or used PCs, 37

purchasing preconfigured home automation PC, 37

shared computer option, 35

circuit breakers, household electrical power, 23

circuit loading, 21

circuits, turning off, 8

clock timers, 29

collecting data from Internet, 262-268

coloring, wire colors, HVAC, 211-212

COM ports, 90

  voice portal modems, 200

Comcast Xfinity, 295

comments, 103

commitment terms, monitoring services, 291

Common Connections, HVAC, 210

communication based events and actions, 61

computer cases

  desktop, 38

  small form factor, 38

  towers, 38

computer operating systems, 38-39

computers

  all-in-one, 38

  choosing, 34-35

    dedicated computer option, 35-36

    having home automation systems professionally installed, 37

    networked computer options, 36

    purchasing new or used PCs, 37

    purchasing preconfigured home automation PC, 37

    shared computer option, 35

  Ethernet ports, 42

  I/O ports, 41

  memory, 40

  monitors, 42

  optical drives, 41

  processors (CPU), 39-40

  setting up, 45

    battery backup, 56-57

    creating recovery media and diagnostics, 56

    surge protection, 56-57

    updating operating system software, 45

    updating security software, 51-54

  sound cards, 42

  storage drives, 41

  video cards, 41-42

  Windows-based computers, 33-34

Configuration Properties window, 108

configuring

  control module identities in HALbasic, 148

  voice mail, 202

connecting

  control adapters to the PC, 90-92

  UPB control adapters to PCs, 145

  voice portal modems to operating systems, 197-199

connections, wiring UPB controls, 143

contracts, monitoring services, 291

control adapters, connecting to the PC, 90-92

control communication, 62

control devices

  installing, 299

  selecting, 298

control methods, 59-60
  automated control, 60
    communication based events and actions, 61
    event-based actions, 61
    need-based events, 60
    time-based actions, 60
  protocols, 62
    imposing messages on physical media, 63-64
    INSTEON, 65
    physical-layer communication, 62-63
    UPB (Universal Powerline Bus), 64-65
    X-10, 64
    Z-Wave, 65-66
  standards, 62
control module identities, configuring in HALbasic, 148
control modules
  costs, 94
  hard-wired outlet control modules, setting up, 98-100
  plug-in control modules, setting up, 95-98
  setting up, X-10, 93
control points for lighting, taking inventory of, 130
controllers, 236
controlling HAL
  enabling HALids, 274-275
  with smart phones, 274
  smart phones
    Android devices, 281-284
    iOS, 275-280
  with tablets, 274
  over the Web, 270-271

controls
  time-based routines, 115-121
  voice commands, 122-125
converters, 19
  alternative power sources, 30
  household electrical power, 19
    AC wiring and devices, 19
    arc fault breakers, 24
    cable TV/satellite, 25
    circuit breakers, 23
    circuit loading, 21
    fuses, 23
    GFCI (ground-fault circuit interrupter), 21-22
    GFI (ground-fault interrupter), 21-22
    ground/bonding wire, 20-21
    hot wire, 20
    household low-voltage wiring types and devices, 24
    infra-red remotes, 24
    microphones, 25
    motors (electric), 24
    neutral wire, 20
    phones, 24-25
    relays, 23
    solenoids, 23
    surge suppressors, 22
    thermostats, 25
  legacy electric controls
    clock timers, 29
    dimmer switches, 25-29
    dimmers, 25-29
    heat sensor switches, 30
    motion sensor switches, 30
    switches, 25-28
    timers, 29

cooling degree day (CDD), 209

copper, wiring, 10

copying

    CDs, 251

    music and sound to hard drives, 243-245

costs

    control modules, 94

    HALdmc (Digital Music Center), 242

    headsets, 122

    installation costs, monitoring services, 289-291

    of installing thermostats, 216

    sound reproduction equipment, 242

    voice modem, 192

    Z-Wave, 231

crimp tool, 160

cross talk, 18

customizing playlists, 253

D

data

    collecting from Internet, 262-268

    viewing Internet data collected by HAL, 268-270

data setups, 299

DC (direct current), 11

dedicated computer option, 35-36

degree day, 209

delta-connected three-phase transformers, AC (alternating current), 14

Design and Do list, 297-299

design steps for adding new automation actions, 297-299

desktop cases, 38

Device Control, 271

Device Controller window, 221

device installation, testing, 105-106

Device Manager, 197

Device Wizard, 101

diagnostics, creating, 56

dialing options, 204-205

dials, rotating, 103

Digital Life Service, AT&T, 287

Digital Music Center. *See* HALdmc (Digital Music Center)

digital music file formats, 243

digital sound reproduction quality, 242-243

    digital music file formats, 243

dimmer switches, 25-29

dimmers, 25-29

dimming, 105-108

    lights, types of lights, 129

direct current (DC), 11

downloading music, legally, 244

Droid app, 274

E

E, 211

electrical currents, 10

    AC (alternating current). *See* AC (alternating current)

    DC (direct current), 11

ELK Products M1, 302

energy costs, X-10 adapters, 92

Ethernet ports, 42

event-based actions, 61

events, automation processes, 67

extended warranties, PCs, 37

F

fans, installing (in-line fan controls), 216-217

feedback, voice feedback, 107

feedback loops, communication based events and actions, 61

firewalls, 258

four-way switches, 28, 134

furnaces, 210

fuses, 23

G

G, 211

gang boxes, 129

gauges, heating and cooling systems, 209

GE Concord Hardware/Wireless kit, 302

GE Home Security, 295

General screen, Telephone Config window, 201

GFCI (ground-fault circuit interrupter), 21-22

GFI (ground-fault interrupter), 21-22

Global Cache, 302

GREEN (Getting to Reduced Energy Expenditure Now), 3

ground wires, 20-21

ground-fault circuit interrupter. *See* GFCI (ground-fault circuit interrupter)

H

HA management, 293-294. *See also* monitoring services

future offering, 294

HAL

controlling over the Web, 270-271

controlling with smart phones, 274

controlling with tablets, 274

Internet and, 262

collecting data, 262-268

registering, 86

viewing Internet data collected by HAL, 268-270

HAL DVC (Digital Video Center), 159

HAL HomeNet, 259

HAL Remote Telephone Services configuration window, 200

HAL Setup Type window, 78

HAL Setup window, 77, 227

HAL Setup Wizard, 147

installing voice portal modems, 199

HAL Telephone Services screen, 200

HAL voice portal, 43, 191

HAL VP300 modem, 192

HAL2000 PhonePad, 205-206

HALbasic

acquiring, 69

activating, 82-84

backing up, 184

configuring control module identities, 148

automatic updates, 69

modifying OS security settings, 72-73

pre-installation, 70

security software, 70-71

steps, 75-82

installing, 71-72

navigating, 86

waking, 125

HALdmc (Digital Music Center), 241-242

copying music and sound to hard drive, 243-245

digital sound reproduction quality, 242-243

digital music file formats, 243

installing as an add-on to HALultra, 246

playlists, customizing, 253

Record/CD Player feature, 250-251

setting up, 246

sound reproduction equipment, 242

sound reproduction quality, audio CDs, 243

using, 250-253

voice commands, 254

testing, 254-256

HALdvc, 246

cameras, registering, 173

HALhms (Home Manager System), 37

HALids (Interactive Device Server), 273

Android apps, 274

checking logs, 285-286

enabling, 274-275

iOS app, 274

logs, checking, 285-286

HALultra, 183

activating, 187

camera security actions, 178

installing, 186

potential energy savings, 189

testing, 187-189

upgrading to, 184

video, 157

HALultra Automation Setup Screen window, 237

HALultra-compatible thermostats, installing, 210-216

HALvoices, 43

hard drives, copying music and sound to hard drive, 243-245

hard-wired outlet control modules, setting up, 98-100

HDD (heating degree day), 209

headsets, 122-123

heat sensor switches, 30

heating and cooling systems

deploying gauges, triggers, and sensors, 209

HALultra-compatible thermostats, installing, 210-216

on/off devices, 208

thermostats, 208-209

time-based controls, 209-210

heating degree day (HDD), 209

home automation

benefits of, 2-3

defined1

having systems professionally installed, 37

security software, 302

HomeNet servers, 259

enabling, 259-262

logging in, 262

hot wire, 20

House identifiers, 95

household electrical power

AC wiring and devices, 19

arc fault breakers, 24

cable TV/satellite, 25

circuit breakers, 23

circuit loading, 21

fuses, 23

GFCI (ground-fault circuit interrupter), 21-22

GFI (ground-fault interrupter), 21-22

ground/bonding wire, 20-21

hot wire, 20

household low-voltage wiring types
and devices, 24

infra-red remotes, 24

microphones, 25

motors (electric), 24

neutral wire, 20

phones, 24-25

relays, 23

solenoids, 23

surge suppressors, 22

thermostats, 25

**household low-voltage wiring types
and devices, 24**

**HP Compaq small form factor 4000
Pro SSF PC, 43-45**

human intervention, 59

HVAC, 210, 227

Common Connections, 210

wire colors, 211-212

I

incoming calls, 202-203

infrared, 226-227, 302

infra-red remotes, 24

initiating events, 298

**in-line fan controls, installing,
216-217**

input/output devices, interfaces, 229

**installation costs, monitoring servic-
es, 289-291**

installation location, planning, 43

**installer competence, monitoring
services, 291-292**

installing

cameras, 162

IP Ethernet cameras, 164-171

multiple-cameras, 163-164

one-USB-camera solution, 162

USB cameras, 163

devices, testing installation, 105-106

HALbasic software, 71-72

automatic updates, 69

*modifying OS security
settings, 72-73*

pre-installation, 70

security software, 70-71

steps, 75-82

HALdmc (Digital Music Center), as
an add-on to HALultra, 246

HALultra, 186

HALultra-compatible thermostats,
210-216

in-line fan/light controls, 216-217

UPB controls, 141-142

voice portal modems, 193-195

with HAL Setup Wizard, 199

INSTEON, 65

interfaces, 229

setting up interfaces, 218-223

system add-ons, 300-301

INSTEON USB control, 219

Interactive Device Server. *See*
HALids (Interactive Device Server)

interface modules, selecting, 298

interfaces

HVAC, 227

infrared, 226-227

input/output devices, 229

INSTEON, 229

security, 228

setting up INSTEON devices, 218-223

ZigBee, 225-226

Z-Wave, 229-232

  costs, *231*

Internet, 257-258

controlling HAL over the Web, 270-271

HAL and, 262

  collecting data, *262-268*

HAL HomeNet, 259

modem-router-firewall-switch, setting up, 258-259

viewing data collected by HAL, 268-270

Internet connections, 45

Internet protocol security cameras, 160-161

inverters, 18-19

I/O ports, 41

iOS app, HALids (Interactive Device Server), 274

iOS devices, controlling HAL, 275-280

IP addresses, 259

  assigning for cameras, 171-181

IP Camera Finder tool, 171

IP cameras, 161, 164

IP Ethernet cameras, installing, 164-171

J

jack ports, 242

K

Kanda.com, ProBee, 226

L

labeling wires, 212

Lamp Module, setting up, 103-106

landlines, 191

laptops, Leviton RF Installer tool (Z-Wave), 233-238

legacy electric controls

clock timers, 29

dimmer switches, 25-29

dimmers, 25-29

heat sensor switches, 30

motion sensor switches, 30

switches, 25-28

timers, 29

legally downloading music, 244

Leviton RF Installer tool, using with laptops (Z-Wave), 233-238

Leviton snap-in wall jacks, 167

light controls, installing, 216-217

lighting

fixtures switched from a single location, 131-132

fixtures switched from four or more locations, 134

fixtures switched from three locations, 133

fixtures switched from two locations, 132-133

switching for indoor and outdoor lighting circuits, 128-129

lights

dimming, 105-108

  types of lights, *129*

Lamp Module, setting up, 103-106

multilocation switching, 129

location of installation, planning, 43

location of monitoring center, 292

logging in to HomeNet servers, 262

logs, IDS logs, 285-286

M

macros, camera security actions, 178

market service areas, monitoring services, 288

memory, 40

messages, imposing on physical media, 63-64

microphones, 25

modem-router-firewall-switch, setting up, 258-259

modems, 192, 258

    testing, 205

    voice portal modems, installing, 193-195

modes, 115, 120

modifying OS security settings, 72-73

monitoring services, 294-295

    commitment terms, 291

    future offering, 294

    installation costs, 289-291

    installer competence and tech support, 291-292

    location of monitoring center, 292

    market service areas, 288

    monthly service fees, 291

    PC or controller based, 289

    proprietary technology, 288-289

    support, 291

    what do they monitor, 292

    what is managed versus what is offered, 293-294

monitors, 42

monthly service fees, monitoring services, 291

motion sensor switches, 30

motors (electric), household electrical power, 24

MP3, 243

multilocation switching, 129

multimeters, 8-9

multiple-cameras, installing, 163-164

music

    copying to hard drives, 243-245

    downloading, legally, 244

N

National Electrical Code (NEC), 30, 129

navigating HALbasic software, 86

NEC (National Electrical Code), 30, 129

need-based events, 60

networked computer options, 36

networks, setting up Z-Wave, 233-238

neutral wire, 20

nonhuman intervention, 59

nonmetallic sheathed cable, 19

Norton Internet Security, 51

Norton LiveUpdate window, 52

Norton products, 71

O

O & B terminals, 211

Ohm's Law, power formula and, 15-17

one-off devices, 60

one-USB-camera solution, 162

one-way protocols, 63

on/off devices, heating and cooling systems, 208

on-off sensors, 158

on/off switches, 25

operating system software, updating, 45-

operating systems, 38-39

    security settings, modifying, 72-73

    voice portal modems, connecting, 197-199

optical drives, 41

outlets, adding to the system, 112-114

P

PCs

    connecting control adapters to, 90-92

    connecting UPB control adapters, 145

    extended warranties, 37

    purchasing new or used PCs, 37

phones

    caller ID, 202

    dialing options, 204-205

    household electrical power, 24-25

    incoming calls, handling, 202-203

    landlines, 191

    modems, 192

    requirements for voice modem, 202

    speakerphone mode, 204

    voice mail, configuring, 202

physical-layer communication, 62-63

pigtails, 139

planning installation location, 43

playlists, creating, 253

plug-in control modules, setting up, 95-98

power consumption, 16

power distribution transformers, 17-18

power formula, Ohm's Law and, 15-17

power sources, alternative power sources, 30

preconfigured home automation PCs, purchasing, 37

pre-installation considerations, 70

pressure when installing cards into motherboards, 195

primary controllers, Z-Wave, 232

ProBee, 225-226

process actions, 67-68

processors (CPU), 39-40

processors comparison tools, 40

professionally installed home automation systems, 37

professionals, 208

proprietary technology, monitoring services, 288-289

Protect America, 295

protocols, 62

    imposing messages on physical media, 63-64

    INSTEON, 65

    one-way protocols, 63

    physical-layer communication, 62-63

    UPB (Universal Powerline Bus), 64-65

    X-10, 64

    Z-Wave, 65-66

prototype computer for this book, 43-45

punch-down tool, 160

purchasing

    new or used PCs, 37

    preconfigured home automation PCs, 37

Q

quality
  monitoring services, installer competence and tech support, 291-292
  sound reproduction, 242-243
    digital music file formats, 243
  sound reproduction quality
    audio CDs, 243
    copying music and sound to hard drive, 243-245

R

RAM (random access memory), 40
Record/CD Player feature, HALdmc (Digital Music Center), 250-251
recovery media, creating, 56
registering
  cameras, in HALdvc setup, 173
  HAL, 86
relays, household electrical power, 23
remote wall switches, UPB controls, 156
remoting with IR, 302
resistance, 16
Romex, 19, 211
rotating dials, 103
routers, 258
runners, switches, 27

S

safety, 98
  indoor use products, 128
  tips for, 7-9

SaskTel, 37, 295
Scan All Drives, 254
Schedule Wizard, 115-117
schedules, time-based routines, 115-121
schematic diagrams, 31
security, 228
security actions, cameras, 178
security settings, modifying in operating systems, 72-73
security software, 70-71
  home automation, 302
  updating, 51-54
SecurTek, 37
  SaskTel, 295
semi-proprietary, 288
sensors
  heating and cooling systems, 209
  on-off sensors, 158
serial port connections, 91
Setup Wizard, 302
shared computer option, 35
signal limits, UPB controls, 156
single-location UPB-controlled lighting fixtures, 135
single-phase AC circuits, 12
single-point switches, 26
small form factor PCs, 38
smart phones, controlling HAL, 274
  Android devices, 281-284
  enabling HALids, 274-275
  iOS, 275-280
smoke alarms, children, 158
software upgrades, 183
solenoids, household electrical power, 23
sound, copying to hard drives, 243-245

sound cards, 42

sound reproduction equipment, HALdmc (Digital Music Center), 242

sound reproduction quality, 242-243
  audio CDs, 243
  copying music and sound to hard drive, 243-245
  digital music file formats, 243

speakerphone mode, 204

standard two-way switches, 131

standards, control methods, 62

storage drives, 41

support, monitoring services, 291

surge protection, 56-57

surge suppressors, 22

surveillance cameras, 159
  deciding how many are needed, 162
  Internet protocol security cameras, 160-161
  USB cameras, 159

switch drop, 26

switches, 25-28, 258
  four-way switches, 28
  heat sensor switches, 30
  motion sensor switches, 30
  on/off switches, 25
  runners, 27
  single-point switches, 26
  three-way switches, 26-27

switching
  for indoor and outdoor lighting circuits, 128-129
  multi-location switching, 129
  three-way switches, 130

system add-ons
  INSTEON devices, 300-301
  Setup Wizard, 302

UPB devices, 299-300

Z-Wave, 301

T

tablets, controlling HAL, 274
  enabling HALids, 274-275

tech support, monitoring services, 291-292

Telephone Config window, General screen, 201

Telephone Volume Adjustment, 202

terminal connections, thermostats, 214

terminal designations, thermostats, 210

testing
  actions, 299
  device installation, 105-106
  HALultra, 187-189
  voice commands, HALdmc (Digital Music Center), 254-256
  voice portal modems, 205

thermostats, 25
  costs of installing, 216
  HALultra-compatible thermostats, installing, 210-216
  heating and cooling systems, 208-209
  terminal connections, 214
  voltage, 214-215

three switch locations, 133

three-location UPB-controlled lighting fixtures, 139-141

three-phase AC circuits, 12-13

three-way switches, 26-27, 130

Time Warner Cable, 295

time-based actions, 60

time-based controls, heating and cooling systems, 209-210

time-based routines, 115-121

timers, 29

times, initiating, 298

tools

crimp tool, 160

IP Camera Finder tool, 171

Leviton RF Installer tool, 233-238

punch-down tool, 160

Vizia installer tool, 233

tower cases, 38

transformer connections, AC (alternating current), 13

transformers, 18

power distribution transformers, 17-18

triggers

for automation processes, events, 67

heating and cooling systems, 209

troubleshooting, 114

turning off circuits, 8

two-location UPB-controlled lighting fixtures, 138-139

two-switch locations, 132-133

U

UPB (Universal Powerline Bus), 64-65

UPB control adapters, connecting to PCs, 145

UPB control modules, 127

configuring identities in HALbasic, 148

setting up, 147-148

UPB controls, 127

adapting existing wiring, 135

single-location, 135

three-location fixtures, 139-141

two-location fixtures, 138-139

installing, 141-142

remote wall switches, 156

signal limits, 156

wiring connections, 143

UPB devices, system add-ons, 299-300

updates, automatic updates, installing HALbasic, 69

updating

operating system software, 45

security software, 51-54

upgrading to HALultra, 183-184

USB cameras, 159

installing, 163

user comments, 103

V

verizon Home Monitoring and Control, 295

VGA input jacks, 42

video, HALultra, 157

video cards, 41-42

viewing Internet data collected by HAL, 268-270

Vizia installer tool, 233

voice commands, 122-125

HALdmc (Digital Music Center), 254

testing, 254-256

voice feedback, 107

voice mail, configuring, 202

voice portal modems

connecting to operating systems, 197-199

installing, 193-195

with HAL Setup Wizard, 199

testing, 205

voltage, 16

checking, 215

thermostats, 214-215

W

W1, 211

W2, 211

waking HALbasic, 125

warranties, extended warranties, PCs, 37

watt hours (kWh), 16-17

watts, 16

Wi-Fi, 274

Wi-Fi cameras, 161

Wi-Fi mode, cameras, 167

Windows 7, updating operating system software, 46

Windows installer flag, 218

Windows-based computers, 33-34

wire colors, HVAC, 211-212

wire nuts, 90

wires, labeling, 212

wiring

adapted for UPB controls, 135

single-location, 135

three-location fixtures, 139-141

two-location fixtures, 138-139

connections, UPB controls, 143

existing wiring

fixtures switched from four or more locations, 134

fixtures switched from three locations, 133

lighting fixtures switched from a single location, 131-132

lighting fixtures switched from two locations, 132-133

wiring labels, thermostats, 210

wizards

Device Wizard, 101

HAL Setup Wizard, 147

installing voice portals, 199

Schedule Wizard, 115-117

WMA file types, 243

wye-connected three-phase transformers, AC (alternating current), 14-15

X

X-10, 64, 89, 211

adapters, energy costs, 92

connecting control adapters to the PC, 90-92

control modules

hard-wired outlet control modules, 98-100

plug-in control modules, 95-98

setting up, 93

Y

Y1, 211

Y2, 211

Z

zero crossing point, 64

ZigBee, 225-226, 289

Z-Wave, 65-66, 229-232

   costs, 231

   Leviton RF Installer tool, laptops, 233-238

   primary controllers, 232

   system add-ons, 301

Z-Wave lamp module node, 237

CHECK OUT THESE OTHER
ABSOLUTE BEGINNER'S GUIDES
FROM QUE PUBLISHING

Windows 8

No experience necessary!

Paul Sanna

ISBN: 9780789749932

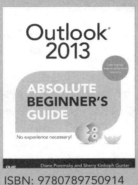

Outlook 2013

No experience necessary!

Diane Poremsky and Sherry Kinkoph Gunter

ISBN: 9780789750914

Project Management

No experience necessary!

Third Edition

Gregory M. Horine

ISBN: 9780133115604

iTunes and iCloud for iPhone, iPad, & iPod touch

No experience necessary!

Brad Miser

ISBN: 9780789750648

iPad and iPad mini

No experience necessary!

James F. Kelly

ISBN: 9780789750990

Wireless Networking

No experience necessary!

Michael Miller

ISBN: 9780133381320

No experience necessary!

quepublishing.com

HOME AUTOMATION Made Easy

Do It Yourself Know How Using **UPB**, **Insteon**, **X10** and **Z-Wave**

DENNIS C. BREWER

FREE Online Edition

Safari
Books Online

Your purchase of *Home Automation Made Easy* includes access to a free online edition for 45 days through the **Safari Books Online** subscription service. Nearly every Que book is available online through **Safari Books Online**, along with thousands of books and videos from publishers such as Addison-Wesley Professional, Cisco Press, Exam Cram, IBM Press, O'Reilly Media, Prentice Hall, Sams, and VMware Press.

Safari Books Online is a digital library providing searchable, on-demand access to thousands of technology, digital media, and professional development books and videos from leading publishers. With one monthly or yearly subscription price, you get unlimited access to learning tools and information on topics including mobile app and software development, tips and tricks on using your favorite gadgets, networking, project management, graphic design, and much more.

Activate your FREE Online Edition at
informit.com/safarifree

STEP 1:   Enter the coupon code: NTTWNGA.

STEP 2:   New Safari users, complete the brief registration form.
            Safari subscribers, just log in.

If you have difficulty registering on Safari or accessing the online edition,
please e-mail customer-service@safaribooksonline.com